APR 0 8 2025

Praise for *Sister, Soldier, Surgeon*

"Sister Dede is an American hero who served her country with devotion and courage from Ground Zero to Afghanistan and back. She is a beautiful personification of the many patriots who draw upon their faith to build and sustain this great country. I hope her powerful story, as told by Dr. Carzon, will inspire a new generation of Catholics and Americans to a life of service."

— **President Donald J. Trump**

"Sister Dede is an inspiration. Her intellect, religious devotion, courage, and grit are a rare and compelling combination. This book will give readers a healthy dose of the hope, encouragement, and humor that's needed now more than ever."

— **Laura Ingraham, Host, *The Ingraham Angle***

"I have the highest regard for both Sister Deirdre 'Dede' Byrne, P.O.S.C., and for Dr. Leisa Marie Carzon. Dr. Carzon's biography of Sister Dede is an edifying and inspiring story of God's grace at work in the life of a soul who completely surrenders to His Truth and Love, known through both reason and faith. It is clear that God guided Sister Dede by a faithful Catholic family and through the spiritual counsel of Servant of God John A. Hardon, S.J.; Saint Teresa of Calcutta, M.C.; and His Eminence James Aloysius Cardinal Hickey to be a *Sister* in our nation's capital, evangelizing for the King of Kings and Lord of Lords; to be a *soldier* for the United States of America, for the Kingdom of God, and for the right to life; and to be a *surgeon* who serves as an instrument in the hands of our healing and merciful God. I highly encourage everyone to reap the fruits of this excellent study of the life of Sister Dede, a coworker with Christ in the Truth (see John 3:8)."

— **Raymond Leo Cardinal Burke**

" 'I can do all things through Him who strengthens me' is a familiar Scripture passage from Saint Paul's Letter to the Philippians. Sister Dede's life of selfless service is a remarkable reflection of these words. Sister Dede has dedicated her life to healing people in body and soul. Known not only as 'pro-life' but 'pro–eternal life,' this modern-day Joan of Arc is an outspoken advocate of the Catholic Faith and the unborn. Dr. Leisa Marie Carzon vividly captures the life and courage of this extraordinary woman."

— **Most Rev. Salvatore J. Cordileone,
Archdiocese of San Francisco**

"These pages tell an amazing story of a doctor, religious woman, and army colonel who has served her country in all three roles without contradiction. She embodies the Catholic tradition of service in truth, and we are enriched by her commitment. Dr. Carzon tells her story well — now it is up to us to learn and to imitate, the highest form of flattery."

— **Most Rev. Timothy P. Broglio,**
Archdiocese for the Military Services, USA

"It is said the opposite of fear is love (see 1 John 4:18). The inspirational courage of Sister Dede Byrne to speak Christ's truth without fear or apology in every aspect of her life is a manifestation of the way she so beautifully loves all she encounters. This incredible, must-read book by Dr. Carzon chronicles the life of one of our nation's finest heroes and shows us what it means to be Christ's hands in a world desperate for His love."

— **Most Rev. Joseph L. Coffey, Auxiliary Bishop,**
Archdiocese for the Military Services, USA

"The remarkable modern-day story of Sister Deirdre 'Dede' Byrne, P.O.S.C., is beautifully told by Dr. Leisa Carzon in this compelling biography. It is hard to put this captivating book down. Combining the courage of a Joan of Arc and the compassion of a Mother Teresa, Sister Dede is the living embodiment of what John Paul II described as the 'feminine genius.' Whether she is in scrubs, camouflage, or her religious habit, Sister Dede proposes Christ to everyone she meets in a winning, joy-filled way, with fearless abandon and determined love. This is a beautiful story of a modern woman that everyone should read."

— **Most Rev. James Conley, Diocese of Lincoln,**
and Episcopal Advisor for the Catholic Medical Association

"Sister Dede Byrne is a hero. Whether in the operating room or in the public square, she exemplifies the feminine genius and demonstrates love in action in all she does. Dr. Carzon's page-turner chronicles Sister's life while revealing her daily life of prayer and charity. This is an inspiring life worthy of attention and, one hopes, imitation."

— **Raymond Arroyo, New York Times Bestselling Author**
and Broadcaster

"One mark of our age's corruption is how little we learn about the saints. The greatest people ever to have lived go largely unmentioned. That sad fact describes not only the canonized dead but also and especially the exemplars of faith and virtue who still walk the earth. In this latter category, none rank higher than Sister Dede Byrne, whose life offers inspiration and a model to emulate. Dr. Carzon's marvelous biography of Sister Dede goes a long way toward helping us get to know one of the very best among us."

— **Michael Knowles, Daily Wire**

"Sister Dede is one of my favorite Catholics. Whether it's the military frontlines of Afghanistan, the medical frontlines of COVID, or the political frontlines of the fight for the unborn, Sister Dede always fearlessly goes where she is needed most. Her story should be heard by more people — so they know what real Christian heroism is like."

— **Charlie Kirk, Founder and President, Turning Point USA**

"Sister Dede's dedication to protecting unborn and eternal life is an inspiring story for all of us on how to live our godly purpose. Thank you, Dr. Carzon, for telling it."

— **Glenn Beck, Host, *The Glenn Beck Program***

"*Sister, Soldier, Surgeon* is a remarkable and inspiring story about Sister Dede Byrne — a woman who boldly confronts adversity and tragedy with strength, humility, and unwavering devotion to Jesus Christ."

— **Ambassador Callista L. Gingrich**

"Sister Dede Byrne brings the love of Christ to all she encounters, and she exemplifies the feminine genius. I hope Dr. Carzon's beautiful story of Sister's heroic service to God, the country, the unborn, and the Body of Christ will move the hearts of young women to consider a similar life of service."

— **Mother Assumpta Long, Foundress,**
Dominican Sisters of Mary, Mother of the Eucharist

"This is an inspiring story of a humble woman born for this time of great divisions and distress in our nation—a modern-day Joan of Arc. While some claim we have already crossed the Rubicon of a dying civilization, Sister Deirdre 'Dede' Byrne is a shining example of how Christians should not despair but should cling to their faith. Despite all the obstacles placed in her path, she relentlessly defends her faith, country, and the unborn. Her weapon of choice is the Rosary. And despite an avalanche of criticism, she publicly proclaimed her steadfast support to the most pro-life president in the history of the United States."

— **Dick Thompson, President and Chief Counsel,**
Thomas More Law Center

"Sister Dede's fearless defense of the unborn is inspirational. This powerful biography by Dr. Carzon highlights Sister's courage and emboldens us to walk proudly beside her in the fight for life."

— **Kristan Hawkins, President, Students for Life of America**

"Dr. Leisa Marie Carzon does a wonderful job detailing the powerful life and most important work of Sister Deirdre Byrne as she serves Him through serving the most vulnerable."

— **Marjorie Dannenfelser, President,**
Susan B. Anthony Pro-Life America

"Sister Dede is a steadfast champion of the Rosary whose life and actions witness the love of Christ to a world much in need."

— **Father Donald Calloway, M.I.C., Author,** *Champions of the Rosary:*
The History and Heroes of a Spiritual Weapon

"As a great admirer of Sister Dede, I am thrilled that Dr. Carzon has put into print this compelling, comprehensive narrative of Sister's life and work. In a world of cynicism and narcissism, this is a story that must be told because it is a tale of good conquering evil, of light over darkness, and of life over death. Dr. Carzon has captured most accurately the heart of this current-day Mother Teresa, and it will be both a delight and an inspiration to everyone who reads this book."

— **Rev. Edward V. Meeks, Pastor Emeritus,**
Christ the King Catholic Church, Towson, Maryland

"A beautiful account of an extraordinary woman and an extraordinary life. Sister Deirdre Byrne's threefold career calling, though unusual, is deeply instructive and exemplary. This timely, uplifting story will bring hope and inspiration to a culture presently much in need. In both the spiritual and terrestrial realms, Sister Dede shines. This book provides the light."

— **Dr. William Bennett, Former Secretary of Education;**
Author, *The Book of Virtues*

"In a moment in history when young Americans yearn for authentic heroes and role models, Sister Dede's story provides a compass for a life lived in service and faith that will inspire and enrich generations to come."

— **John Solomon, Founder,** *Just the News*

"Americans and the rest of the world can always use more stories about the lives of saints and the battles of heroes. Dr. Carzon's book on the indomitable Sister Dede fits the bill."

— **Tom Fitton, President, Judicial Watch**

"A magnificently moving testimonial of one woman's courage, compassion, and commitment. Her life of heroic virtue is filled with lessons for all people seeking to live everyday virtue."

— **Dr. Ray Guarendi, Psychologist, Author, and TV and Radio Host**

"Sisters in black habits are usually not thought of as globe-trotters and powerful political figures. But hold on to your hat because this sister will rattle these generalizations. Dr. Carzon has done us all a favor in bringing the life of Sister Dede Byrne to light."

— **Steve Ray, Pilgrimage Leader, CatholicConvert.com**

"Over the course of two thousand years and in every era of Church history, there have been those who respond heroically to God's call to ministry in defense of life and human dignity. In *Sister, Soldier, Surgeon*, we hear the remarkable story of one such person, Sister Dede Byrne, who has been an instrument of divine mercy in the heat of battle and in the medical clinic. She exemplifies a life of loving service dedicated to healing the whole person in imitation of her beloved Spouse, Jesus Christ. May Dr. Carzon's story of Sister's life inspire many others to respond similarly to the call to service in the vocation of medicine."

— **Steve White, M.D., President of Catholic Health Care Leadership Alliance; Former President of the Catholic Medical Association**

"Courageous love and the recognition of the value of every individual life are embodied by Sister Dede. Grounded in a love of Our Lord, she serves Him and her patients, including speaking with an unapologetic clarity for the voiceless little ones. May we follow Sister's example so beautifully told by Dr. Carzon and fearlessly defend the unborn."

—**Robin Pierucci, M.D., M.A., Neonatologist, American Academy of Pediatrics Pro-Life Chair**

"In *Sister, Soldier, Surgeon: The Life and Courage of Sister Deirdre Byrne*, Leisa Marie Carzon, Ph.D., captures the extraordinary spirit and profound impact of Sister Byrne's life with vivid storytelling and deep insight. This captivating biography, blending Sister Byrne's thrilling experiences as a professed Catholic nun, renowned surgeon, and retired U.S. Army colonel, with her unwavering faith and service, offers readers an unparalleled glimpse into the life of a modern-day heroine. Carzon's narrative not only celebrates Sister Byrne's remarkable achievements across continents and battlefields but also serves as a powerful call to action, embodying the essence of living one's faith courageously in the public square."

— **Anthony DeStefano, Bestselling Author**

"In a nation longing for leaders willing to speak truth without fear or apology, Sister Dede Byrne testifies to the love of Christ and demonstrates the importance of boldly living our faith in the public square. Dr. Carzon's captivating account of Sister's heroic life is an inspiration to all of us."

— **Bob McEwen, U.S. Congressman**

"Sister Dede Byrne's heroic service as a colonel and a surgeon in the U.S. Army alone makes this book worth reading, but her service in the days immediately after 9/11 at the World Trade Center and her deployments to battle zones such as in Afghanistan make Dr. Carzon's book a must-read."

— Steve O'Keefe, President, VSO;
Chairman of the Board, Christendom College

"Sister Dede's love shines forth in everything she does. Whether in the chapel, in the operating room, or on the front lines of battle, her faith and trust in God are inspirational. I highly recommend Dr. Carzon's wonderful book and hope it will help many to realize the impact and incredible life of this courageous sister."

— Julian Heron, O.P., Former Presidential Adviser;
Board Member, Christendom College

Sister, Soldier, Surgeon

Leisa Marie Carzon, Ph.D.

Sister, Soldier, Surgeon

The Life and Courage of
Sister Deirdre Byrne, M.D.

SOPHIA INSTITUTE PRESS
Manchester, New Hampshire

Sophia Institute Press
Box 5284, Manchester, NH 03108
1-800-888-9344
www.SophiaInstitute.com

Sophia Institute Press is a registered trademark of Sophia Institute.

paperback ISBN 979-8-88911-376-8

ebook ISBN 979-8-88911-361-4

Library of Congress Control Number: 2024940870

2nd printing

Contents

Foreword by Most Rev. Joseph L. Coffey. xi

Acknowledgments xiii

Preface xv

Prologue. xix

Part 1: The Life and Courage of Sister Dede Byrne

1. Family Life and Early Years 5
    The Family: The Garden for Vocations. 10
    Dede's Childhood Years. 14
    Catholicism Was Part of the Byrne Family Identity 16
    My Vocation to Serve Started in Utero. 18
    College Years 22

2. Sinai, Korea, and Young Adulthood 29
    The Sinai Peninsula — On Holy Ground 29
    Jesus Had Already Spoken for Her 30
    Deirdre Byrne Is a Force to Be Reckoned With 32
    The Sunshine Club 35
    Saint Catherine's Monastery 36
    Korea 39

Sister Philip Marie: You're Jesus' Doctor Now, Dede 40

Lourdes Water in Her Rucksack. .43

Had I Walked Away, Love Would Not Have Been Conveyed 43

Time at Saint Agnes 44

The Eucharist Was My Lunch 47

The Ripple Effect of Sister Dede 47

Humility and "Holey" Shoes. 50

Pledging Allegiance in the Front Yard 50

Holy Land Pilgrimages 53

3. Three Major Influences and Serving Others 55

Holding Cardinal Hickey's Heart .55

Mother Teresa's Doctor 56

Keep Your Eyes on the Cross 56

Father Hardon's Influence 58

The Poor Deserve Our Firstfruits, Not Our Leftovers 59

Lord, to Whom Should I Go? 60

I'm Your Girl, Whatever Direction 61

Time with Dad 63

4. September 11 and Finally Finding Her Fit 69

I'm Sure We Breathed in Human Remains 69

Head-Butted by an Israeli Soldier 71

Seeking God's Will. 72

The Little Workers of the Sacred Hearts. 73

All They Felt Was a Little Breeze .74

Attuned to God's Tweeting and SMSs and Finding Her Fit 75

The Power Is in the Veil. 75

First Vows 76

The Military: A Mission Field for Vocations 77

Contents

Scrubs, Camouflage, or Habit? 77

Second Deployment. 78

A Speed Bump on the Journey. 78

Haiti. 80

5. Serving Overseas 85

Afghanistan — Operation Enduring Freedom 85

The Nun with a Gun: Serving at Camp Salerno 85

Called to Be a Fifth Gospel. 88

Nuba Mountains 89

Spina Bifida Repair for Dummies .93

I'm Sorry, but You Can't Have Your Blood Back 94

Operation Unified Response 95

6. Final Vows and Continued Mission Work 99

A Fourth Vow: Free, Loving Medical Care for the Poor 99

Third Tour in Nuba 100

Ministering to the Kurds 102

A Modern-Day Mother Cabrini Witnessing to the Faith. 106

Recognition from the President. 107

The Vocation of Medicine 108

7. COVID — The World Closed 111

COVID Cataracts 113

8. Republican National Convention 117

I'm Your Gal, Lord. 118

The Four Minutes That Changed My World 119

It Wasn't about Politics 120

The Womb Is Ground Zero 123

My Life Took a 180-Degree Turn. .123

A Battle Cry for Christians Worldwide 124

Waking the Faithful 125

9. The Feminine Genius and Continued Impact 129

The Vocation of Motherhood 130

The Influence of Strong Women 130

Our Feminine Cry and Maternal Hearts 132

Helping Overseas from Her Convent 133

10. Medical License Revoked and Lawsuit against D.C. 137

Nun Sues D.C. 138

License Restored 140

Defending What Is Right 141

Part 2: A Week in the Life of Sister Dede Byrne

11. The Convent (Setting the Stage) 147

An Interesting Library 148

The Clinic Area 149

Faith-Based Health Care 151

Additional Ministries 151

Grandma's House Times Ten 153

Taking Christ to the Streets 154

The Patriotic Rosary 155

The Rosary Is Our Weapon of Love 155

12. Day 1: Clinic Day 159

Sending Us Your First-Born Daughter 161

Sister Dede's Loving Care for All 166

13. Day 2: Abortion Clinic Day 169

I Can Reverse Your Abortion 170

Contents

Have Altar, Will Travel 170

Supporting Pro-Life Colleagues. 171

14. Day 3: Abortion Pill Reversal 175

God Will Forgive You. . . . Will You Forgive Yourself?. 177

We Flood These Moms with TLC 179

15. Days 4 and 5: Maintenance Days 183

Finally, Someone We Can Be Proud Of 184

It's Who She Points to That Really Makes Me Pay Attention 185

Jesus' Donkey. 185

Speaking the Truth in Love. 187

16. Day 6: Abortion-Pill-Reversal Follow-Ups 189

And What's Wrong with the Valley, Father?. 189

Emma's Follow-Up. 190

Congratulations! You're Expecting a Hamburger!. 191

Preserving Purity 192

Let Me Tell You How to Find a Good Man 195

I'm Not Judging Them; I'm Loving Them. 196

17. Day 7: Sister's Faith in the Public Square 197

Witness to Love. 198

Euthanasia Prevention 200

Part 3: Living Our Faith in the Public Square

18. The Problem That Ails Us. 205

19. The Remedy That Heals Us. 211

Speak the Truth Even When It's Difficult 211

20. Dr. Dede's Prescriptions 215

21. A Call from the Upper Room 231

    Our Inspiration and Sister Dede's Place in History 232

    A Call into the Public Square 234

    It Is Not Enough to Discuss; It Is Necessary to Act 235

    It Is the Hour to Awake from Sleep (Rom. 13:11) 236

    For Such a Time as This (Esther 4:14). 237

    Bibliography 239

    About the Author 251

Foreword

As a bishop and shepherd of souls, I greatly desire to see the spiritual children entrusted to my care become saints. Too rarely do I see this as clearly as in the life of Sister Dede Byrne.

As auxiliary bishop of the Military Archdiocese, I take seriously my obligation to share publicly the love of Christ and those truths that set us free. It was for this reason that I was impressed on the evening of August 26, 2020, to see an unknown sister in full habit hold up her rosary on national television in defense of life and utter those unforgettable words: "I'm not just pro-life, I'm pro–eternal life." I was grateful for her clarity and fearlessness.

While the Second Vatican Council warned that "the split between the faith which many profess and their daily lives deserves to be counted among the more serious errors of our age,"[1] it was clear that this courageous sister understood the calling of all members of the Body of Christ to proclaim the truth of Christ in all aspects of life — including in the public square — and I was determined to meet her.

While Sister and I share similar biographical elements, few are as important as our common calling to defend life, and we echo Cardinal Raymond Burke, who states: "In considering 'the sum total of social conditions,' there is . . . a certain order of priority, which must

---

[1] Second Vatican Council, Pastoral Constitution on the Church in the Modern World *Gaudium et Spes* (December 7, 1965), no. 43.

be followed. Conditions upon which other conditions depend must receive our first consideration. The first consideration must be given to the protection of human life itself, without which it makes no sense to consider other social conditions."[2]

Sister and I have been involved in several pro-life activities together, some of which, such as the opportunity to celebrate Mass in front of an abortion clinic, are detailed in the pages to come. Her exhortations to remain in the state of grace, to cultivate a well-formed conscience, to frequent the sacraments, to pray the Rosary daily, to be a voice for the unborn, to engage in works of mercy, and to share and defend the Faith publicly are especially important for the modern Christian.

In *Sister, Soldier, Surgeon*, Dr. Carzon provides us with an inspiring account of this modern-day heroine. Her page-turning biography offers an inside glimpse into Sister's daily life of prayer and service. May these moving accounts of Sister's love, determination, humility, and continual self-giving encourage all to imitate her virtue and courage and to become saints.

— Most Rev. Joseph L. Coffey
Auxiliary Bishop
Archdiocese for the Military Services, USA
August 15, 2024

---

[2]   Most Reverend Raymond L. Burke, *On Our Civic Responsibility for the Common Good*, no. 20, EWTN, https://www.ewtn.com/catholicism/library/on-our-civic-responsibility-for-the-common-good-3658.

Acknowledgments

I wish to express gratitude to the many people whose insights and assistance made this book possible. Unless otherwise noted, reflections herein have been drawn from interviews and conversations with those below, as well as an abundance of materials supplied by Sister Dede. Certain names have been changed upon request.

Sister Deirdre Byrne, P.O.S.C.

Bishop Bill Byrne

Bishop Joseph Coffey

John Byrne

Mary Byrne

Gloria Byrne

Sue Byrne Rust

Sister Elias

Evelyn, Lea, and Melani

Father Ed Meeks

Dr. John Stewart

Father Vincent Woo

Dr. Tom Catena

Deacon Jack Cheasty

Dorinda Sears

Trish Palumbo

Denise Douglas

Lisa Bailey Dorr

Jackie Smith

Father Francline Javlon

Dr. Ed James

Howard Walsh

Jennifer Tulaine

Andy Coulter

Mother Iliana

Dr. Aaron Epstein

Clinic friends and employees

Sam Lee

Preface

The first time I heard of Sister Deirdre (Dede) Byrne was when she addressed the Republican National Convention the evening of August 26, 2020, in anticipation of the upcoming presidential election. There are certain addresses that stand out as memorable in one's life and garner national attention: Martin Luther King Jr.'s "I Have a Dream" speech; Ronald Reagan's 1987 "Tear Down This Wall" speech; Mother Teresa's 1994 National Prayer Breakfast speech when she defended the unborn before pro-abortion legislators; John Paul II's 1979 homily in Warsaw's Victory Square when he called down the Holy Spirit on a communist-oppressed people; and, to many people of faith, Sister Deirdre Byrne's address in 2020.

On the national stage at this time, Justices Gorsuch and Kavanaugh had recently been appointed to the Supreme Court and the impending presidential appointment of a new justice after Ruth Bader Ginsburg's passing on September 18, 2020, raised the temperature on an already heated presidential race. Attempts to boycott committee hearings and stall the nomination of Amy Coney Barrett to replace Ginsburg added to the dissension.

On the global stage, the COVID pandemic had shut down the world. Churches were forced to close, and people were not permitted to attend Mass or receive the sacraments. COVID-19 vaccines were in their infancy — mandates just around the corner — and hate crimes against Christians were also rampant. One news outlet reported nearly five hundred hate crimes against European Christians in 2019 alone.[3] Priests were attacked, churches were set on fire, the Eucharist was stolen, and pregnancy centers and religious statues were vandalized. Similar crimes were perpetrated in the United States.[4] This time of uncertainty, turmoil, stay-at-home orders, curfews, quarantines, masking, social distancing, and virtual workdays reshaped the nation and served as a backdrop for the 2020 election cycle. Notably, the Democratic National Convention, held August 17–20, featured two Catholic religious figures: Father James Martin and Sister Simone Campbell.

It was in this cultural context that Sister Deirdre Byrne's words first struck a chord with millions of people worldwide on that evening in August 2020. While people of faith nationwide had long been storming Heaven for more religious leaders willing to defend publicly the pro-life message, an unknown sister from Washington, D.C., took her place on that national stage. People glued to their TV screens wondered who this sister was, as her words "I'm not just pro-life but pro–eternal life" rang out across the nation. She was a voice not only for the unborn but also for so many of us who longed for a modern-day hero. It was her Esther moment (see Esther 4:14)!

> While we tend to think of the marginalized as living beyond our borders, the truth is the largest marginalized group in the world can be found here in the United States. They are the unborn.... It is no coincidence that Jesus stood up for what

---

[3] "More Than 500 Hate Crimes against Europe's Christians Recorded in 2019," *Catholic World Report*, November 20, 2019, https://www.catholicworldreport.com/2020/11/17/more-than-500-hate-crimes-against-europes-christians-recorded-in-2019/.

[4] "Arson, Vandalism, and Other Destruction at Catholic Churches in the United States," United States Conference of Catholic Bishops, https://www.usccb.org/committees/religious-liberty/Backgrounder-Attacks-on-Catholic-Churches-in-US.

was just and was ultimately crucified because what he said was not politically correct or fashionable. As followers of Christ, we are called to stand up for life against the politically correct or fashionable of today. We must fight against a legislative agenda that supports and even celebrates destroying life in the womb.[5]

When I first approached Sister Dede and asked for permission to shadow her for the purposes of writing this book, she laughingly responded that I must be writing a comic book. When she asked if I could wait until she was dead, you can guess my response: "No, Sister, unfortunately, we can't wait." Borrowing from Cardinal Sarah: "Christians are trembling, wavering, doubting. I want this book to be for them. To tell them: do not doubt! Hold fast to doctrine! Hold fast to prayer! I want this book to strengthen faithful Christians."[6] In a culture hostile to the gospel message, we need courageous witnesses to love and truth now more than ever.

Inspired by Christ's words — "Go therefore and make disciples of all nations" (Matt. 28:19) — Sister now travels the globe speaking to one person and one group at a time, just as Christ did. After spending decades healing people's physical wounds, she now heals spiritually as well. Her messages are simple. She beckons us to stay focused on God — never to go ahead of Him but to go with Him. She reminds us that life begins at the moment of conception and must be protected until natural death. She encourages us to frequent the sacraments and,

5   Sister Dede Byrne, "Full Text: Sister Dede Byrne's Speech at the 2020 Republican National Convention," Catholic News Agency, August 26, 2020, https://www.catholicnewsagency.com/news/45617/full-text-sister-dede-byrnes-speech-at-the-2020-republican-national-convention.

6   Cardinal Robert Sarah, *The Day Is Now Far Spent* (San Francisco: Ignatius Press, 2019), 13.

most importantly, stresses that we must always — *always* — be in the state of grace.

Dubbed the Mother Teresa of D.C., Sister Dede Byrne lives an inspirational life of joyful service that serves as a call to both virtue and action. Mindful that if the apostles had remained hidden in the Upper Room, we would not have a Church today, let us follow her beyond prayer and into the public square to courageously live out our faith and infuse the culture with an unapologetic defense of Christ's beauty, truth, and goodness.

Prologue

One mass casualty I will never forget was when a mother and her children arrived at Mother of Mercy [Hospital] in a rickety vehicle. Her children who accompanied her were missing fingers and she had half her face blown off, yet was still able to breathe through what appeared to be bloody swollen lips. One of [her] legs had been sheared off above the knee and her other foot was completely missing. She had sharp shards of metal throughout her torso and I had to use a Foley (urinary) catheter to drain a sucking chest wound filled with blood and air, as there was no chest tube available, a common piece of emergency equipment found in any emergency room in the United States.[7]

Near death, Imani looked up through her swollen eyes to glimpse the kind, gentle face of the small-framed female physician so desperately working to save her life. As the only hospital to service more than one million Nuba people, Imani was fortunate to have even made it there alive. As she clung to life, little did she know that the doctor working so hard to save her was also praying for her soul.

[7] Sister Dede Byrne, "In the Service of Christ: My 'Tours' in the Nuba Mountains," in *Sudan's Nuba Mountains People Under Siege: Accounts by Humanitarians in the Battle Zone*, ed. Samuel Totten (Jefferson, NC: McFarland, 2017), 72.

Sister, Soldier, Surgeon

Imani's doctor was not only a surgeon but also a soldier and a professed religious sister.

When not wearing scrubs, she wore a U.S. Army uniform; and when not in uniform, she wore the religious habit of the Little Workers of the Sacred Hearts. Such is the threefold calling of Sister Dede Byrne: sister, soldier, and surgeon.

Sister, Soldier, Surgeon

Part 1

The Life and Courage of Sister Dede Byrne

1

Family Life and Early Years

Sister Deirdre Mary Byrne was born into an Irish American family that has a rich history of faithful immigrants who proudly and courageously brought their religion with them to the States. Huge, beautiful Catholic churches and manufacturing were the norm in Massachusetts and New York at that time. Catholicism was ubiquitous. It was in this cultural milieu that Dede's parents, Mary Largent and William Byrne, were born.

William Draper Byrne was born in 1924 in East Orange, New Jersey; he was the sixth of ten children born of Thomas Ryan Byrne and Ruth Eberhart-Byrne. Descended from immigrants who came to the United States after the Civil War, they were a culturally and spiritually faithful Catholic family of German and Irish lineage and also one of prominence. Bill's siblings included John (later Father John Byrne, a priest in the Archdiocese of New York), Mary, Tom (later an ambassador to Czechoslovakia and Norway), Dorothy, and Ruth. When Thomas's mother, Julia Nunning-Byrne, once visited, she so strongly impressed the value and blessing of a large family upon her son and his wife that they subsequently expanded their family to include Danny, David, Marie (Mimi), Ann, and Ann's twin, who, sadly, died in utero.

The Byrne family greatly appreciated the value of a college education. Bill's Grandma Julia graduated with a degree from Saint Mary's College in South Bend, Indiana, at the turn of the century, well before Notre Dame admitted females. His mother, Ruth, a strong-willed Germanic woman, also strongly reinforced the value of higher education in her children such that Bill and all his siblings attended college. While three of his brothers discerned vocations to the religious life, one even eventually becoming a priest, Bill never felt drawn to the priesthood and knew he was called to the vocation of marriage.

Bill grew up in New Rochelle, New York, attended twelve years of Catholic school, and was a scholarship student at Iona Prep High School. In his late teens, he worked a summer job driving a beer truck. One route took him down a New York parkway where he underestimated the height of an overpass and clipped the truck's roof. Beer barrels spilled across the parkway, and Bill was left to pick up and reload every single one. Exhausted after the ordeal, he vowed he would never make a living using his back; he wanted to use his mind instead.

Bill received a football scholarship to Notre Dame, where he played tackle for two years, was fast-tracked into Georgetown medical school on a navy scholarship, and graduated magna cum laude in 1948. Looking to earn extra money during his years as a resident, he took a second job working in the cafeteria. He was always amused at his patients' reactions when they discovered that their physician also manned the hot dog station at lunch.

He carried many fond memories of his Fighting Irish years and returned fifty years post-graduation, when all those who had been fast-tracked into wartime medical programs were awarded degrees in a moving college ceremony. Bill was born to be a surgeon, and throughout his career, he used his healing hands as instruments of God's mercy and love to others. He was shy and scholarly by nature, so he didn't date much. In an attempt to draw him out of his shell, his sister bought him ten lessons at an Arthur Murray Dance Studio.

While Bill could delicately suture veins together, he was quite uncoordinated on the dance floor. When he reluctantly attended his final lesson, he found that he had a new instructor: Mary Largent. Little did he know she would be the love of his life.

Mary Largent Byrne was born to the Largent family in Baltimore, Maryland, on March 19, 1923. Her family tree includes members of the Daughters of the American Revolution. Of French lineage, her father, Vance (born in 1900), was an electrician from West Virginia, and her mother, Anastasia St. Ruth Costello (a.k.a. Ruth, born in 1901), was a Catholic from Cork, Ireland. The two met when Ruth was spending a summer vacation with her aunt, who ran a boardinghouse in New York City. The family jokes that just about the time Grandma Ruth came through Ellis Island, Our Lady of Fátima was making her way to Portugal.[8]

While Vance never drank anything stronger than warm milk, for Ruth, happy hour began at 5:00 p.m. She was a smoker, played the horses, and was annoyed when priests who, after absolution and having recognized her Irish brogue during Confession, would inevitably ask, "So Ruth, how are the kids?" Ruth never missed a daily Mass or a daily Rosary, however, and refused to marry Vance until he converted to Catholicism. He joyfully embraced the Faith, entered the Church, and was a devoted husband, father, and grandfather.

Weekly Mass was nonnegotiable in the Largent family, and Vance would wake their four girls every Sunday morning to be sure they were never late. Ruth's attendance at daily Mass was a strong example for her girls, and a practice that her daughter, Mary, continued and witnessed to her own children as well. As the oldest of four girls, Mary has fond memories of living a normal Catholic life growing up with her three sisters, Grace, Gloria, and Fran. She never felt a call to religious life and admittedly enjoyed clothes, makeup, and dating boys from Georgetown. Her sister Grace eventually married Bill's roommate, who also

---

[8]   The Blessed Mother appeared to three shepherd children in Fátima, Portugal, in 1917, about the same time Grandma Ruth would have come through Ellis Island.

became a Georgetown doctor and was chosen to be NFL coach Vince Lombardi's personal physician.

Mary and her friend Irene Hagen attended Strayer's Secretarial School, a path frequently chosen by women in the 1940s for whom college was not yet the norm. As a young adult, she moved to Silver Spring, Maryland, and was a dance instructor for an Arthur Murray Dance Studio. This is where she first met Bill when he arrived for the last in a series of his ballroom dancing lessons. "He was just a nice guy all the way around, and we enjoyed each other's company very much. Besides, he had money for a night on the town, and few men did back then!" jests Mary.

Thus began a lasting courtship, and the couple married on August 21, 1948. With both grounded in faith, and with love of God as their priority, this was a strong, faithful union. Bill's first navy deployment as a married man was to Detroit, where the couple relocated for his gynecology residency and welcomed their first child, Sue. Shortly thereafter, they moved to Ohio, where Bill served in the Air Force Medical Corps at Wright-Patterson Air Force Base.

Bill's search for a medical specialty that suited him was a long journey. He began as a general medical officer in West Virginia; trained in gynecology at Detroit's Mount Carmel Mercy Hospital from 1949 to 1950; was resident and later chief resident of general surgery at Georgetown University from 1952 to 1956; and completed a fellowship in colorectal surgery at Stanford University Hospital from 1957 to 1958. After deciding to train in thoracic and cardiovascular surgery at Highland Alameda County Hospital in Oakland, California (1959–1961), and moving his family back to the D.C. area to finish his studies, Mary gently grabbed him by the scruff of the neck and declared, "This is it! No more training! We have baby mouths to feed!"

Mary's parents, Vance and Ruth, lived in a small house in Silver Spring, Maryland, and when Bill made his final move back to the D.C. area, he, Mary, and the children all moved in with them. Vance loved having the grandchildren around and even built them a tree fort. Bill never forgot his in-laws' generosity, and years later, he repaid the favor by buying them a large cattle farm in Round Hill, Virginia. Vance was in his element, and Bill assisted with the books.

Bill's return to Georgetown also afforded him the opportunity to train under renowned surgeons Dr. Charles Hufnagel and Dr. Robert Coffey. Dr. Hufnagel pioneered and implanted the first artificial heart valve in a human patient and participated in the first kidney transplant. Bill was also part of a surgical team that cared for a meat-packing supervisor whose two hands were severed at the wrists by a meat chopping machine. The poor man's coworkers placed his severed hands in plastic bags, packed them in ice, and dashed their colleague and his hands to the hospital. The cutting-edge surgery performed by Dr. Bill's team proved to be a hallmark case that not only garnered news attention but also informed subsequent reimplantation surgeries.

Finally, after many years and multiple relocations, Bill had definitely found his fit amid such challenging and rewarding surgical opportunities. The Byrne family settled in McLean, Virginia, where Bill practiced as a thoracic and cardiovascular surgeon for more than forty years in the Fairfax County and Washington, D.C., areas. In addition to being chief of cardiovascular surgery, he was an associate clinical professor of surgery at Georgetown University. Even after his retirement, he continued to volunteer his surgical services at the Spanish Catholic Center in Washington, D.C., and eventually completed many medical missions with Sister Dede in the Caribbean, East Jerusalem, Jamaica, the Dominican Republic, and Haiti.

Bill was very close to his older priest brother, Father John. Father served as a real mentor to Bill throughout his life and once recommended that he balance his medicine with a well-rounded routine of spiritual reading — especially books by Hilaire Belloc and G. K. Chesterton — so that he would be a broad-minded doctor rather than one focused solely on his work as a physician. Bill took this to heart, became an avid reader of both authors, and was frequently surrounded by books. In fact, he once filled his suitcase with so many books that there was no room left for essentials. During one trip to England, he was delighted to discover a Chesterton book with hand-stenciled images signed by the author and stuffed in the middle pages. So vast was Bill's book collection that upon his death, it was donated to the John Paul II Seminary in D.C. In addition to being a member of the Thomas More Society and the Knights of Malta, Bill cofounded the G. K. Chesterton Society of Northern Virginia.

Bill and Mary had eight children: Susan, Tom, Kevin, Pat, Dede, Gloria, John, and Billy Jr., the baby of the family. John, now an orthopedic surgeon with ten children, thought he was surely going to be the last child in the Byrne family. Already four years old at the time, John was *not* happy when Billy came home from the hospital with Mom and Dad. So disturbed was he over the rude awakening that he broke the leg off his toy camel during a temper tantrum on the day his new brother arrived home. "The joke is that my parents said a novena to Saint Joseph to be blessed with children. After the first several arrived so close in age, they went back and prayed for Saint Joseph to slow things down!" Sister Dede relates.

Of course, John and Billy are now very close — even best friends. In fact, when Billy was later ordained a deacon in Rome, the family held a celebratory dinner at a nearby restaurant. When John stood up to toast his brother, he got as far as, "To my brother Bill," choked up, and couldn't finish. Dede jumped in to finish the sentiment. They are a tight-knit family to this day.

The Family: The Garden for Vocations

But just how did Bill and Mary cope with the demands of raising such a large family coupled with a chief of surgery's grueling schedule? Both were daily communicants at Saint Luke's in McLean. Bill attended the 6:45 a.m. Mass before work, and Mary attended the 9:00 a.m. Mass, after she got all eight children off to school. "My husband prioritized Mass daily, regardless of anything else he had going on. He rose early, attended Mass, and headed to the hospital for his surgeries — seven days a week," Mary fondly recalls. "He led by example, and that was an influence on all of us."

Both parents' daily reception of Holy Communion positively impacted their family life in lasting and formative ways. The couple even planned family vacations by mapping out, in advance, where they would attend daily Mass. The religious commitment and example of her parents and siblings shaped the lens through which young Dede viewed life and demonstrated the importance of prioritizing Christ, the Mass, and the Eucharist.

While Mary was a stay-at-home mom raising a large family, she still managed to find time to volunteer regularly at Saint Luke's for a program called So Others May Eat, an interfaith project supported by the parish that prepared food for delivery to the needy of Washington, D.C. It was in this environment of Bill's and Mary's self-giving and continual service to others that the Byrne children grew and were formed.

Though not a requirement for the eight kids, Bill would entice them to accompany him to daily Mass during their summer breaks by promising breakfast at a restaurant afterward. Sunday Mass was, of course, nonnegotiable. Young Billy, now a bishop in Springfield, Massachusetts, fondly recalls stopping for breakfast at the Holiday Inn at Tysons Corner after Sunday Mass and the pancake-eating contests that ensued. With so many children, getting to Mass required two cars, and Bishop Billy now laughs at having been left behind at the restaurant once. Such are the memorable happenings of life in a big family.

Bill's influence in the lives of his children was evident in more ways than one, and his example stirred their natural curiosity. As children of a thoracic surgeon, they were accustomed to the more unusual elements of daily life. Bill once brought home a human heart in a jar for the kids to take to school for show-and-tell the next day. Imagine their surprise to open the refrigerator and find a human heart on the shelf next to the eggs! Another fond memory includes a call late one night indicating that Bill was immediately needed at the hospital. Dede secretly crawled into the back seat of the car to accompany him. When she finally made her presence known, Bill just laughed and eventually found a place for her to watch during the surgery.

Bill loved being a surgeon and helping people. His joy and satisfaction obviously impacted his children's career choices, as three of the eight — Kevin, Dede, and John — also chose to pursue medicine. Dr. Kevin Byrne became a radiologist, Dr. John Byrne an orthopedic surgeon, and Dr. Deirdre Byrne a family medicine physician and general surgeon. Far more important than medicine, however, was Bill's concern for his children's faith life, and he prayed for vocations every evening during family prayer. "My father was a strong spiritual leader. Every night we prayed the family Rosary, around my parents' king-size bed. Some of us would kneel, some would lie down," Sue comments. "But we were all there — every single one of us. We just knew it was expected."

With eight children and Bill's busy schedule, the older Byrne brothers were the ones primarily responsible for assisting with things such as the annual Pinewood Derby races, coaching sports, supervising young Billy when he joined Cub Scouts, and various other childhood activities.

Daily family dinners were happy pandemonium, and the children learned that the faster they ate, the more they got. John was notoriously the family clown who cracked jokes and made a big mess at the table. But meals were a joyful time of family conversation and bonding. Mary, being a former dance instructor, taught the children how to dance. While Bill Sr. still had two left feet, Billy Jr. was quite a dancer.

He and his mother frequently commanded the dance floor together at family weddings.

Other memories with extended family include an interaction that evidences Bill's strong beliefs as well. After one particularly lively political discussion on the front lawn between Bill and his brother Ambassador Tom, Dede, with great admiration for her father and respect for his convictions, recalls stating, "Dad, I'm so glad that you're my dad!"

Whenever possible between their busy schedules, Bill and Mary enjoyed loading up all the kids and heading to their vacation home in Bethany Beach, Delaware, a two-and-a-half-hour drive from home. Other fun family vacations included visiting their uncle Father John's home in the Hamptons to go clamming. Father and his two sisters, Mimi and Ann, jointly owned a beach home that they jokingly claimed was run by "two gulls [girls] and a buoy [boy]," and they occasionally hosted the Byrne family.

Uncle Father John was a holy priest and colorful character whose influence was not only evident in his brother Bill's life but also set the stage for Billy Jr.'s subsequent religious vocation. He also strongly defended what he believed to be just. As a priest in Cardinal Spellman's diocese during the 1949 Calvary Cemetery strike, when union gravediggers felt they were being treated unfairly, Father used a radio show he hosted as a platform to publicly oppose Spellman's decision to dispatch a hundred Saint Joseph Seminary students to serve as strikebreakers. Father's opposition and public stance resulted in his reprimand and, according to later accounts, made him one of the first canceled priests of his time. Father John's engagement in the public square evidences the strong conviction and leadership woven into the fabric of the Byrne family lineage and also interestingly foreshadows Sister Dede's public influence.[9]

---

[9] There is a possible, though unconfirmed, Byrne family link with Cardinal John Carberry, a holy cardinal appointed to the Archdiocese of

Dede's Childhood Years

Deirdre Mary Byrne was born on October 1, 1956, the same year that Bill and Mary had their home blessed in honor of the Sacred Hearts of Jesus and Mary. When asked whether there was anything particularly notable about Dede's birth or delivery, Mary playfully jokes, "Well, let's see … Susie, Tommy, Kevin, Pat, Dede … Dede was the fifth one, so I wasn't even paying much attention!"

Though not immediately apparent after birth, Dede was later found to have a congenital dislocated hip after Mary noticed that she wasn't walking properly. To correct the anomaly, Dede had to spend a year and a half in a spica cast to immobilize her thigh, hip, and pelvis. Her legs resembled frog legs hanging out of a cast, and her siblings marveled at how she learned to crawl, maneuver, and even eventually walk in her body cast. They commonly rode the back of her cast like a horse and used it as a step stool to reach things on the counter. Sister now jokes that "sometimes allowing people to step on you is actually a chance to lift them up."

Dede was a happy, carefree child with an even temperament. When things didn't go her way, she typically laughed them off, Mrs. Byrne recalls. Her favorite pastimes included collecting empty soda bottles for money to spend on candy at the local 7-Eleven, climbing trees, riding her bike, playing in the creek, watching tadpoles and frogs, and playing baseball, football, and ring and run with the neighborhood kids. She and her siblings enjoyed gathering the coins that collected

---

Saint Louis in 1969 who not only established the Archdiocesan Pro-Life Commission, which incentivized the pro-life movement in Saint Louis, but who also publicly opposed post–Vatican II abuses and other progressive cultural influences at the time. Donald R. McClarey, "Cardinal Carberry and the First Conclave of 1978," *American Catholic*, August 2, 2021, https://the-american-catholic.com/2021/08/02/cardinal-carberry-and-the-first-conclave-of-1978/.

in the back of the car or that fell out of Bill's pockets when he took a nap on the couch.

Once, having found a snake's skin that had been shed and thinking the snake must have died, Dede held a funeral service for it. She further reminisces: "There was a hill with a creek and lots of trees right beside our home. We'd spend hours catching minnows back in the days when little parental supervision was needed. There was very little drama growing up in the seventies, and things were much simpler. My brothers also taught me how to throw a spiral football."

With few electronic distractions, they spent summer days outdoors and rode their bikes for miles. The Byrne family owned the same TV for more than thirty years, and the change from black-and-white to color was about the only electronic upgrade they recall. Their home was at the end of a cul-de-sac, and neighborhood kids played hard and late into the hot summer evenings. With a large, lighted basketball court in the backyard and a nine-foot fence on either end, the Byrne home was often the place where neighborhood kids gathered to play. "Kids would just come by, flip on the light switch, and play basketball late into the evening, whether we were home or not," Sue adds.

The Stewart family lived next door, and John Stewart, now a pathologist at MD Anderson in Houston, has many fond memories of growing up next to the Byrne kids. Four years older than John, Dede was sometimes asked to keep an eye on things. She frequently joined the packs of boys for tag football, basketball, flashlight tag, and other memorable summer games that mark one's youth. They enjoyed a very innocent childhood characterized by the absence of malice. "Granted we were living in a privileged and protected environment at that time, which made it a bit easier, but we were always, presumably, in the state of grace," John reflects.

Dede helped assemble a makeshift baseball field in the park area one summer and was "a better athlete than any of us boys," John affirms.

"For that reason, we respected her. There was a natural deference to her. She also always made sure that we didn't get into trouble and was someone we all looked up to and followed. I had a very happy childhood, in part, because of Dede's involvement in our lives."

Catholicism Was Part of the Byrne Family Identity

John further recalls the positive influence of Bill on the Byrne children. "Dr. Byrne was a quiet, gentle man whose life was oriented very much toward Catholicism. He took his Faith very seriously, and it was very much a part of the Byrne family identity. Since Catholicism was important to him, it must, therefore, be important to the kids. That was just part of who they were." It wasn't until after Bill's death in 2011 at the age of eighty-six that a young surgeon who attended the funeral further shared with the family that it was Bill's great faith and example that brought him back to the Catholic Church. He was an inspirational presence in many lives.

While Mary was often the disciplinarian in the family, the children appreciate that she never publicly criticized or ridiculed them for their misdeeds. One memory includes an incident involving Dede in the fifth grade when she had a crush on an eighth grader named George Franklin. "George is a nut, and he has a rubber butt," Dede teased. "Every time he turns around he goes putt, putt." While other children found it amusing, Mary had to put a stop to it more than once: "That's enough, Dede," she insisted, gently but firmly. At home, Mary explained that "dirty mouths need cleaning," and put a bar of soap in Dede's mouth.

Also in her early elementary years, Dede read a children's book about a Christian family in Germany during World War II who helped rescue Jewish children. The little girl in the story saved her chocolates to give to the people they were hiding, and the sweet story greatly impacted young Dede. She used to wonder, even at that very tender age, how one society could harm another. So moved was she by the idea of helping those in need that, on hot summer days, she and her brother Pat played in the neighborhood sewer system, where they pretended to rescue Jews by hiding them underground.

Once past the low sewer entryway, they could stand erect and sit on the cement ledges between the support beams. Leaning against the walls with one leg back, as if to imitate the mysterious characters in trench coats they had read about in books or conjured up in their childhood imaginations, they role-played various rescue scenarios. Monsignor McMurtrie, a beloved priest, once walked by and shouted, "Are you Byrne kids in there? Come on out!"

Another childhood memory includes Dede's fifth-grade volunteer initiative that turned frightful. The principal, a religious sister, asked for students willing to stay after school to assist with table assembly for the upcoming science fair. Dede was quick to volunteer, so Sister handed her the school keys. On one trip back into the building to retrieve a table for transport to the gym, an older male student followed her in and ransacked the gift-shop area. He grabbed Dede by the collar, shoved her up against the wall, and threatened, "If you tell anyone, you'll be sorry!" Terrified, Dede returned the keys without saying a word. Shortly after the principal discovered the crime, she visited the Byrne home to question Dede, who was so distraught by that point that she buried her head against the sister and sobbed. "Yes, Sister, I saw who did it, but he threatened to harm me if I told you!" she cried. The culprit was never caught.

Dede attended a K–4 public elementary school before transferring to Saint Luke's in McLean for middle school. She spent her freshman and sophomore years at Bishop O'Connell High School in Arlington and her junior and senior years at Langley High School in McLean. Her sister Gloria recalls that Dede was an above-average student and was competitive and athletic by nature. While the girls on her high school basketball team were accustomed to competing against other girls, Dede was used to playing against her five brothers and all the other neighborhood boys; this made her even stronger. "She could punt a football forty to fifty yards with no problem!" John recalls. Her athletic talent gave her a particular edge when playing and led to her being named MVP. "She always had a baseball cap on sideways and was definitely a tomboy," Sue and Gloria recall. "Having five brothers made her very competitive. She was strong and could certainly handle herself." Frequently sporting her jeans and baseball cap, Dede was once even mistaken for a boy when she went with her brothers to the local 7-Eleven to cash in her Coca-Cola bottles. "What do you boys want?" the clerk asked as they walked up to the register. "I'm not a boy; I'm a girl," Dede gently corrected. From that day on, she wore dresses to school every day.

The Byrne kids also belonged to the local swim club where Dede loved to swim and dive. She once traveled to New York for a diving championship and won first place. Her photo is still displayed at the swim club. She frequently ventured so deep into the Atlantic Ocean during family vacations to their Delaware Beach house that the lifeguards, fearing for her safety, would signal her back.

In addition to sports, Dede enjoyed books and movies that featured religious sisters. Four times in the course of just two weeks, she dragged her father with her to see *The Sound of Music* and was strongly attracted to the religious theme.[10] "She was also very artistic and could draw well, work with clay, and paint. She even made a big [decoupage mosaic] of Jesus out of small pieces of magazine pages," John mentions.

My Vocation to Serve Started in Utero

Dede's servant heart was evident from a very early age. "Mom said my vocation and call to serve others started in utero," Sister now reflects.

---

[10] Dede Byrne, "Defend Life Lecture Tour," Saint Philip Neri Parish, YouTube video, 17:10, May 7, 2021, https://www.youtube.com/watch?v=wuJie6JaSJI.

"When you have many children, you can see some are geared this way, some other ways. I guess I was geared towards a life of service."

Dede was always tending to animals and people in need. The family didn't initially own pets, as Bill was not particularly fond of them. The neighbor's dog, Prince, didn't help matters by continually dragging dirty tennis shoes to the Byrne home. Not surprisingly, Dede had to beg her dad for permission to keep a stray mutt she brought home one day. Knowing the dog was scared, she slept in the basement with him to comfort him.

Bill eventually relented, and they named the dog Virginia. Little did the family know, however, that this was only the beginning of Dede's bringing home strays — both canine and human! "We never knew what random person she would bring home for Thanksgiving," Sue recalls. And they quickly learned that traveling anywhere with Dede required budgeting extra time, as she would routinely stop to assist anyone in need along the way. "Helping people was just part of her DNA, even from her high school years," John reflects.

What was it that nurtured in Dede such a loving heart for service? Many factors were in play, but given the Byrnes' generous philanthropy, religious organizations frequently mailed them newsletters or magazines. Particularly impactful in young Dede's life were the Maryknoll missionary magazines, and she would leaf through them for hours. She was convinced at an early age that serving others like the sisters in the magazine photos she saw was exactly what she wanted to do with her life. "While she never tried to be outwardly pious in any way, it was obvious that there was an inward piety growing in Dede. And this was manifested in the way she treated others," Gloria comments.

Also formational in young Dede's life were visits to her Aunt Ruth, a third-grade Catholic school teacher in New York City. During her summer vacations, Auntie ministered to children with Down syndrome. She was a saintly woman whose example was influential.

Dede's high school years were filled with other service-related activities as well. She met a wonderful Catholic religious named Sister Frederic Niedfield, a surgeon who studied with her father at Georgetown and graduated at the top of her class. Dede spent a short time helping Sister in India and found her life as both a surgeon and a religious very intriguing. She enjoyed their conversations, frequently questioned her about medicine, and found in her an inspiring example of how medicine and a religious vocation could be merged in service to God and others.

Probably the biggest inspiration in Dede's formative high school years, however, was Mother Teresa. Malcolm Muggeridge's book on the life of Mother Teresa convinced Dede that she wanted to imitate Mother and serve the poor in much the same way. From then on, Mother had a tremendous impact on Dede's life and discernment.

In addition to having a heart for service, Gloria recalls that Dede showed leadership traits at a very early age. She was a "take-charge person, but in the kindest, nicest way." While there were always many chores that needed to be done in such a large family, she'd see a need and tend to it without her parents even having to ask.

Like all high schoolers, Dede was excited to get her driver's license. One evening, when Bill and Mary went out for dinner, Dede was eager to drive somewhere and asked Sue's permission to take the car. Knowing well by that point how Dede was accustomed to bringing home strays, Sue carefully instructed, "Okay, but it's late and dark. So, whatever happens, do *not* pick anybody up.' Well, wouldn't you know it, Dede ran into a family of four whose car had broken down on a side road, and she just had to stop and help them. In fact, she brought the entire family of four back to our home for dinner. That's just the way she was."

Gloria also recalls a time when she was in the passenger seat with twenty-year-old Dede behind the wheel. Stuck in traffic, they took an exit off 495 and made a U-turn onto an alternate route; a line of vehicles followed them. Looking back, Gloria laughs and describes this story as analogous to Dede's whole life. She paves new paths, and people follow: "I realized very early on in my life just how courageous Dede was. She had a kind of Joan of Arc conviction in everything she did — she was fearless."

The daily prayer of faithful Catholic parents is that their children will eventually become saints in Heaven. Such was the case for Bill and Mary in raising their eight children. While Bill always prayed for religious vocations in the family, Mary particularly prayed that one of her sons would become a priest. Little did the couple know that not only would their daughter eventually be called to witness to the love of Christ as a religious sister but that their youngest son, Bill Jr., would become a priest and a bishop.[11]

When asked if he recalls fighting with Dede growing up, Bishop Bill laughs that he wouldn't have had the nerve to fight with her. "She does things I would never do!" he states. He is proud of his sister's strong faith and her great ability to combine laughter with faith. Despite his elevated position in the Church, the good bishop teases that he still gets introduced as "Sister Dede's brother."

Sister and her bishop brother sometimes speak together at large events. In fact, both addressed the 2024 National Prayer Breakfast attendees in Washington, D.C. Bishop Bill's keynote address regarded the necessity of the Eucharistic revival currently underway. Referencing

---

[11] Born in 1964, Billy Jr. was eight years younger than Dede. He attended Mater Dei and Georgetown Preparatory Schools in Maryland and later completed collegiate studies at Holy Cross College in Massachusetts and the Pontifical North American College and the Angelicum in Rome. Father Byrne was ordained a priest by Cardinal James Hickey in 1994 and appointed the tenth bishop of Springfield, Massachusetts, on October 14, 2020.

self-identified Catholics who, in relying on their own personal ethics rather than the Catholic Church for guidance, fail to recognize the beauty and power of their Baptism, the good bishop reaffirmed the critical need for Confession, the Eucharist, and bringing Christ to the world.[12] After Bishop Bill's address, Sister spoke on behalf of imprisoned pro-lifers who have given their freedom to defend the unborn. The two together make quite a dynamic duo.

College Years

Dede attended Virginia Tech as an undergraduate from 1974 to 1978 with her dog, Virginia, in tow; the two were inseparable. They hitchhiked together around the small college town of Blacksburg, Virginia, and Dede even sometimes sneaked her companion into the library with her.

Struggling with reservations related to the challenges and rigor of medical school, she briefly considered the possibility of a social-work major. But thoughts of her father, his example, and his love of medicine and service had so inspired Dede that she remained undeterred. She decided to pray, trust, and put the matter in God's hands. "Lord, if You really want me to be Your spouse [by becoming a religious sister], you'll get me into medical school," she bargained.

She further promised to provide free medical care to the poor and even documented the deal she struck with God by writing her commitment on paper, tucking it in a book, and revisiting it during times of uncertainty. "Quite honestly, I didn't think I'd ever get in. Then I thought I'd definitely be off the hook for becoming a sister! I

---

[12] McKenna Snow, "Bishop at Catholic Prayer Breakfast: Fauci Perfectly Shows Need for Eucharistic Revival," CatholicVote, February 8, 2024, https://catholicvote.org/national-catholic-prayer-breakfast-fauci -perfectly-explains-need-eucharistic-revival/.

never forgot that promise." Trusting that God would make up for her deficiencies, she declared a biology major and proceeded with hope.

Finding like-minded peers with whom she could share the Faith during her college years was important. She connected with the campus's Newman Center, which provided the spiritual support and service-oriented community for which she longed. Among many other volunteer initiatives, she enjoyed answering calls for Birthright, a pro-life organization dedicated to helping abortion-minded women choose life.

To help pay her tuition, Dede worked a summer job as a swim instructor. Another college student, an architecture and urban affairs major by the name of Jennifer Tulaine, was teaching tennis at the same location. While the two eventually became roommates and good friends, Dede's dog, Virginia, was admittedly more popular on campus than the two combined, and she accompanied at least one of them to lectures on a regular basis. The professors welcomed the mellow, wolf-looking mutt, and he became somewhat of a campus celebrity.

The very small Catholic community at Virginia Tech made Dede's attendance at 4:00 p.m. daily Mass noteworthy. While Jennifer changed her major several times, Dede was singularly focused on her admission to medical school, and her daily routine reflected the same. "With the exception of a short break on Saturday nights, Dede ran full throttle, seven days a week, toward med school," Jennifer recalls. "She was generally very quiet, and it impressed me that she shunned attention and lived very simply."

"There was a humility about Dede, and everyone loved her. In fact, much to my chagrin, all the guys liked her rather than me," Jennifer further recalls with a chuckle. "But much to *their* chagrin, she allotted limited time for socializing amid her intense study schedule. Many hearts were broken, I'm sure, but that girl was clearly on a mission."

Dede drove an old stick-shift Jeep, and life with her was always an adventure, Jennifer reminisces. To save on auto repairs, Dede parked on hills so she could pop the clutch and start the vehicle every morning. Her plea, "Help me find a hill!" became a running joke between the roommates.

But while Dede often sacrificed her own material comforts, she was extraordinarily generous with others. For example, when Jennifer couldn't afford a college graduation ring, Dede funded it. Jennifer was also shocked the day Dede picked her up in the Byrne family's yellow Cadillac convertible that she had borrowed for a weekend trip to their Delaware Beach house. "I couldn't believe she lived so simply when it was obvious her family came from wealth," Jennifer comments. "There is zero pretense with Dede. She takes all people as they are and is the most authentic person I know."

Dede's leadership, kindness, and advocacy for others continued throughout her college years. Jennifer incurred an injury playing volleyball that left her unable to perform several required swim-class activities. Because Jennifer was reluctant to approach the instructor, Dede privately did so on her behalf. It was Dede's charity and genuine concern in the smallest details of daily life that impacted Jennifer and made Dede greatly beloved among all those who knew her on campus.

Jennifer stayed in touch with Dede after graduation, and the two remain good friends to this day. When Jennifer was diagnosed and hospitalized with cancer in 2017, Sister Dede (having, by that time, already taken religious vows and become a physician) visited her almost daily in the hospital. She brought Sister Licia to serenade the patient with Italian songs, and closely tracked Jennifer's medical condition to offer insights. This continual self-giving and love of others, coupled with her willingness to mentor countless medical students and physicians, profoundly impacts people, both spiritually and professionally. "Not only is she fearless and smart, but there is a humility and a servant's heart that accompanies everything she does — never judgment, always love."

Looking back, Jennifer now characterizes her college years spent with Dede as a spiritual awakening that helped her differentiate the truth of Christ from the cultural lies to which she had temporarily succumbed. While many lose their way during their college years, Jennifer found hers, thanks to Dede. She entered college as someone who supported abortion, and by the time she graduated, she was engaging in pro-life work together with Dede at Birthright. "Dede changed me. She awakened a goodness in me and made me want to be a better person," Jennifer states. "I knew that, to be a better person, I needed to stop messing around. Her friendship was important to me, and I knew that, when I was following her example, I was on the right track."

After four years of perseverance in pre-med classes, Dede graduated from Virginia Tech in 1978 and, by what she deems a "miraculous event," was accepted to Georgetown Medical School, her dad's alma mater. She jests that while some graduated summa cum laude and others magna cum laude, she graduated "Thank ya, Lawdy [Lordy]!" and attributes her achievements entirely to God's intervention. "Sometimes, we are our own worst enemies. I never thought I was very smart. But you have to have a positive and tenacious attitude. To go into medicine, you have to want it very, very badly — unless you're brilliant and things come naturally; but for most of us schmucks, we had to work very hard to make it through."

To this day, when young people share with her their insecurities and doubts about attaining ambitious goals, she responds that without God's grace and intervention, it would, indeed, likely be impossible, but that she is living proof that God can work through our human deficiencies.

Not wanting to burden her parents financially, Dede joined the military to get an army scholarship that would help pay for her medical education. While there was limited free time for socializing amid the busy hospital schedule and long work weeks, she became friends with and eventually dated a dental-school student named Joe. Shortly after graduation, she shared with Joe that the Lord was still tugging, quite strongly, at her heart.

"Joe, I really think God is calling me to be a religious sister," Dede commented one day when she was compelled to share the fruits of her prayer.

"Well, maybe he's calling me to be a priest," Joe replied, somewhat tongue-in-cheek.

"You'd actually be a fantastic priest. You're such a good and devout man."

The two remained friends, and Dede doubled down on her spiritual discernment. She found her strength from daily reception of the Eucharist and time spent in prayer in the hospital chapel during breaks.

She was eager to learn from her dad and frequently "scrubbed in" to assist him with surgeries. As a first-year med student, Bill once allowed Dede to scrub in for a hysterectomy. So profuse was the blood that she began to sweat heavily and nearly fainted. After Dede left the OR to get fresh air and rest in the hallway on the hospital floor, Bill came out to question what happened.

"Dad, I'm sorry. I hope I didn't embarrass you."

"Oh, that just means you're going to be a good surgeon!" he lovingly assured her.

But though her dad was supportive, her brother John teased her mercilessly for years. He'd walk by her waving a fan and ask, "Oh, Dede, do you feel faint?" He continued to find it hilarious until years later, he too — all six feet, five inches of him — fainted at the sight of blood as a first-year med student in the OR and even knocked over the Mayo equipment stand. The fall was so bad that Dede didn't have the heart to tease him in return.

Two years later, as a third-year med student, Dede was privileged and eager to learn from Dr. Hufnagel, the physician with whom her dad trained so many years earlier. Knowing she was Bill's daughter, Dr. Hufnagel would sometimes joke with Dede when she scrubbed in to assist.

"Do you even know *how* to scrub in?" Dr. Hufnagel teased.

"Yes, I learned from an expert!" Dede replied, referring to her dad.

"Do you know what an ex-pert is?"

"No, what?"

"It's an old drip! Ex-spurt."

Dede later scrubbed in when Dr. Hufnagel was doing an axillofemoral bypass. After watching what she deemed a rather crude approach for bringing the prosthetic tubing through the subcutaneous area of the patient's body, Dede offered, "Dr. Hufnagel, there's got to be a better way than this. This looks pretty harsh."

A dismayed, wide-eyed chief resident who was also present conveyed a look of caution. Unperturbed, Dr. Hufnagel humbly responded: "And what would you suggest, Dr. Byrne?"

"Well, let me think about it tonight, and I'll let you know tomorrow," she replied.

After Dr. Hufnagel scrubbed out, the stunned chief resident asked, "Dr. Byrne, do you know what they call that maneuver you just witnessed?"

"No, what?"

"The Hufnagel maneuver!"

Mortified at having questioned a pioneer in his field, Dede planned how she might recover from the situation when again asked.

"So, did you come up with a better idea?" Dr. Hufnagel inquired the next day.

"I thought, and I thought, and I thought, and I can't think of any better way than yours!"

After graduating medical school in 1982, Dede went on to complete her family-practice residency from 1982 to 1985 at Dewitt Army Hospital at Fort Belvoir, Virginia. While her next deployment was supposed to be to Germany, the army was also searching for volunteers interested in deployment to Egypt's Sinai Peninsula. As enticement, they offered potential volunteers the opportunity to take a course in tropical medicine, and this caught Dede's attention.

Professors from all over the world were brought in to lecture at the Walter Reed Army Institute of Research (WRAIR), including specialists dealing with leprosy and other exotic diseases. Dede was confident the education would well equip her for the missionary experiences for which she longed. Besides, the more that worldly matters, such as hiking and skiing in Germany, began to occupy her thoughts, the more convinced she was that a desert experience would be more conducive to serious vocational discernment.

2

Sinai, Korea, and Young Adulthood
Late 1980s–Early 1990s

The Sinai Peninsula — On Holy Ground

One of Dede's first assignments as a full-time officer during her army-scholarship payback period was as a family medicine doctor in the Sinai Peninsula for thirteen months, from October 1985 through November 1986. She was assigned as a physician to the Logistics Support Unit to provide medical support for the Multinational Force and Observers (MFO). The MFO was a peacekeeping force that was in the region to supervise the implementation of the security provisions of the Egypt-Israel peace treaty.[13]

The desert heat was so miserable that, when Dede arrived, the physician she was there to relieve asked, "So, who did you upset to get stuck with *this* assignment?" It took only a week or so in the oppressive heat for her to realize fully what he meant. Additionally, she was one of only twenty-five women in the entire camp of one thousand men — and the only female *officer* at that! This proved to be a rude awakening, and one that made her toughen up quickly. "Even if you were only a U.S. 0, you become a Sinai 7 fast!"[14] Sister stated, referring to being the rare female in a sea of men.

---

[13] "Mission," Multinational Force and Observers, https://mfo.org.

[14] Sister Deirdre Byrne, "Preparation for Battle," YouTube video, 12:31, January 21, 2023, https://www.youtube.com/watch?v=GqPb4ePrKVY.

Given her love of the sport, Dede swam daily in the Red Sea. It was common for sharks to approach, so wearing swim shoes was necessary for protecting feet when jumping to safety atop sharp coral reefs. It was in Sinai that she met John, a Catholic West Point graduate who had been a quarterback for the academy's football team. The two developed a strong friendship and sometimes threw a football back and forth on the shores of the Red Sea during free time.

"I've never met a girl who could throw a football like you!" John coyly bantered.

"Well, that's because I have so many brothers!" she confessed.

Though John was romantically interested in Dede, she had previously made a personal commitment to cultivate purely platonic friendships in Sinai, not only because it would be difficult to trust the sincerity of a relationship when she was the only female officer among so many men, but also because she was determined to use the desert experience to further discern God's will for her life. Getting distracted might cloud her judgment.

While she wore her military uniform around base, she occasionally opted for a green, zip-up jacket that her pilot friend gave her. "You're out of uniform and desecrating military ground, Dede," John sometimes teased. As the only woman captain in the camp who also happened to be the men's physician, she would sometimes wear a lab coat over her uniform so that men coming for care would feel more comfortable confiding in her about their medical concerns. "See, I don't have a rank today; you can tell me anything you want. You're not going to get into trouble," she reassured, pointing to her white lab coat.

Jesus Had Already Spoken for Her

It was during this time that Dede first met Chief Warrant Officer (CW3) Jack Cheasty. Jack was assigned to the Second Battalion, 504th Parachute Infantry Regiment of the Eighty-Second Airborne Division and had just arrived on his third Sinai tour. He was a slim, fit physician's assistant who was there as part of the MFO's peacekeeping initiatives and fondly recalls his first interaction with Dede.

When he entered the clinic in South Camp, Jack found Dede, then a young captain, in conversation on the phone, sitting in what had been his office during his two previous tours. He was looking to drop his rucksack.

"Hey, you're sitting in my office!" Jack challenged.

"Nice glasses!" she replied with a smile.

They were wearing almost identical round gold frames. Dede was Jack's new supervisor, and she had very good people skills. Two minutes into their conversation, Jack found her likable, and the two immediately hit it off.

"Some docs I've worked with had ego issues," Jack said. "Some could be full of themselves. Army PAs weren't officers at the time, so the docs outranked us. Dede proved to be a competent physician without an ounce of ego. She was a real people person and was always looking out for her patients. There was one major who was interested in Dede, but it was clear that Jesus had already spoken for her."

Jack and Dede quickly became good friends. He was a master scuba instructor and taught her how to dive. Her athletic and fearless nature lent nicely to scuba diving, and she enjoyed it very much. Among many things, she learned proper techniques for preventing the bends, a decompression sickness so named because nitrogen bubbles resulting from too quick an ascent after a dive can leave a person bent over in severe pain.

Lieutenant Colonel Jack Hook, the commander of the Second Battalion, 504th, was Catholic, as were the command sergeant Major Rath and the executive officer Major Tom Gibbony. They started calling the tactical operations center (TOC) "the Vatican" and referred to Dede as "Sister Dede," even though she was not yet a nun at that time.

Jack recalls that he wasn't the only person impressed with Dede — everyone was.

On Monday evenings, the MFO chaplain, a priest with an Irish brogue, flew down from North Camp to offer Mass and attend to the unit's spiritual well-being. Dede was a lay Eucharistic minister, and the Blessed Sacrament was left in her care between chaplain visits. Because Mass was offered only once a week, she planned and led Eucharistic prayer services on weeknights. Despite being a fallen-away Catholic, Jack decided to attend. "She had a pretty fair voice and played guitar well." Needless to say, when Dede discovered Jack's twenty-year spiritual separation from the Church, she was concerned and determined to assist.

Deirdre Byrne Is a Force to Be Reckoned With

Every morning, Dede and Jack would run three to six miles together around the South Camp perimeter road, and Dede used the opportunity to engage Jack in discussions about his spiritual life. He always wanted to argue religion with her and formulated one excuse after another for leaving the Church. Dede refused to let him off the hook. She insisted that Jack should meet a Jesuit priest friend of hers who was on sabbatical in Jerusalem, as she thought he could assist.

After a week or two, Jack finally relented, and Dede arranged to have Sergeant Bruggemeier, a medical noncommissioned officer, drive them to see the priest. Dede had been to Jerusalem previously and stayed at the Notre Dame, a pilgrim hotel run by the Church. The Jesuit in question, Father Myer Tobey, was staying at the hotel. He was a Jewish convert to Catholicism and also a penitentiary chaplain in Maryland.

When they crossed over into Israel from Sinai at the Taba checkpoint in Eilat, someone passed them a message warning them not to go to Jerusalem, as Ramadan had begun. "[Dede] was obviously suffering from selective hearing, so we kept going," Jack recalls.

They drove north through the Negev Desert, up along the Dead Sea, past Jericho, and arrived at Notre Dame around dusk. The run took seven hours in total. Sister Nora Rispoli, the Italian nun who managed the Notre Dame Hotel, instructed them to park their truck in the basement garage. Given the hotel's location just across the street from the New Gate, everything was then within walking distance.

When they were finally able to meet with Father Myer, Jack was still on the fence about the whole situation. "There was my pride, twenty years away from the sacraments," Jack recalls, "and I kept wondering what I would tell my wife, Christine, an Evangelical, if I reverted. Without warning, Father Myer excused himself and said, 'I have a confession to hear.' As he was leaving the table, he touched me on my arm, and we left for the chapel. The confession he had to hear was mine! I hadn't been to Confession in twenty years. A couple of hours later, I came out of the confessional a new man. This was all Dede's doing."

When Jack's wife, Christine, met him at the airport in Tel Aviv a few weeks after his confession, Jack told her about his return to the Faith. She felt betrayed and held Dede responsible for her part in it. The next day, Dede, Jack, and Christine drove up to Jerusalem and had dinner with Father Myer, and Father invited the couple to Mass the next morning. Jack believes this was the beginning of Christine's journey into the Faith as well. Christine eventually converted and came into the Church in 1991 — as a result of what Dede had set into motion.

"It was a wonderful journey for the both of us," Jack reflects. "Our children were baptized, our marriage blessed in the Church, and . . . after the Easter Vigil Mass, with tears flowing down her face, Christine confessed, 'I've come home.' Dede first grabbed me. And that led my wife, my two kids, and I can't tell you how many others since then [as a result of my diaconate and RCIA ministry] back into the Catholic Church. There is a ripple effect Sister Dede Byrne has in the lives of so many people."

In addition to facilitating spiritual healing, Dede was determined to help physically wherever possible — particularly when it came to the marginalized and the needy. Jack recalls being on the way out the door one evening with antibiotics for a civilian who had an infection. The problem was, policy prohibited them from treating civilians. Feeling he had no choice, he grabbed antibiotics and an IV bag and was jumping into the jeep when he ran into Dede.

"Whatcha got there?" Dede asked.

Jack was elusive and didn't want to answer.

"Whatcha doing?" she persisted.

"You really wanna know, Dede? I'm goin' downtown to start an IV on a patient with a systemic infection."

Aside from the MFO, medical care in the local area was severely lacking. While they frequently referred patients to the hospital in Eilat, not everyone could cross the border. In these situations, Jack and Dede were the only medical professionals around. Relieved and grateful to have found a kindred spirit, Dede confessed that she, too, had been secretly providing civilians with emergency care. They jokingly referred to their off-duty practice as their "malpractice." Dede and Jack were of the same mind. They partnered to provide continued care to those in need and never charged a fee.

Jack and Sister Dede remain friends to this day. In fact, Jack was present for her first vows in the crypt at the Basilica of the National Shrine of the Immaculate Conception and for her final vows at Saint Peter's on Capitol Hill. He even served as an acolyte for (then) Father Bill when Sister took her final vows.

"Deirdre Mary Byrne is a force to be reckoned with. She is a faithful daughter of Holy Mother Church, and a selfless servant who puts others before her own needs," Jack shares. "On top of all this, she is an outspoken, unashamed, and uncompromising advocate for the unborn."

The Sunshine Club

It bothered Dede that it was such a struggle for many men and women in the Sinai Camp to live chastely. To help them better understand their dignity and identities, she began what she called the Sunshine Club. She persuaded one of the enlisted men to lend her his pickup truck, secured food from the mess hall, and drove the women along the Red Sea to a private cove where they could sunbathe and relax on Sunday afternoons. "I spoke to them about their dignity as women and the importance of preserving their purity — kind of a Theology of the Body before I ever even knew there was such a thing. I really wanted to help those who were struggling with their femininity, chastity, and self-worth." Dede, then in her late twenties, was the same age as many of the women. They all looked forward to her talks and esteemed her as a role model.

But it wasn't only women whom Dede impacted. Many of the men in her medical unit were so deeply moved by her influence in their lives that when her tour was nearing an end, everyone from the clinic workers to the lab and X-ray technicians compiled a farewell booklet filled with photos of their time together and notes of gratitude: "Your caring attitude is an inspiration to all of us," wrote one. "Thank you for all the help you have given me in both my work and spirit," another commented. "I have worked with [many] physicians in my career, but none have shown the compassion that you have shown toward the troops here," a third stated.[15] While shared experiences and intense hardships in the military cultivate unique bonds and strong friendships, Dede returned all the glory to God and to the inspiration of the Holy Spirit in the lives of the soldiers.

---

[15] Gabriella Boston, "Nun Serves God and Army," *Washington Times*, January 25, 2009, https://www.washingtontimes.com/news/2009/jan/25/working-miracles/.

Saint Catherine's Monastery

It was also during this time that Dede served as the liaison for the Greek Orthodox monks who lived at the base of Mount Sinai, at Saint Catherine's Monastery. The monks have lived in this location since the fourth century. The site also houses the relics of Saint Catherine of Alexandria, which were found after one of the monks had a vision related to their whereabouts.[16] Dede was privileged to pray with and care for the monks and Bedouins of the area.

The monastery was about a three-hour drive from the base and could be accessed by traveling along the coastline of the Red Sea and then eventually cutting inland, or, on occasion, via helicopter. Dede and her military group would climb Mount Sinai as a day trip — one of her favorite pastimes in Sinai. The Bedouins for whom she cared were Muslim Arabic-speaking inhabitants of the area who lived and worked peacefully, side by side with the monks. The reciprocity and respect between the groups and their support of one another are manifested in many ways, not the least of which is their weekly tradition of making bread together.[17] As such, Dede never felt any danger in the area and found her time there incredibly rewarding.

Dede was initially forbidden from entering the interior of the monastery when she made her monthly sick-call visits. As time progressed, however, the monks eventually welcomed her, provided a tour, and sometimes allowed her to sit in on services that were celebrated in the Chapel of the Burning Bush. This historical chapel sits atop the roots of the burning bush where God spoke to Moses for the first time

---

[16] "Mount Sinai Monastery," Mount Sinai Monastery, https://sinai monastery.com/index.php/en/.

[17] "The Bedouin and the Monastery," Mount Sinai Monastery, https://sinaimonastery.com/index.php/en/the-bedouin/the-bedouin-and-the-monastery.

(see Exod. 3:1–6). To this day, and in keeping with God's command to Moses, pilgrims remove their shoes to enter this holy place.[18] The strong connection with God and such important biblical history was deeply meaningful to Dede and fortified her spiritual longings.

As a scholar and an avid reader, Dede distinctly recalls how the Sinai Library, renowned worldwide and temperature-controlled to prevent deterioration and mold, houses one of the oldest handwritten copies of the *Iliad* and the *Odyssey* on Earth. Theologians often frequent the historical site to view its many treasures, including mosaics, engraving prints, over half of the world's Byzantine icons, and many writings dating back to the time of Christ.[19]

Saint Catherine's remains are enshrined in a reliquary at the south side of the sanctuary and are exposed for veneration by the faithful on special occasions. To this day, they continue to emit a sweet fragrance and bring about many miracles.[20] Dede was privileged and grateful to receive oil-soaked cotton from Saint Catherine's tomb, gifted to her by one of the monks.

One hot afternoon, Dede was called to the monastery to provide medical attention to a Greek monk with colon cancer. She walked up a steep, narrow staircase to the upper level, and a monk shooed away the bystanders. Though she knew no Greek and the poor monk knew no English, "a smile goes a long way," she remarks. After providing needed medical care, the old, gentle monk capped off the appointment by pouring glasses of hundred-year-old cognac that the two shared.

[18] "Holy Bush," Mount Sinai Monastery, https://sinaimonastery.com /index.php/en/description/the-monastery/holy-bush.

[19] "Treasures," Mount Sinai Monastery, https://sinaimonastery.com /index.php/en/treasures.

[20] "Saint Catherine," Mount Sinai Monastery, https://sinaimonastery .com/index.php/en/history/saint-catherine.

Dede specifically recalls one Greek Orthodox monk named Father Makarios who was stationed in Sinai. Father was originally from Chicago and had a brown robe, cap, and ponytail. Because military protocol prohibited treating or providing medication to those on the outside, Dede and Father needed to find another way to care for the Bedouins. With the support of their commanding officer, she and Father were permitted to sign them in as guests so that they could come on post to receive needed medical care. As had been her lifelong habit, when Dede found a person in need of assistance, she found a way to help, regardless of obstacles. She loved her time and work on the Sinai Peninsula. While she was sorry to see the thirteen-month assignment come to an end, she felt strongly that God would bring her back to that sacred place.

Upon her return to the States, Dede applied for service on the *Hope* military ship, which was voyaging to the Pacific Islands for medical missions. While her initial application was approved, the major in charge of making the final selection was *not* one of the military's finest men. Already having tried to ruin the career of another physician who registered a formal complaint about him, the major needed his path forward paved with yes-men and as few red flags as possible. He had already been passed over more than once, and any additional reports could cost him his promotion.

As such, Dede was not the only soldier who bore the brunt of the major's wrath. When he learned that Dede had been previously reprimanded during her deployment in the Sinai for giving a small refrigerator to a missionary friend — the daughter of one of the founders of the American Colony Hotel in Jerusalem, who desperately needed it for storage of vaccines — he denied her approval for deployment on the *Hope* ship. Thus, instead of serving in the Philippines, Dede spent one year as a family-practice doctor in Aberdeen, Maryland, admittedly one of her least exciting career assignments.

Korea

In 1987, Dede volunteered to serve in Korea, where she was stationed in Seoul to practice family and emergency medicine. Being assigned to run the emergency room and scrubbing in to assist surgeons on a vast array of cases provided her with the hands-on experiences she was seeking.[21]

Before she left, a Dominican religious sister asked if Dede would look up a friend of hers named Tim who was also deployed to Korea and discerning a vocation to the priesthood. Given Dede's own serious discernment, she was delighted to make the connection.

When Dede and Tim met, however, there were instant sparks, and the two developed a strong friendship and dated a bit. When she later learned he was to be deployed elsewhere, they made the mutual decision that the separation was for the best, so that both could continue their discernment. Interestingly, after her later return to the States, she was praying in the chapel at Saint Luke's in McLean and saw a man she was certain was Tim — only to have him quickly disappear. To this day, she wonders if Tim was an angel God put in her life to test her commitment to a religious vocation.

As a diversion from the pressure of daily medical care in Korea, Dede played guitar in a group with ten other musicians. In such a large group, mistakes went unnoticed, and she could even sometimes "air-play" through difficult passages — after all, there was little practice time available with such a grueling medical schedule. This worked fine until one day her bluff was called. Cardinal Kim was coming to celebrate a Confirmation Mass, and Dede was the only person who showed up to play that day. "No more 'air-playing' for me!" she recalls thinking. "Aside from the piano player, I was the only guitar player at that Mass.

---

[21] Jeffrey Donahoe, "Sister Dede Answers the Call," *Georgetown University Health Magazine*, October 16, 2016, https://today.advancement.george town.edu/health-magazine/2016/sister-dede-byrne/.

I remember someone teasing me afterwards, asking, 'Isn't there more than just one chord in that song, Dede?'"

One cold, snowy day in Korea, Dede and her ob-gyn friend were both on call. As they were chatting, they received a call from the demilitarized zone (DMZ) that a woman in labor was being helicoptered down. "I've got this one," Dede said, thinking she would serve as a simple escort for the patient en route to the hospital.

Approaching under the moving helicopter blades, she ran to the poor woman, who was screaming in the chopper. The first thing she saw was a prolapsed cord! "Oh, no!" Dede gasped. She quickly threw on her gloves and was attempting to get the cord back in place when the baby was delivered right on the helicopter — blades still spinning.

"Clamp, clamp, cut! I then just wrapped the baby in the warmest thing I could find. I hadn't delivered the placenta yet because we just needed to get her to the hospital fast."

It was then that Dede noticed that the baby wasn't breathing, and she administered chest compressions and mouth-to-mouth as they loaded both mother and baby into the ambulance. Thanks to Dede's quick intervention, both mother and child survived the life-threatening emergency. Nonetheless, the harrowing ordeal left her later joking, "Well, that's what I get for saying, 'I've got this.'"

Sister Philip Marie: You're Jesus' Doctor Now, Dede

In 1988, nearing what Dede thought was going to be the end of her military medical career, she met an incredible Lebanese missionary named Sister Philip Marie, who was giving retreats about the Holy Spirit all over the world. The date of the retreat at Dede's church was distinctly memorable because the Summer Olympics were being held that year in Seoul, and Dede greatly enjoyed sports.

At that time, almost every military base had a space that could be easily adapted for Mass. Some bases used the local nondenominational church, but Dede's base was fairly large and included a Catholic church. Sister Philip Marie had just come from a mission in Australia and was worn out from the travel. She contracted a parasitic infection and pneumonia during her stay in Korea, and Dede nursed her through them. Sister recuperated for an entire month in the little dwelling where they had contrived a makeshift chapel. While Dede was deeply inspired by Sister Philip Marie, Sister quickly recognized and began to nurture Dede's religious vocation.

Now working three or four fifteen-hour shifts followed by three or four days off, Dede began using her free days to travel with Sister Philip Marie, pass out booklets or rosaries, and assist with retreats. Feeling somewhat constrained by the schedule, Dede eventually became an inactive reservist and took a year off from surgical training to complete her medical research. This flexibility of schedule afforded her the opportunity to travel more frequently with Sister Philip Marie. Such were the promptings of the Holy Spirit now at work in Dede's heart.

Sister Philip Marie taught Dede to pray the Liturgy of the Hours, encouraged her in her discernment, and provided much spiritual guidance. She also reinforced the importance of daily Mass and a daily holy hour, which, thanks to the influence of her parents, Dede had readily understood since childhood. Over the years, her devotion to the Blessed Sacrament continued to grow, particularly during the time she later spent with the Missionaries of Charity. She still fondly recalls when Sister Philip Marie, in conversation with a CEO businessman, recommended he spend one hour a day in adoration. "I'm *very* busy, Sister," the man stated, insinuating that he didn't have time. "Oh, then you need two hours a day," Sister replied. Such comments and interactions were formative.

Dede considers her time spent in prayer with Our Lord as essential for feeding her spiritual life. At Sister Philip Marie's promptings, she also completed the forty-day spiritual exercises of Saint Ignatius. This proved to be incredibly fruitful for helping discern God's will for her life.

During her long stay in Korea, Sister Philip Marie gave Dede some Lourdes holy water and instructed, "You're Jesus' doctor, Dede. Use this holy water to bless others." From that moment on, Lourdes water could be found alongside Dede's stethoscope. Dede also began asking priests to bless the IV fluids she prescribed for patients, so that holy water would course through the veins of each ill person. In this way, Dede practiced truly holistic health care by tending to patients' bodies, minds, and spirits. Mindful that each person was a temple of the Holy Spirit, she allowed Christ, the Divine Physician, to use her as His instrument to bring healing and love to His suffering children.

When Sister Philip Marie had finally recovered from her illness, she returned to her hometown of O'Fallon, Missouri, where her community's motherhouse was located. Shortly thereafter, she developed a corneal abrasion that landed her in the community's infirmary. Preferring Dede's medical care, Sister reached out to her for help, but Dede wasn't sure how to assist.

Finally, an opportunity for visiting the States presented itself. Dede received a call from her commanding officer asking if she could medevac a patient — Ann, the mother-in-law of a soldier — from Korea back to the States. The patient had a brain hemorrhage, was on a ventilator, and had been in a coma for more than a month. The poor woman was then loaded onto a C-130 air ambulance with constant, jarring movements and noise so loud that earplugs were necessary. They first flew from Korea to Japan to refuel, and then to Hawaii to pick up and drop off patients. It was a three-day journey in total, and the goal was to land in California, get the patient to an intensive care unit, and then head on.

Lourdes Water in Her Rucksack

Dede, Ann, Ann's daughter (Connie), and about seventy-five other very sick patients were preparing to leave. Dede's requests to get Ann boarded first fell on deaf ears, as protocol granted priority to military personnel over even critically ill civilians. While en route, and praying all the while, Dede suddenly remembered the Lourdes water in her rucksack, dug deep inside to pull it out, and blessed Ann with it.

Uneasy about the prospects of potentially having to reintubate Ann in a moving C-130 if she did happen to come out of the coma, Dede prayed first for the woman's recovery and next that she wouldn't kill her if the endotracheal tube came out midflight and required reintubation. Sure enough, after thirty days in a coma, shortly after the blessing with Lourdes water, and somewhere in the air between Hawaii and California, Ann woke up. She was lucid and, as feared, began fighting intubation. "Quick, hold her hands down, or she'll pull the tube out!" Dede shouted over the deafening noise of the plane.

Fortunately, they were able to keep Ann intubated until they reached California. A week later, she was taken off the ventilator and made a full recovery. Dede attributes the miraculous recovery to the Lourdes water. This experience proved to be impactful in her life and affirmed her desire to continue ministering to others as Jesus' doctor on earth.

Had I Walked Away,
Love Would Not Have Been Conveyed

During one of their retreat visits to Maui, Dede and Sister Philip Marie met Dorinda Sears, a faithful Catholic wife and mother. The trio became fast friends. Dede shared with Dorinda that she always knew, even from an early age, that she had a calling to religious life. Though she wasn't sure which direction God was leading, she was open to whatever path He desired. "The thing that always amazed me about Dede was that it was incongruous in my mind to see such a gentle soul in someone who had gone all the way through medical school, was in the military, and was always putting herself in harm's way. *Passive* is *not* an adjective that would describe Dede," Dorinda reflects.

Dede's naturally strong yet calm disposition in the face of pressure and conflict was certainly further honed in the heat of battle and the demands of the emergency room. Her pure heart also sometimes renders her oblivious to ulterior motives, and she truly sees every personal interaction as an invitation from God.

On one occasion after a church event, a twenty-minute conversation with a particularly difficult woman who approached to speak with Dede left Dorinda asking why she had not ended the interaction more quickly.

"You could have ended that conversation a lot sooner. Why didn't you?" Dorinda asked.

"Yes, I guess I could have. But the message is love. Had I walked away, that message of love would not have been conveyed," Dede responded.

After her time in the army reserves, Dede spent one year doing missionary medical work, including work in India with Sister Frederic Niedfield, the surgeon from Georgetown who had so greatly impressed her years earlier. Sister Frederic was training nurses for a hospital she had opened in India, and Dede was honored and excited to assist. Once again, Sister Frederic's vocation and witness reaffirmed for Dede how religious life and medicine could beautifully complement each other.

Time at Saint Agnes

In 1990, Dede was assigned for several years to Saint Agnes Hospital in Baltimore. She requested the assignment because of its location near a religious order she was considering at the time. A sister from the order had become a distant acquaintance, and Dede wanted to investigate the order's charism further. She was not prepared for what she discovered, however: one of the nuns was reading and distributing tarot cards!

Troubled, to say the least, she sought out the counsel of Father Larry Gesy, a diocesan exorcist who was stationed in Baltimore, just three minutes from Saint Agnes.

"If you had a three-year-old child and the child was ready to fall into a cobra pit, what would you do?" Father asked Dede.

"I would jump in to save the child, even though jeopardizing my own life," she replied.

"The cobra, in this case, is the devil tied to those tarot cards," Father cautioned.

Satisfied that she had the answer and the guidance she needed, Dede scheduled a visit with the sister and shared Father's wisdom regarding the dangers of the tarot cards.

"How *dare* you talk to a man about our order!" the sister furiously replied with a gruff voice.

"Do you mean the priest? Father Gesy?" Dede asked, puzzled.

"Yes! I mean the priest," the combative sister continued.

Greatly disturbed after this interaction, Dede knew this was definitely not the order for her and severed all ties to it.

It was also during her time in Maryland, however, that she met Lisa Bailey Dorr and Denise Douglas, two young nurses who were working in the medical oncology unit at Saint Agnes Hospital. Dede had just begun her surgical residency, and a mutual friend, an ER nurse, introduced the three to each other.

Though Lisa and Denise were cradle Catholics, their faith had not yet fully blossomed, and they were on a journey toward something deeper. The more they were around Dede, the more intrigued they were by her spirituality. As a surgical resident, Dede worked the entire hospital, so Lisa and Denise frequently saw her during rounds. On call

24/7, she would often show up exhausted to assist with whatever was needed. It wasn't only her medical skills that impressed everyone but also the way she interacted with and treated patients.

Somehow, Dede had a way of attracting people and was frequently found praying with patients, staff, and even visitors. Many immediately felt at ease and shared their crosses and concerns. This same witness to the love of Christ dramatically influenced Lisa and Denise and affected their spiritual lives in ways that forever changed them. "She helped us grow in our spiritual lives, simply by the way she lived and practiced her own faith. It wasn't uncommon for her to call us to a patient's bedside to pray. 'John has a tumor. Would you pray with me for him, please?'" they recall.

Dede frequently invited Lisa and Denise to her Fell's Point three-level brownstone, the top level of which she had converted into a chapel. It was in her home chapel that Dede taught her friends to pray the Chaplet of Divine Mercy and encouraged regular recitation of the Rosary. They also began attending Sister Philip Marie's retreats together whenever Sister came to town.

Ever busy, Dede frequently ate on the run and rarely sat down at work. The mandates of juggling so many roles sometimes made her late, as she tirelessly gave of herself in so many ways. In addition to her 24/7 on-call service at Saint Agnes, she worked one weekend a month in the reserves at Walter Reed Medical Center, ministered to the Missionaries of Charity, and volunteered with Project Rachel to assist post-abortive women in her spare time.

When Lisa inquired about Dede's ability to maintain a strict daily prayer routine amid such a grueling schedule, Dede confessed that she employed a practice that Sister Philip Marie taught her. "On occasion, I hold my rosary in my hands at night and pray, 'Blessed Mother, I'm really sorry to have to ask you this, but would you please finish the Rosary for me if I accidentally fall asleep?'"

The Eucharist Was My Lunch

What kept Dede energized? For as long as she can remember, daily Holy Communion was her source, summit, and strength. Not one day passed during the ten-year span of her chief residency without her receiving Holy Communion. She attributes this commitment to the faithful example her parents set for her and her siblings. Because there was so little time in her busy day, she attended Mass during her lunchbreak when others went to the cafeteria. This apparently didn't sit well with the chief of surgery, who voiced concerns about how Dede spent her break time.

"Dr. Byrne, you weren't in the ICU. Where were you?" the chief of surgery queried.

"I left to go to Mass. Why, were there complaints about mismanagement or neglect of patients in my absence?"

"Well, no," replied the chief.

He eventually left her alone.

The Ripple Effect of Sister Dede

Dede planted in the lives of her coworkers seeds that grew and blossomed even years later. Just as she had influenced Jack Cheasty, who became a deacon and, in turn, brought dozens more into the Church, Dede impacted people at Saint Agnes in such a way that their spiritual growth subsequently affected many others and even the hospital itself.

Saint Agnes had always enjoyed a wonderful reputation for its strong Catholic identity. "In fact, we used to direct patients to the Radiology Department by telling them to walk down to the Sacred Heart statue and follow His right hand," Lisa and Denise lightheartedly recall.

But during the early 1990s, committees were formed to reevaluate both spiritual and physical hospital practices. Unfortunately, in what was deemed the spirit of ecumenism, crucifixes and statues were removed; pews were nowhere to be found in the new chapel's construction plans; and, in place of a centralized crucifix, a small art deco cross was to be placed off to the side.

In addition to the manger scene, interior holiday displays celebrated Kwanzaa and other non-Christian religions. Laypeople on the hospital's spirituality committee were instructed to refrain from visibly making the Sign of the Cross when praying with patients, and EWTN was removed from TV offerings in favor of an ecumenical religious channel. Needless to say, Dede, Lisa, and Denise were concerned over the hospital's new direction. "Why don't we go to Emmitsburg?" Dede proposed.

Emmitsburg, Maryland, was where Sister Mary Louise, a faithful daughter of the Church and the former hospital president, was living at the time. They prayed that Sister's intervention might help stop the purge. "Now, *that* ruffled a few feathers, I can assure you!" Lisa reflects. While the faithful trio had no idea what consequences might await them for challenging hospital administration, they strongly believed it was their duty as faithful Christians to intercede. Their conversations about the matter were overheard by other Catholic physicians who, in the absence of a properly appointed chapel, also threatened to withhold funding.

In the end, the visit to Emmitsburg to expose the wrongdoing paid off and eventually resulted in a restoration, over time, of the hospital's identity — not the least of which was an almost immediate modification of the chapel plans to include the addition of kneelers. EWTN was restored, and crucifixes were rehung.

Today, thanks to what Dede helped set into motion, as well as the faithful intercession of Lisa, Denise, faithful Catholic physicians, and new administrative leadership, the hospital's Catholic identity is strong, and the large lighted outside cross is clearly visible, even from the highway. Such is the ripple effect of Sister Dede Byrne. Her bold example positively impacts others, who, in turn, go on to inspire others to action as well.

This was not the only connection Dede had with Sister Mary Louise, however. Sister was a faithful religious who believed in holding legislators accountable for failing to uphold the truth of Christ in the public square. As such, she frequently wrote letters to a Catholic Maryland senator who happened to live near Dede at the time. Given her proximity, Dede frequently served as the carrier to deposit Sister's letters in the wayward senator's mailbox.

Dede frequently spoke of her favorite saints and encouraged Lisa and Denise to incorporate a regimen of regular spiritual reading. Two of her favorite saints were St. Faustina and St. Edith Stein. St. Faustina's devotion to the Blessed Sacrament and St. Edith Stein's strength and perseverance amid suffering and persecution were examples and inspirations for young Dede. This zeal, in turn, inspired Lisa and Denise.

As Dede nurtured the spiritual growth of her friends, they wanted to share the fruits of their joy more fully. Lisa began carrying holy oil in her pocket to anoint and pray with the terminally ill for whom she cared. She became a youth minister at her church, thus impacting many others, and even worked with the radiation nurse to make rosaries and prayer pamphlets available to patients at the registration desk. The rosary basket was frequently empty and had to be replenished regularly because the terminally ill were seeking solace in their suffering. It was common to see even non-Catholics wearing rosaries around their necks in the cancer ward.

Dede, Lisa, and Denise have remained friends over the years. Even after her service at Saint Agnes, Dede continued to provide medical care in memorable ways — sometimes even bringing patients from overseas who wouldn't otherwise have been able to obtain or afford needed medical care. Lisa recalls how Dede once flew a poor couple from South America to the States for treatment. The unfortunate patient's gangrenous leg required daily cleansing. Dede paid for all their needs, changed the wound dressing multiple times a day, and, after more than a year and a half, was finally able to stabilize the leg and provide the needed surgery.

Humility and "Holey" Shoes

Lisa and Denise also recall Dede's simplicity and humility. "She never wore makeup, nail polish, or flashy clothes," Lisa remembers. "Her hair was simple, and she always drove a used vehicle. But an image that was really ingrained in our memories was when we attended her final profession in 2011 and she was lying prostrate on the floor. It was only at that moment that a large hole in the bottom of her shoe was visible!"

Such examples of humility, mortification, and sacrifice were impactful in the lives of Lisa, Denise, and many others. She believes in avoiding waste and making use of things for as long as possible. She was even known to sometimes transport soon-to-be expired U.S. meds — those that might otherwise be thrown in the trash — to third-world countries, where undersupplied physicians were grateful to receive them to save lives.

Other qualities that impressed her friends were Dede's authentic feminism and her example of what real strength in a woman of faith should look like. In particular, they admire her fearlessness, endurance, persistence, joy, great sense of humor, and the way she so beautifully loved and cared for all whom she encountered at St. Agnes. "Dede was never afraid to defend her Faith and encouraged others to do the same. She was not fond of lukewarmness!" her friends recall. "She is a kind of modern-day heroine that women and the world so desperately need right now."

Comforting the Sick and Pledging Allegiance in the Front Yard

During the 1990s, Dede accompanied Sister Philip Marie to Calcutta, India, for a mission Sister was leading for the Missionaries of Charity. It was there that Dede first became acquainted with Mother Teresa's secretary general, Sister Priscilla, a wonderful, faithful Anglo-Indian sister who opened Missionaries of Charity homes in both the Bronx and San Francisco and who later played a role in Dede's discernment and vocational journey.

One evening in the fall of 1991, Dede and Sister Philip Marie attended Mass and a healing service at Saint Mark's in Catonsville, Maryland, where the priest blessed people with relics that Sister had brought. Here they met a young woman by the name of Trish Palumbo who was providing music for the service.

When Dede discovered that Trish had recently been diagnosed with a rare liver disease requiring transplantation, she convinced her to move her United Network for Organ Sharing (UNOS) transplant wait time from Johns Hopkins to Fairfax, where Dede's brother and dad were doctors at the time. Dede wanted Trish's medical care in good hands and knew that Dr. Bill and Dr. John would closely monitor her progress when the time for surgery arrived.

At one point during her long transplant waiting period, Trish was hospitalized with coagulation and kidney issues. She was in intense pain, but nurses were afraid to treat her, for fear of compromising her liver or jeopardizing her spot on the UNOS list. She was weak, frail, and out of her mind with pain, yet nobody seemed able to help. When Dede heard Trish was hospitalized, she went immediately to provide comfort and assistance.

Within five minutes of implementing Dede's suggestions, Trish's pain was gone. "Dede knew exactly what to do," Trish states. This common theme repeats itself even today as physicians who know Sister Dede indicate that when all else fails and when they've tried every treatment plan without success, they send their patients to Sister, as "she'll figure out how to help."

After being on the transplant list for almost two years, Trish finally received a call on Epiphany 1994 that a liver was available and that she was to come to Fairfax Hospital for the surgery. As planned, both Dr. Bill and Dr. John checked in on Trish daily. In fact, Trish's entire transplant team was Catholic and even played Trish's original music during the long surgery.

"It's so odd to see a friend on the operating table, cut open. I don't think I could ever operate on a friend," Dede commented as she watched the surgery from the gallery.

Not more than five minutes after she made that comment, the surgeon, weary after more than eight hours of surgery and in need of a break, asked her to scrub in to help remove the gallbladder. In the end, Trish's transplant was a success, and she kept in close contact with the Byrne family, even vacationing with them at their Delaware Beach house.

Times at the vacation home were filled with love, spiritual reading, games, and big family tables at which to gather and visit. The family very much enjoyed cooking and eating together. Trish recalls that, if anyone left food on a plate, Dede would collect it and eat it, as she believed nothing should go to waste.

Trish has many other fond memories as well. "Every morning and every evening at the beach house, Dede would take my kids outside, teach them the proper way to raise, lower, and handle the U.S. flag, and have them say the Pledge of Allegiance in the front yard." Sister Dede was eventually even featured as a singer on one of the CDs Trish recorded[22] and also sang both backup and select lead vocals on Sister Philip Marie's scriptural Rosary CD.[23]

But it wasn't just Trish's medical care that Dede took so seriously. She tended to all patients with the same love and concern, making

---

[22] Mario and Trish Palumbo, *Jesus Christ Is Alive*, The Orchard, 2010, compact disc.

[23] Sister Philip Marie Burle, *Praying the Scriptures of the Rosary for Family Healing*, CD Baby, 2015, compact disc.

them feel as if they were the only people in the room at the time. When Sister Marta, a tiny sister in the Little Workers, was hospitalized at Sibley Memorial, Dede packed up pasta, sauce, Italian bread, and wine to provide a feast in Sister Marta's hospital room. "Mangia, mangia!" Dede joyfully exclaimed, as Sister Marta's color returned. Trish reflects that the love of Christ is tangible through Sister Dede: "People just feel it. She has a gift of putting people at ease, and everyone who meets her instantly loves her."

Holy Land Pilgrimages

Trish also reflects on the annual Holy Land pilgrimages that Sister Philip Marie led for the feast of the Epiphany each year — more than forty trips in total. Dede was grateful to assist in more than twenty-five of them. This, in addition to Dede's previous military deployments and missionary work there, equipped her with a vast knowledge of the area. Whether walking down the street or waiting for a dinner table in Jerusalem, she was and often still is recognized and joyfully greeted by seminarians and locals in the region.

During her many travels, Dede frequented the poor part of Jerusalem, also known as the Old City, where a historical home once owned by a famous physician, Dr. Avraham (Albert) Ticho, and his wife, Ann, had been transformed into a restaurant art museum. Dr. Ticho was a renowned ophthalmologist who pioneered a treatment for trachoma, an eye disease that was widespread in Jerusalem during his years of practice.[24] As a physician herself, Dede was intrigued by this. She eventually went on to open and run her own eye clinic in the

---

[24] Judy Siegel-Itzkovich, "The Days and Years of the Tichos," *Jerusalem Post*, February 21, 2015, https://www.jpost.com/israel-news/health/the-days-and-years-of-the-tichos-391744.

basement of the Little Workers' Washington, D.C., convent and named it after convert Dr. Dan Finkelstein.

After Sister Philip Marie's death, Dede assumed leadership of the Holy Land pilgrimages. The group stays at Jerusalem's Notre Dame Hotel, departs at five o'clock each morning, and proceeds down the warmly lit streets to the Holy Sepulchre. Walking the Via Dolorosa, visiting the empty tomb, spending quiet time at Calvary, and touching the true Cross are life-changing highlights for the pilgrims Sister leads every year.

3

Three Major Influences and Serving Others
1994–2000

In 1994, when Dede was a third-year resident at Saint Agnes, Dr. Russ Nauta, the residency director at Georgetown University Hospital, offered her a third-year residency spot. While taking a third-year spot meant an additional year of training, Dede jumped at the chance, as it also afforded her the opportunity to work with her father. It was around this time that the influence of three holy people greatly impacted her life and finally illuminated her vocational path: Cardinal James Hickey, Mother Teresa, and Father John Hardon.

Holding Cardinal Hickey's Heart

In 1996, Dede was a senior resident on the cardiac surgery service at Georgetown University Hospital when His Eminence Cardinal Hickey came in with crushing chest pain. He had just returned from a visit to Lourdes, and Dede was the surgical first assistant on his case. She helped open his chest, harvest his veins, and daily manage him post-op in the ICU. She was honored — and one of the only people on earth — to have literally held His Eminence's heart in her hands during surgery. Given Dede's vigilant care and the grace of God, the cardinal survived and became her spiritual director.

Mother Teresa's Doctor

A year later, in 1997, Dede had the opportunity to provide medical care for Mother Teresa when Mother visited Washington, D.C., on June 5 to accept the Congressional Gold Medal in recognition of her humanitarian and charitable activities. Then eighty-six years old, Mother Teresa was in frail health. Sister Priscilla of the Missionaries of Charity contacted Dede to ask if she would be "Mother's doctor" and provide medical care during Mother's five-day visit. Given that Dede was on call 24/7, her supportive hospital colleagues agreed to cover her shifts in exchange for Dede bringing them a medal from Mother Teresa. Dede slept in the room next to Mother and accompanied her everywhere she went. It was one of her greatest blessings in life to care for and spend time with the hero she had esteemed since high school.

During Mother's visit, Dede's bottom unfortunately gained a level of notoriety! Dede was in the front row on the day Mother received her medal, so as to be close in case any medical needs arose. At one point, Sister Priscilla slapped Dede on the back and exclaimed, "She's gonna fall. Get her!" Dede lunged onto the stage, at which point all the cameras zoomed in to get a close shot of the commotion. Fortunately, the mishap was averted, but Dede had to endure the subsequent teasing. Mrs. Byrne received a call from her two sisters-in-law, Dede's aunts, who were watching from New York.

"Is Dede in D.C. with Mother Teresa?" her aunts asked.

"Yes, why?" said Mrs. Byrne.

"We saw her bottom!" her aunts replied.

"So that's my claim to fame," Sister now jokes.

Keep Your Eyes on the Cross

During Mother's Washington, D.C., visit, Sister Priscilla and Sister Philip Marie encouraged Dede to approach Mother with the idea of adding a medical branch to the Missionaries of Charity. A wealthy Catholic woman was flying Mother out of Washington, D.C., on one of her Learjets, and a group came early to await Mother's arrival. Once inside the plane, Dede was able to steal a few private moments with her. "Mother, what are your thoughts about someone like me providing medical care and being able to help in your community?" Dede asked.

"Keep your eyes on the Cross," Mother replied.

"I think she might have misunderstood what I was trying to ask," Sister reflects. "But now I just tell everyone I meet that Mother Teresa's message to me, that I now share with you — that is 'from a saint, to a sinner, to all you future saints' — is 'keep your eyes on the Cross,' no matter what happens. That's a very good message from Mother to all of us, and I will never ever forget it."

Dede was scheduled to meet with Mother a few months later in the fall of 1997 for a second discussion about this idea, but Mother unfortunately passed away before the meeting. Nonetheless, Dede proceeded with plans for her trip to Calcutta to meet with Sister Nirmala, who was the second superior general for the Missionaries of Charity (MCs). On the way to the airport, however, Dede received a call that one of the MC sisters had been hit by a car.

"Please, Dede, will you stop by the hospital to evaluate Sister's condition before heading to the airport?" Sister Nirmala asked.

Dede was fresh out of residency and had received a great deal of trauma training at Georgetown. She was well equipped to evaluate Sister's situation, and she headed to the hospital to assist. She also learned that one of the MC sisters in Canada had recently died of meningitis and that her death might have been prevented with earlier diagnosis and treatment. In her conversations with the MCs, Dede mentioned these as examples of how their community could greatly benefit from a sister who was also a physician.

Despite Dede's convincing evidence, however, Sister Nirmala confirmed that Mother Teresa never intended another branch for the MCs. Mindful that when doors close, windows open, Dede took to prayer in front of the Blessed Sacrament. She simply wanted to do God's will, not her own. "Well, Lord, do You want me to give up the idea of religious life and be a lay missionary instead?" Dede asked in prayer.

For the moment, she knew it was God's plan for her to move on. Interestingly, though, God did later fulfill her dream in a different way with the Little Workers of the Sacred Hearts. The convent, now transformed to include a medical clinic that ministers to the poor, frequently provides care to members of the MC community.

Father Hardon's Influence

It was also about this time that Dede met Father John Hardon, S.J., for the first time. Father was Mother Teresa's spiritual director and regularly provided retreats for the MCs. He was a faithful, humble son of the Church, world-renowned for his clear teaching and spiritual guidance. Given the connection, Sister Pietra, the MC superior in D.C., recommended that Dede speak with Father for guidance about her vocation, especially in light of the sisters' clear vision that the order was not to include a medical branch. "Father, I'm thinking about quitting medicine. I know it's a gift from God, so I will simply give it back to Him. I'll quit medicine and become a sister with the Missionaries of Charity."

After so many years of Dede's uncertainty in prayer and discernment, Father Hardon's reply was immediate, crystal clear, and an answer to her prayer: "No. You will not quit your medicine, and you will not enter the MCs," Father Hardon instructed. "We need faithful Catholic doctors, and God gave you a gift that you shouldn't throw away. God will show you the way, but it's not with the Missionaries of Charity."

"I love when someone is that clear with me!" Sister now gratefully reflects.

The Poor Deserve Our Firstfruits,
Not Our Leftovers

Despite many obstacles along the way, one thing was always apparent during Dede's vocational journey. She wanted to be able to provide the poor with the best medical care possible. This was, in fact, the prominent motivating factor that drove her decision to pursue her certification as a fellow not only in family medicine but also in the American College of Surgeons. The poor deserve our firstfruits, not our leftovers.

By 1997, Dede had finished her general surgery training and was required to practice for two years before sitting for written exams. She moved to California and practiced family medicine from 1997 to 1999 at Ventura County Medical Center, which was renowned for its residency program. She was within walking distance of a church for daily Mass and just two minutes from the hospital. Her time there proved to be an incredible, growth-filled experience.[25]

She also knew Ventura County was famous for sending well-prepared practitioners into the mission field. Hungry to expand her knowledge base and acquire new, cutting-edge surgical techniques for subsequent mission work, she eagerly embraced the new assignment. Given her heart for truth and service, however, the experience was

---

[25] One month after arriving in Ventura, stories of a brave, young, pro-life woman were still circulating through the hospital. Angela Baird, a sophomore at Thomas Aquinas College in Santa Paula, California, had been hiking with her friends, fell sixty feet into a ravine, and had to be helicoptered to Ventura County Medical Center. During her suffering, she stated, "Don't worry about me. I'm offering my sufferings for the unborn." Sister Dede recounted this story at an Aquinas College fiftieth anniversary address she delivered in D.C. She is still struck by Angela's beautiful defense of the unborn and the impact she had on the lives of Ventura County employees.

not without obstacles. "Sister bumped heads with some of the powers that be at Ventura," Dorinda recalls. "She frequently volunteered her services by offering free care to the indigent in the city. Of course, this sent hospital management into a fit. They didn't want her bringing people into the clinic and offering free care."

Another problem was that family doctors at Ventura commonly prescribed contraception. This posed a real problem for Dede; in conscience, she could not comply. She knew that contraception is not a life-giving method and only facilitates behavior that leads to a dead end. Fortunately, Cardinal Hickey was a steady guide who nurtured her soul and vocation. Having a spiritual director and sounding board as she dealt with various standards of care that sometimes conflicted with Church teaching was an immense grace that she treasures to this day. "He was a real spiritual father in this way, and that's what our bishops need to be," Sister states.

To this day, removing contraceptive progesterone implants remains one of Sister Dede's most rewarding outpatient procedures. Women in her current client base consist primarily of refugees, many of whom have been persuaded by their former Central American physicians to have the implants placed. When a woman seeks removal of an implant on Sister's assigned clinic day, Sister never misses an opportunity to evangelize. Furthermore, any Catholic pre-med students who have the good fortune to shadow Sister on the day in question will be instructed not only about implant removal procedures but also about *Humanae Vitae*, Theology of the Body, and why contraception does not support God's design for human life. Such is the experience of a medical student under the tutelage of the faithful, pro-life Dr. Dede Byrne!

Lord, to Whom Should I Go?

After Dede's two-year assignment in Ventura, Cardinal Hickey advised her to return to Washington, D.C., serve the poor, and further discern where God was calling. The transition was an easy one, especially given that her brother, Father Bill, was then a priest assigned as the chaplain for the University of Maryland's Catholic Student Center in College Park, just a short distance from Washington, D.C. Dede and Father Bill had always been close, and she welcomed the opportunity to see him more frequently.

Now in her early forties, Dede had already completed her family medicine residency, four years of military payback, a surgical residency combined with research, and a transfer to Georgetown Hospital, all of which meant an additional seven years of medical training. Her long, ten-year journey included not only training in family and surgical medicine but also overseas surgery for Catholic medical missions in Kenya, Haiti, and Saint Lucia — certainly ample time searching and discerning!

All the while during this period of her life, her prayer remained, "Lord, to whom should I go?" She continued to seek a religious order that would best help her deepen her love for Christ, and she was waiting for the Lord to reveal His plans for her life. She continued to investigate various religious medical communities but found them all lacking — some even distributing contraception. She earnestly prayed for the right fit.

I'm Your Girl, Whatever Direction

An additional unwelcome obstacle at this time was related to her military ranking. While lieutenant colonels with a ranking of O-5 could remain in the army until retirement, the military's promotion system afforded majors such as Dede (O-4) only two attempts for promotion to a higher rank. Failure to be promoted required resignation of military commission.

Hopeful that she would soon enter a religious community, she reasoned that forgoing promotion and its benefits would be an unintended and regrettable consequence. Even so, in both prayers and dreams, she frequently envisioned herself descending hospital steps wearing a military uniform. Though never fully understanding these images, she was convinced that God intended both a military and a religious calling for her life. She continued to question what God was asking of her. "Father, are You calling me to the religious life to do missionary work, or do You want me to stay in the military? I'm Your girl, whatever direction!"

So there she was, around the year 2000, having been passed over twice, when a friend learned of Dede's situation. The woman was an air force captain, a devout Catholic, and a former speechwriter for a secretary of state. The letter of recommendation she wrote on Dede's behalf was such a strong endorsement that Dede was promoted just three weeks later. Shortly thereafter, Dede joined the Walter Reed unit as a lieutenant colonel (O-5) and stayed in the military long enough to become a colonel (O-6).

At one point during Dede's long discernment process, Cardinal Hickey recommended that she maintain a daily routine of half a day in prayer followed by half a day of serving the poor. She received permission to move in with the Missionaries of Charity at their Gift of Peace House, an AIDS hospice in Washington, D.C. She had humble accommodations in the basement and a simple mattress on which to sleep. Here she could help with the sisters' night duties and care for the patients as a physician and nurse. The Missionaries' in-house chapel not only enabled her to attend Mass each morning before dashing off to the medical clinic but also provided opportunities for the additional prayer time so necessary for her vocational discernment during this period of uncertainty.

Dede had a strong network of friends, some of whom offered advice. After one particularly sacrificial holy hour spent kneeling with Dede on the hardwood floor in the MCs' chapel, Dorinda commented: "I love you and would never desert you as a friend, Dede, but my knees can't take this. They want you to clean toilets here, but you are a doctor. I don't think this is the right place for you."

Sister Philip Marie also had ideas for Dede's future, including the formation of a new order that would provide medical care for the indigent. When she outlined a very strict daily regimen, including lights out at 9:00 p.m., Dorinda commented that adherence to a strict daily routine would be difficult for a physician like Dede, who would be tending to patients, intervening at a moment's notice, and making time-sensitive life-and-death decisions. Dede took this all to heart and was very discerning.

Shortly thereafter, Cardinal Hickey phoned Dede early one morning with exciting news. He offered her the use of an abandoned convent on the south side of Washington, D.C. Though the building was in great disrepair, it would at least afford the opportunity to consider the possibility of establishing a new medical religious community there. Astonished and grateful, she moved forward in trust and began thinking about renovation plans for the old building. One thing was clear at that point, however. Given Father Hardon's prior guidance and God's direction since that time, the door to religious life with the Missionaries of Charity had been permanently closed.

Time with Dad

Dede's frequent mission trips afforded many opportunities to operate with her father. One such instance was in 2000 when Dede received a call from Jack Cheasty, whom she had met in Sinai. Still practicing as a physician's assistant, he, like Dede, found himself intercepting some very interesting medical cases in the service. Jack had recently met a wealthy Haitian man whose bodyguard had suffered a serious gunshot wound. Though first flown to Cuba for medical care, he subsequently developed a fistula between an artery and a vein and ended up under Jack's care back in Haiti. In need of assistance, Jack called Dede in a panic. "I need to get this guy back to the States for surgery. Can you help?" he asked.

"Not likely. But how about if I get a vascular surgeon to you in Haiti?" Dede responded.

"Yeah, of course, but who?"

"My dad's the best vascular surgeon around! The two of us will be on the next flight out."

While in Haiti, Dede and her father performed countless surgeries together. She enjoyed not only honing her skills and gaining experience with new and difficult cases but also the opportunity to operate side by side with her dad — the biggest blessing of all. "Dad could do anything!" she fondly recalls.

Another surgery the father-daughter team performed together was on a large Haitian woman with a prolapsed uterus. While neither Bill nor Dede were ob-gyns, Bill felt equal to the task. Dede, less confident but not wanting to object, knew that with Dad at the helm, all would be well. They discovered that her cervix was stretched over her massive, twelve-pound uterus — larger than a football. At one point undersedated, the woman began to move her hand toward her open abdomen.

"Now, Roseline, we don't need your help! Back to sleep, please!" Dede responded, as the nurse anesthetist intervened.

They were finally able to remove the huge mass and save the woman's life. During another mission in the Dominican Republic later that year, Dede and Bill, each with little former colorectal surgical experience, successfully operated outside their specialty areas to save a man from serious colonic incontinence.

Another medical mission trip to Israel with her father in March 2000 was also particularly memorable. John Paul II was making his historic five-day pilgrimage to Israel at that time, the first pontifical visit in almost forty years. Dede and Bill were working at Saint

Joseph General Hospital in the Sheikh Jarrah neighborhood in East Jerusalem. It was run by the Sisters of Saint Joseph of the Apparition and served East Jerusalem, the West Bank, and the Gaza Strip. A Franciscan priest there who was also a surgeon would frequently scrub in with Dede and Bill. The trio made quite a dynamic medical team and saved many lives.

Dede heard that John Paul II would be saying Mass at the Church of the Holy Sepulchre during his visit, and she wanted to see and meet him. The church was filled to capacity. After Mass, the pope was escorted down the narrow streets in a special cart for the short ride to the Latin Patriarchate of Jerusalem. There was a place where select pilgrims could greet or approach the dignitaries, and Dede was determined to make her way to the front. Bill always wore a suit and tie, so he could easily pass as a dignitary or a man of importance.

But how could Dede arrange for the two of them to work their way up the long line? She noticed an elderly cardinal — well into his nineties and entirely alone — and concocted an idea. "Dad, if we look like we are part of the support crew, we might get closer! Let's help out this elderly cardinal. Follow me!" Dede instructed.

Dede grabbed the arm of the old cardinal and began making conversation. "Your Eminence, let us help you. Where are you from?" Dede began.

When others took notice, she engaged him further, with hopes that their presence in line among the dignitaries might seem natural. Who, after all, would intrude upon or question seemingly good friends of great importance in the procession line?

In the end, and with a little help from the good cardinal, the plan worked. Dede and Bill finally made their way to the Latin Patriarchate as part of the pope's escort. All told, she met him four times — in Jerusalem, in Tiberias, in Bethlehem, and during a private meeting in Rome when he blessed her habit shortly before her religious profession. She marks these occasions as some of the most memorable of her life.

Later in 2000, Dede traveled to northern Kenya for another three-month medical mission trip. Each of her many return trips to Africa over the course of her career inevitably presented challenging medical cases. Women's labor and delivery often proved very dangerous. Most pregnant women delivered their babies in the African bush and endured very intense labor. If one did end up in Dede's medical ward, it typically meant she was in acute danger. Such was the case with one patient who had ruptured her uterus in the bush and was brought to Dede on a stretcher made of various kinds of bamboo and palm leaves.

The poor woman was barely alive and had almost no discernable blood pressure. Her baby had died in utero, and she was so dehydrated that placing an IV was nearly impossible. After multiple attempts, Dede resorted to placing a central line in the woman's neck and took her straight to the operating room to repair her uterus. Learning how to perform Cesarean sections on women in remote missionary locations was essential. The woman was near the point of bleeding to death, but Dede's quick intervention saved her life.

For older Kenyan men, benign prostate disease was a common problem, and many needed prostatectomies. Failure to treat the condition could result in obstruction or rupture and death, so Dede needed to learn quickly. Fortunately, a skilled Dutch surgeon there at the time taught her how to perform these surgeries, which proved very helpful for her subsequent mission work in the Nuba region.[26]

It is not surprising that, with vast worldwide travels and experiences under dire and stressful circumstances, Dede formed many lasting friendships along the way. Besides Jack Cheasty and countless others,

---

[26] Byrne, "In the Service of Christ," 73.

she met an Italian female family physician who provided medical services alongside Dede in Kenya and even adopted a young abandoned bush child with severe disabilities. After tending to and saving many lives during their missionary trips, the two became friends and remain in touch.

Baby Dede in her body cast

First Communion

Dede with her father at the beach (in college)

College graduation

Dede in her twenties

After a swim in the Red Sea (left); hiking in Jordan (right)

Sinai Peninsula, 1986

Multinational Force and Observers, Sinai Peninsula, 1986

With a Bedouin gatekeeper at Saint Catherine's Monastery,
Sinai Peninsula, 1986

Korea: Dede playing the guitar (left); with Sister Philip Marie (right)

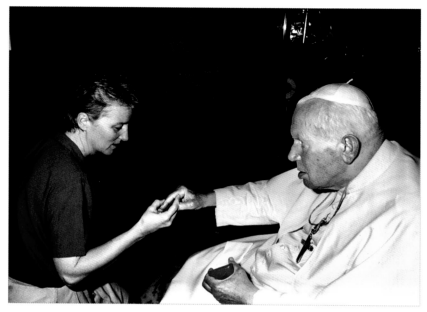

Vatican chapel (private meeting): Pope John Paul II
blessed the habit Sister was soon to wear.

With Father Francline Javlon (left) and Father Ed Meeks (right)

With Father Donald Calloway: two Champions of the Rosary

With childhood neighbor Dr. John Stewart

With Cardinal George Pell and Raymond Arroyo

With Jack Cheasty, now a deacon

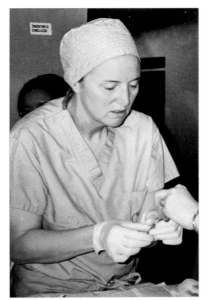

Dominican Republic: Dr. Dede Byrne and Dr. Bill Byrne
in minor surgery

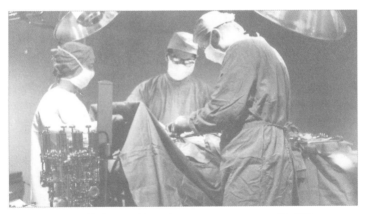

Dr. Bill Byrne (front) in major surgery (1956)

Convent chapel

With Commander Andy Coulter in Haiti after
the 2010 earthquake (Operation Unified Response)

With Bishop Bill and Mrs. Byrne

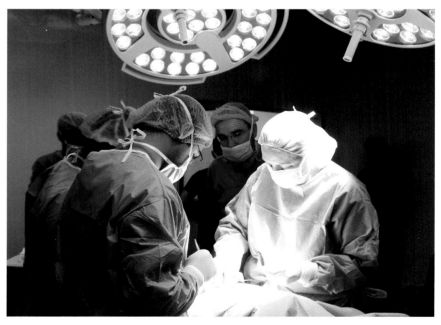

Surgery in Erbil, Iraq

Nuba Mountains in Sudan

At the 2020 Republican National Convention

THE WHITE HOUSE

WASHINGTON

August 23, 2019

Sister Deirdre Byrne, LWSH
Washington, D.C.

Dear Sister Dede,

Thank you for being my guest at the Salute to America celebration. It was an honor to share your inspiring story of selfless service and faith.

As a military officer, physician, surgeon, and sister with the Little Workers of the Sacred Hearts, you have devoted your life to the physical and spiritual well-being of others. In every aspect of your distinguished career and religious vocation, you have brought hope and healing to people worldwide. Your humility, compassion, faith, and generosity of spirit represent the very best of American values.

Melania and I are grateful for your ministry and pray that God continues to bless you in your ongoing service to others,

Sincerely,

Salute to America letter from President Trump
to thank Sister Dede for her service

"I'm not just pro-life, I'm pro–eternal life....
You'll find us here with our weapon of [love]: the Rosary!"

With Sister Licia

Clinic day in 2023

Ministering at the Spanish Catholic Center in D.C.

SACRED HEARTS MEDICAL CLINIC
DEIRDRE BYRNE, M.D.
3620 15TH STREET NORTHEAST
WASHINGTON, DC 20017-3005

(202) 746-7672 TEL.
(202) 529-4643 FAX

DEA # BB 0995768
LIC. # MD21880
NPI # 1144310392

NAME _____ DOB _____

ADDRESS _____ DATE _____

TAMPER-RESISTANT SECURITY FEATURES LISTED ON BACK OF SCRIPT

R̵

Confession ASAP

dx: spiritual deprivation

☐ 1-24
☐ 25-49
☐ 50-74
☐ 75-100
☐ 101-150
☐ 151 and over
_____ Units

Refill NR 1 2 3 4 5

_____
(Signature)

To ensure brand name dispensing, prescriber must write 'Brand Necessary' on the prescription.

♻ 000075

3D10FP0183281

Prescription for Confession (diagnosis: spiritual deprivation)

4

September 11 and Finally Finding Her Fit
2001–2005

On September 10, 2001, shortly after Dede's return from Africa, Sister Priscilla was visiting the United States and accompanied Dede on a trip to Manhattan. Sister Pietra — the Italian MC who had introduced Dede to Father Hardon — had recently undergone open-heart surgery and needed a follow-up echocardiogram near the sisters' New York convent. And so it was on that fateful day, the morning of September 11, 2001, that Dede was at a hospital near Harlem with Sister Pietra. The day that the Twin Towers fell is forever impressed on Dede's memory.

When Dede arrived at the sisters' New York convent, one of them anxiously exclaimed, "Dede, officials are looking for doctors, and specifically surgeons!"

Sister now soberly recalls, "The atmosphere was absolutely surreal. You could see the base of Manhattan in flames, and I walked to a police precinct, where the police then drove me to Saint Luke's Hospital on Fiftieth Street. I waited and waited, hoping to be able to help, but nothing happened! I stayed till 5:00 p.m. near the operating room, but nobody was brought in. There were absolutely no casualties. It was difficult to comprehend."

I'm Sure We Breathed in Human Remains

Since Dede wasn't able to offer any help at the hospital, Sister Priscilla called her back and recommended that she and two other sisters proceed to the base of the World Trade Center to offer food and water to the firefighters. The sisters picked up Dede, and they tried making their way to Ground Zero. The entire city was empty — completely devastated. The trio had a big box of food and got as far as Tenth Street.

With all the restrictions, they were fortunate to have made it even that far, but for Dede with her medical license and two habited sisters, the police opened up all the barricades. The air was so thick with smoke and debris that they could barely see. "I'm sure we breathed in human remains. We were there for hours and hours breathing it all in. Even to this day, I get short of breath. So many devastating memories remain from that day," Sister recalls.

"My wife was here, but she's gone! I can't find her!" one man cried out to Dede. There was little to do but comfort the living.

Dede worked in the first-aid tents, dispensed supplies and water, and cared for and supported the first responders. She tried to offer relief to some of the exhausted firefighters: "Boy, you guys go to extremes to get water and hoagies from sisters!" she said, trying to lend comfort.

Two Europeans in the neighboring building erected a makeshift first-aid station to serve the wounded. Nobody came — not one person. Everyone was dead.

A Jewish female police officer called Dede over to the body of a dead pregnant woman. "Can you do something? Can you please pray for her?" the officer asked Dede and the sisters.

So they did. They prayed for the deceased, thanked the officer for her service, and handed her a Miraculous Medal.

"Oh, that's a beautiful little trinket. Thank you," she replied.

"No, it's not a trinket," Dede corrected. "This is another Jewish woman who is the mother of all mothers. She is the Blessed Mother."

The officer was very touched and clasped the medal to her heart.

Dede and the sisters remained at the base of the Towers until eleven o'clock that night but never intercepted any casualties.

The next morning, New York officials were calling for flashlights, blankets, and other supplies. Sister Philip Marie had been with a group of sisters not far from New York City, so Dede drove there to pick her up and secured five hundred dollars' worth of supplies to take back to Ground Zero. By the next day, authorities had heavy barricades in place and refused to let anyone approach. Unable to assist, Dede and Sister took all the supplies to a nearby church that was serving as a drop-off station. Prayer was their only remaining means of support.

After that dark day of human destruction, Dede returned to Washington, D.C., forever changed. "The world was a very different place post–September 11," she reflects. "The two towers had fallen, and the United States was at war. I felt very torn because I wanted to continue serving my country." Uncertain where God was leading, Dede moved forward in trust.

Head-Butted by an Israeli Soldier

Many months later, Dede returned to Israel and volunteered to help at Holy Family Hospital in Bethlehem. Among other things, it was a maternity hospital that cared for women in the area, and the Knights of Malta had asked her to spend time tending to patients there.

While in Israel, Dede and another laywoman named Sophie, who also subsequently became a religious sister, were in an ambulance tending to a seriously ill victim of breast cancer. Desperate to transport the woman to the hospital for urgent medical attention, they were trying to get from Palestine across the Israeli border into Bethlehem. The Israelis had blockaded the road and refused to let the ambulance pass. Dede exited the ambulance and approached the Israeli soldier, who was standing guard.

"I have a very ill patient in the ambulance and need to get her to the hospital. She needs immediate medical attention," Dede firmly established.

"No! You will not pass!" the Israeli guard shouted.

"But I must pass! This patient will die if I don't."

The soldier head-butted Dede and shouted, "As I said, you will not pass!"

Sophie got out of the ambulance to lend support. "Let us by. We have a sick patient here, and if you don't let us pass, we will call the American Embassy! What's their number, Dede?"

At that moment, a huge explosion erupted from a house bombing in Bethlehem, leaving Dede and Sophie shaken. As the explosion settled, they were finally given permission to pass.

Commenting on her courage under pressure, her brother John offers that "Dede would take a shot herself before she let something bad happen to someone else."

Seeking God's Will

In late 2001, Dede received news that shaped her vocational journey. She was disappointed over the November 21, 2000, resignation of her close friend and spiritual director, Cardinal Hickey, who had served as archbishop of Washington, D.C., for twenty years. While she learned that his successor would be Cardinal McCarrick, she had no idea of the obstacle that would come her way during his 2001–2006 tenure.

When Dede was completing a three-week surgical mission trip in Jerusalem, she received a long-distance call informing her that she would have to leave the Washington, D.C., convent. McCarrick had apparently decided to reconsider his predecessor's commitment to give Dede the old convent. Instead, he gave the building to a different order of sisters and provided them with a large sum to purchase a second building as well. Although the news was another speed bump in Dede's discernment process, she remained docilely open to God's will.

Shortly after leaving the convent that she thought was to be hers, she was introduced to Father Robert Falabella, a holy priest who then lived in the home on the south side of the convent of the Little Workers of the Sacred Hearts in Washington, D.C. Once a chaplain in the Vietnam War, he was now a faithful worker priest who was leading adoration and Mass for the three Italian Sisters next door — Sister Licia; her blood sister, Sister Salvatrina; and Sister Marta.

Sister Philip Marie had recently run into Father Robert at the local Franciscan gift shop, mentioned that Dede was seriously discerning religious life, and asked if he would be willing to speak with her. Father Robert subsequently introduced Dede to Sister Licia, and the three sat down to talk.

"What would you like to do?" Sister Licia inquired.

"I think God wants me to give free surgery to the poor and to offer Him religious life as well," Dede humbly answered.

Sister Licia's face lit up. "That's exactly what our foundress wants us to do — to be present to those in need."

While the Little Workers of the Sacred Hearts comprise about 80 percent teachers and 20 percent medical workers worldwide, the Washington, D.C., convent was entirely education focused at that time. Sister Licia affirmed that medical services would be a welcome addition to their ministry. Dede felt a great sense of peace and wanted to learn more about this beautiful order.

The Little Workers of the Sacred Hearts

The congregation of the Little Workers of the Sacred Hearts was founded in Italy by Blessed Francesco Maria Greco and was approved by the Holy See as a pontifical institute in July 1940.[27] The sisters serve

---

[27] "Our History," Little Workers of the Sacred Hearts, https://littleworkersofthesacredhearts.com/our-history/.

in the United States, Albania, Argentina, Haiti, the Holy Land, India, Italy, and Iraq. Their U.S. locations include Philadelphia; Riverdale, Maryland; Connecticut; and Washington, D.C.[28]

Sister Salvatrina and Sister Agedia arrived in D.C. in 1954 and worked at the Ukrainian Catholic Church near the Shrine of the National Basilica for a dollar a day. Sister Licia and Sister Marta arrived four years later, through Ellis Island, on a naval warship that had been converted to a civilian liner. In 1973, the sisters opened a preschool in the convent and eventually expanded to add a music school led by a concert pianist who offered to teach area children.

The Storm of Vatican II Blew, and All They Felt Was a Little Breeze

Dede was attracted to the Little Workers for many reasons. She was immediately impressed with Sister Licia, who was a very holy sister and was definitely a force to be reckoned with. There was nothing subtle about Sister, and her straightforward personality was well matched with Dede's. Dede also greatly admired the sisters for remaining faithful to their vows and way of life after Vatican II. "The storm of Vatican II blew over their heads, and all they felt was a little breeze," she now recalls. "When they were instructed to modify their habits after Vatican II, the extent of their modification was the mere removal of a thin red stripe from the cuffs of their sleeves."

Dede was further attracted to the Little Workers' rich devotion to the Eucharist, including daily adoration. The need for additional divine protection during the COVID pandemic later inspired Sister to increase Eucharistic adoration to three times daily, a practice they maintain to this day.

---

[28] "Mission Locations," Little Workers of the Sacred Hearts, https://littleworkersofthesacredhearts.com/mission-locations/.

As an added blessing, Mother General was very supportive of Dede's desire to continue serving in the army during her religious formation. The sisters' fond childhood memories of U.S. Air Force liberation after the Nazi invasion of their small Italian village left them with a sense of gratitude and love for the U.S. military. Encouraged that God had provided new direction, Dede was grateful and stepped forward in hope.

Attuned to God's Tweeting and SMSs and Finding Her Fit

Thus, on the feast of the Sacred Heart 2002, board-certified Dr. Dede Byrne began her religious formation with the Little Workers of the Sacred Hearts. After a long journey of discernment and questioning God's plan for her life, she now had an answer. It was when she finally emptied herself of her own will and allowed God to lead that she found the Little Workers of the Sacred Hearts. She points out that the process of dying to oneself evolves over time, and when she got out of God's way, she was better able to discern His will. "It's not that God's will changed over time; it's just that I became more attuned to his tweeting and His SMSs over time." Dede had finally found her fit!

The Power Is in the Veil

During her pre-profession retreat, Sister Licia suggested that Dede wear the habit to become accustomed to it. It is common for the devil to prey on and play havoc with one's weakness, and Dede was no exception. For some reason, wearing her veil during this initial period proved to be a real obstacle and became a source of great agitation.

"My veil was constantly coming off — sometimes when I'd go for a walk and once when I was in a store. It even fell off during chapel, and I didn't realize it. Sister Licia commented on my obvious agitation during Evening Prayer one day, all of which I attributed to wearing that veil!"

Father Bill phoned Dede during the retreat and asked: "How's your retreat going?"

"I'm doing just fine, but it's the veil that's the problem! Somehow this veil is causing me a great deal of trouble."

"Dede, don't worry. The power is in the veil. You'll do fine." The good bishop was a great source of guidance and consolation.

"The moment I made professions with full habit and veil, the problem was solved," Sister recalls. "I could probably have done cartwheels at that point, and it would have stayed on. The devil was just taunting me to make things difficult and put obstacles in my way. He particularly hates sisters who wear their habits."

First Vows

After fruitful spiritual formation and growth, Sister Dede completed her canonical novitiate and professed her first vows on September 15, 2004, the feast of Our Lady of Sorrows, at the Basilica of the National Shrine in Washington, D.C. The Bible passage that most strongly guided her vocational journey during those many years of searching and finally brought her to this day was this: "If anyone wants to be a follower of mine, let him renounce himself and *take up his cross every day and follow me*" (see Luke 9:23, emphasis added).

Sister's military deployments continued soon thereafter. These were primarily stateside missions. In total, she was deployed three times over the next six years — twice stateside and once overseas to Afghanistan for three months. She also continued her military medical and mission work, sometimes as long as six weeks at a time, to Africa and other places throughout the years. While the military showed to her "man's inhumanity to man,"[29] it also often brought out the best in people.

---

[29] Byrne, "Defend Life Lecture Tour," 25:55.

The Military Is a Fantastic Mission Field
Where Many Vocations Are Born

Sister Dede's first stateside deployment was scheduled to be to West Point to cover surgery, but by the time she arrived, she was no longer needed and was conveniently reassigned to Walter Reed Army Hospital, just fifteen minutes away from the convent. This turned out to be her first military deployment as a religious sister. "The military is a fantastic mission field where many vocations are born," Sister reflects. "Many are devout Catholics who go above and beyond the call of duty and continually put themselves in harm's way for others."

Scrubs, Camouflage, or Habit?

In addition to being reassigned locally to Walter Reed, Sister Dede was also able to complete the stateside deployment by working just one weekend every month. This greatly facilitated the marriage of religious and military life for her. She could maintain a regular and rigorous religious and prayer life while still serving her country.

"You're not going to wear *that* when you operate, are you?" the chief of surgery asked Sister the first time she arrived at Walter Reed wearing her religious habit.

"No, I'll change into scrubs," Sister assured.

Her deployment at Walter Reed holds many fond memories. There were incredible trauma teams that consisted of an anesthesiologist, a general surgeon, an orthopedic surgeon, and three nurses each, all of whom provided outstanding care to the trauma patients who came from far-off places. "I'll never forget the story of the Iraqi soldier who threw a hand grenade into the tent of a bunch of American officers," Sister soberly recalls. "They were our first group of casualties at that time: there were other casualties coming in from Germany too. Even if we weren't on call, we were always ready and available to come help if they needed us."

Second Deployment

Sister Dede's second military deployment as a religious sister was to Fort Carson, Colorado, in 2005. This time frame was specifically memorable for her because of Pope John Paul II's passing and Benedict XVI's election while she was serving there. Her Colorado deployment was a wonderful experience. As at Walter Reed, she signed in wearing her habit and then changed into her scrubs or her army combat uniform.

"I mostly just lived in scrubs, but on Sundays I wore my habit to help Father distribute Holy Communion to the patients. I remember once shopping in the military commissary and two little girls greeted me by saying, 'Hi, Mary.' My veil and long habit apparently reminded them of the way the Blessed Mother dressed, so I replied, 'I'm not Mary, but we *are* good friends!'"

Sister Dede found her time on post to be a real ministry. Young couples with children would frequently invite her to dinner, and she developed close friendships with many of them. "There's a real thirst in the military for the Faith, and their faith is very strong. I mean, imagine, they're looking at the end of their lives all the time."

Medically speaking, Sister Dede was like a sponge at this time in her career, and she devoted every free moment to shadowing various surgeons and learning new skills. To this day, she still uses surgical techniques acquired at Fort Carson, including one for treating lower-extremity varicosities.

A Speed Bump on the Journey

Sister Dede continued her religious formation through the years and was greatly anticipating her final vows. With the full support of her community and superiors, she wrote a proposal for a new medical branch of the Little Workers. It was under review for final approval when, in 2007, she received a call from her mother general. Sister was on a medical mission in Haiti in the middle of a surgery at the time, when a call from Mother was patched through: "Sister Dede, we've got a problem! The Vatican contacted me to say someone has complained about you."

Unfortunately, a religious sister who held a prominent position during McCarrick's tenure learned that Sister Dede operated periodically in army hospitals and was about to make her final vows. She had a letter written in Italian and sent to the Vatican with a warning that Sister should not be permitted to continue plans for the new branch within the Little Workers. "You have this sister here in D.C. . . . If you agree that she needs to be told to leave, I'd be happy to do that for you," Sister now recalls as a rough summation of the letter.

"I'm afraid it appears you have a choice to make, Sister — either leave our community or start all over again as a member of our current community," Mother General stated.

Sister, briefly stunned, wondered why a religious from another order would be at all concerned about what she was up to. She had spent so many years discerning and finally finding her way, only to now be met with another obstacle. "Well, I think God really wants me to be with you. Men change their minds, but God doesn't, so I know He wants me here. If you'll still have me, I'll stay and start all over."

The complaint, it turned out, was from a religious who was not Sister Dede's biggest supporter. "Some religious sisters, especially those who might be anti-military, think we are all warmongers. At least, I think that's probably how she saw me. But I explain to people all the time that I'm on the healing end of the wars. I'm a physician on the other side of the battles, taking care of our brave soldiers who have done so much. We sleep at night while they are awake, and they're awake all night so that we can sleep without any fear."

Mother General and Sister Licia knew what motive likely drove the complaint and were fully supportive of Sister Dede. Nonetheless,

Sister was unable to make her final vows in 2007, as originally planned, and she repeated her years of formation.

It was also during this time that Sister Dede met Catholic University of America (CUA) nursing school graduate Motria Lonchyna. In an attempt to settle a lighthearted dispute about whether Hildegard of Bingen was better known for her ancient medical skills or her musical composition, Motria e-mailed her former CUA Spirituality of Nursing professor, who, in response, invited her to attend Evening Prayer and dinner with Sister Dede and the Little Workers of the Sacred Hearts at their convent, just a few miles from CUA.

Motria fell in love with the community and began visiting the convent on a regular basis. While she had previously felt a calling to the married life, she sensed something attractive about the religious life while she was in nursing school. That attraction grew during her time spent with Sister Dede at the convent. "Just by being there and praying, I was becoming who God wanted me to be," she recalls. "You become what you admire. And I admired Sister Dede and the Little Workers."

When Motria later encountered last-minute logistical difficulties related to her admission to graduate school, Sister Dede's counsel and redirection motivated her back into action, and this change eventually led to Motria's meeting her spiritual director. "Through Sister Dede's intervention, I eventually found my way — both to graduate school and to my spiritual father. I am forever grateful to her for this."

Sister further recommended that a medical-mission-trip experience could also be helpful for Motria's educational and spiritual growth and invited her to accompany her to Haiti. The trip proved to be extraordinarily impactful in the young woman's life.

Haiti

Sister has traveled to Haiti for mission work several times over the years. Members of the Knights of Malta invited her to volunteer her surgical services at Hôpital Sacré Coeur, a large private hospital in the town of Milot, Haiti, that the Knights support. As one of the poorest nations in the Western hemisphere, Haiti is rampant with malnutrition and resultant infection, disease, cognitive damage, and death. Sister is always eager to offer her assistance, and she arranged for Motria and her to travel to Port-au-Prince. From there, they took a smaller plane into Cap-Haïtien for subsequent travel to the hospital. The tiny plane shook and dropped several times during their descent in the mountainous region, and the harrowing landing is still a vivid memory.

The well-organized volunteer program for Haitian mission trips relied on American doctors who arrived in specialty teams: one week, a team of urologists might come; the next week, a team of orthopedic doctors, and so on. They not only provided medical care to suffering patients but also worked with local doctors to equip them with needed medical skills. In Sister's case, she was honored to teach general surgery techniques to the local Haitian physicians so that they could operate and manage patient care after she was gone. Empowering local doctors to care more effectively for their own people is a blessing for all involved.

Sister and her colleagues saw as many as fifty patients during a one- or two-week period. She assessed their need for surgery and performed upwards of six surgeries a day, including breast biopsies, hernia repairs, thyroidectomies, colon surgeries, and the like. The dedicated work of the volunteer surgical teams continues to improve standards of care and profoundly impacts the lives of the Haitian people.

As a pediatric nurse in the States, Motria was accustomed to working in Level 1 Neonatal Intensive Care Units (NICUs) where everything modern medicine has to offer was at her disposal. She was unprepared for the devastation and poverty she encountered during her time with Sister in Haiti, where the lack of access to quality health care presented what she deemed to be one impossible medical case after another.

One patient they treated was a teenage boy whose infected knee lesion had so long been neglected that it had grown to more than twelve inches in diameter. With no other medical option available, Motria held his hand as he underwent spinal anesthesia and Sister Dede amputated the poor boy's leg. Mindful that prosthetics would never be available in such destitute conditions, they could only hope to find crutches or a wheelchair as added assistance.

Given the daily usage of machetes in Haiti to both facilitate chores and protect against gang violence, related injuries are also common. Sister's medical team saw a patient with exposed hand ligaments and bones after a machete injury. Such a case would have required advanced surgery in the United States, but, sadly, no such option was available to him in poverty-stricken Haiti.

Despite many obstacles amid the suffering, however, Motria was grateful that "Sister Dede continually thought outside the box" and searched for ways her medical mentees could learn and grow. Mindful that Motria's specialty was pediatrics, Sister encouraged her to visit the pediatrics ward in between their surgical schedule. One young malnourished girl, her lungs flooded with fluid, and her body filled with worms, was in the last stages of septic shock. Unable to administer the most basic of medications or interventions, Motria, via a translator, asked the patient's stoic mother if she would like to hold her dying daughter. Motria placed the limp child in her mother's arms as the poor woman watched her daughter draw her last breath. The mother, who had walked two long days to bring her dying daughter to Sacré Coeur, was then left to begin her long journey back home — alone. At Mass that evening, Sister and Motria prayed for their patients and shared their frustration amid such poverty and suffering. "If we only had anthelmintics [antiworm medications], antibiotics, Lasix, Dopamine, or medical devices, such as a ventilator, we could have helped her. If we were only back in the States, we could have saved her life!" Motria now soberly recalls.

Before their trip to Haiti, Motria had known Sister only as a friend and a mentor. But in these desperate circumstances, she witnessed Sister's leadership skills as a surgeon and colonel for the first time. "She could immediately organize a room, remedy a problem, and take control by providing others with needed direction," Motria recalls. A huge hole in the OR wall that was supposed to have been previously fixed led to an interruption of surgical services. Mindful that lifesaving surgeries would have to be postponed because some people had neglected their responsibilities, Sister Dede was intent on correcting the problem. Her confidence, clear vision, and direction led to a swift resolution that made it possible for surgeries to continue.

Sister was also resourceful and creative in emergency situations—a gift that is particularly critical in destitute mission locations where there is a shortage of medical equipment and supplies. On one occasion, a woman with life-threatening injuries presented with an open abdominal wound. Motria watched Sister quickly improvise a wound VAC (vacuum) using Kerlix (gauze) wrap, Tegaderm transparent medical dressing, and nasogastric tubing to provide negative wound pressure therapy.

While Motria was initially influenced by Sister Dede's love for others, particularly the elderly for whom she so beautifully cares, she is now also struck by Sister Dede's courageous willingness to be countercultural and her humble self-giving in religious life. "Sister Dede never pressured me in my discernment in any way. She simply loved me and allowed me to experience the Little Workers' spirituality and daily routine. That was really important to me." The blessing of allowing her vocation to be nurtured in God's time was exactly what Motria needed to discover God's will for her life. When she eventually shared with Sister Dede that she felt God's call to religious life, Sister wasn't at all surprised and even helped her discern various religious orders.

By God's grace, His continued call, and the quiet influence of Sister Dede, Motria offered her generous fiat and received the name Mother

Iliana on December 8, 2018, as a life-professed nun of Christ the Bride-groom Monastery, a Byzantine Catholic monastery in the Eparchy of Parma.[30] Mother now states, "Sister Dede's constant example and guidance redirected my steps and helped me find God's will during many important, key moments of my life." Not only will Mother be forever grateful for Sister's loving, steady, and courageous presence in her life, but she believes that Sister's beautiful witness will positively influence other young women in today's world to generously offer their fiats in religious life as well.

---

[30] Mother wrote a book about encountering the Father's love amid our weakness: *The Light of His Eyes*.

5

Serving Overseas
2008–2011

Afghanistan — Operation Enduring Freedom

During the years of her long backtrack in 2008, Sister Dede was deployed overseas to Afghanistan as a military surgeon for Operation Enduring Freedom. With no churches, no Blessed Sacrament, and only five priests in all of Afghanistan who had to travel between bases to serve all the troops, soldiers had to facilitate their own worship services. Sister and five airmen from Saint Louis made a commitment to hold daily prayer services with Bible readings, the Rosary, and the Divine Mercy Chaplet. Occasionally, a priest might be available to celebrate Mass. This became a very difficult, "desert-like experience" for Dede — one in which she was unable to receive Our Lord regularly.

The Nun with a Gun: Serving at Camp Salerno

This was the only time in Sister's military career when she carried a sidearm. The joke was that she was the nun with a gun, but she carried it only in case she needed to protect a patient.[31] Sister never had to use

---

[31] J. W. Dellinger, "Meet the 'Nun with the Gun' Honored at the 2019 White Mass," Angelus News, October 15, 2019, https://angelus news.com/local/la-catholics/meet-the-nun-with-the-gun-honored -at-the-white-mass/.

her gun and jests that her real job was to patch up the Taliban so they could be interrogated.

As part of the military trauma center on the front lines during Operation Enduring Freedom, Sister was stationed in a bombproof hospital at Camp Salerno, six miles from the Pakistan border. They often heard missiles overhead, and nearby bombings were a frequent occurrence. There were two levels of wire around the complex, and entry beyond the inner wire required a helmet. U.S. soldiers provided protection within the inner wire, and Afghani soldiers worked in tandem within the second set. Unbothered, Sister Dede routinely walked the inner perimeter for exercise.

The facility had four beds with ample space for expanding to accommodate many additional wounded. There were two stations in the large operating theater, which made it possible to handle two surgeries at the same time, and they were even equipped with a CT scanner to facilitate effective combat casualty care.

By the time of Sister's arrival, the United States had been in Afghanistan for many years, and most of the casualties were civilians. Prior to 2003, no organized trauma system existed.[32] Modeled after civilian trauma care, the Joint Theater Trauma System was established to provide essential care and help reduce morbidity;[33] such robust trauma care capabilities in place at the time were a blessing. While Sister jokes that she had long identified with Hawkeye, the surgeon character from the TV series *M*A*S*H*, her pre-deployment training and Clinical Practice Guidelines (CPGs)[34] were insufficient for preparing her for

---

[32] Donald Trunkey et al., *Military Trauma System Review US Central Command* (2010), 9, https://jts.health.mil/assets/docs/assessments/Afghan-Trauma-System-Review-18-Mar-2010.pdf.

[33] Trunkey et al., "Military Trauma System," 5.

[34] "Clinical Practice Guidelines — Joint Trauma System," Department of Defense Center of Excellence for Trauma, https://jts.health.mil/index.cfm/PI_CPGs/cpgs.

the devastation she encountered, the worst of which was routinely performing surgery on maimed six- to twelve-year-old children.

"We had kids playing with what they thought were flying saucers but were really Russian land mines. They'd arrive with blown-up arms and legs. It was just awful. One patient was out in the field and a missile misfired. The flare ricocheted and went right through his head. Sadly, he was dead on arrival."

One of Sister's long-term wound patients was a woman whose legs had been amputated after a bombing. Deeming the crippled patient no longer useful as a wife or mother, the woman's husband abandoned her, leaving her devoted brother to carry her around everywhere they went. Moved by the suffering of the faithful woman and commitment of her brother, Sister Dede called Sister Licia for permission to purchase a wheelchair for the woman. Sister's seemingly simple solution and intervention completely changed the lives of both the patient and her brother. To this day, she recalls this simple story as transformative: "We take so much for granted, while others suffer so deeply."

While facing life-and-death situations on a daily basis both strengthened and formed Sister Dede, the loss of U.S. soldiers was particularly devastating. One of her compatriots had died, and they were flying his body back to his family in the United States. The pilots stopped at Sister's base for the night to rest and refuel. The chilling intercom alert, forever burned in her memory, signaled soldiers on the base to honor their fallen. Soldiers lined the streets on both sides and saluted as the casket was carried to the morgue for the night. For just a moment, the world stopped to mourn the loss.

The oddity of being a Catholic sister and soldier in a country composed almost entirely of Muslims was also no small curiosity and afforded many unique opportunities for Sister to share her faith. While the Americans were forbidden to initiate conversations about their faith, when inquisitive Afghans who had never met a Christian, let alone a Catholic nun, commented on her kindness, she was able to explain her role as a Catholic sister and provide a reason for the hope within her (see 1 Pet. 3:15).

"You seem different," one of the Muslim physicians with whom she was working commented.

"Well, I'm a Catholic sister. So was Mother Teresa. Do you know who Mother Teresa is or what a sister is?"

Surprised that her colleague had heard neither of Mother Teresa nor of religious sisters, Sister shared a bit more.

"That's amazing! I've never heard of that," the physician replied.

"For those who don't know Christ, it's meaningless to tell them that I am married to Christ," Sister later explained. "Instead, I give a simpler explanation. I say that I have given my life to God and that I serve everyone He brings to me. That's often all that's needed to open their hearts."

Called to Be a Fifth Gospel

While Sister experienced incredibly devastating traumas of the Afghan people, she also witnessed many beautiful things. Her daily prayer services steadily attracted more and more soldiers who came to pray, find comfort amid such suffering, and invoke God's protection of their compatriots and ministering priests who were continually in harm's way.

So moved were others in the camp who witnessed the phenomena that by the end of her three-month stay, more than a hundred others were joining them in daily prayer, and locals even began converting to Catholicism. Some of the converts weren't even previously Christian! "This was an affirmation for me that we are all made for love. And the ultimate [object] of this love is Our Lord. For people who may be thirsty for the love of God, we may be their only fifth Gospel," Sister Dede states.

Hearts so desperate for the love of Christ had found it in the work and fruit of Sister's hands, and they simply wanted what she had. As she ministered both physically and spiritually to hurting people, hers were the hands and feet of Jesus.

After having seen several war fronts, Sister Dede finally retired from the army in 2009 with the rank of colonel (O-6). Sister Colonel Byrne was honored to have served beside so many incredible men and women in the military and devoted more than twenty-nine years of dedicated service to her country.

Nuba Mountains

Later in 2010, Sister embarked upon her first trip as a missionary surgeon to Gidel, a town in the Nuba Mountains in South Sudan. She traveled there three times — in 2010, 2011, and 2013 — not only to serve Christ in the hidden disguise of the poor[35] but also to assist and relieve her Catholic physician friend Dr. Tom Catena, a lay missionary who is the medical director of the Mother of Mercy Hospital and has devoted his life to providing medical care for the suffering and forgotten Nuba people.[36] The dangerous, war-torn region, rife with bombings, dangerous fauna, malnutrition, and rampant disease, is not for the faint of heart.

"Where Mother of Mercy [Hospital] is situated, the terrain is dry, desert-like, and it at times experiences extremely heavy rainfall — torrential, in fact. It is infested with horrible snakes, scorpions that love to hang out in one's boots, and mosquitoes and the malaria they spread. It is not easy to endure physically, but people are generous and grateful," Sister states.[37]

---

[35] Donahoe, "Sister Dede Answers the Call."

[36] "Everything You Need to Know about Dr. Tom," Catholic Medical Mission Board, https://cmmb.org/everything-you-need-to-know-about-dr-tom/.

[37] Byrne, "In the Service of Christ," 71.

Dr. Tom first met Sister Dede when their time working in northern Kenya overlapped in the early 2000s. She arrived in the town of Kakuma to relieve Dr. Kevin Flanagan, and Dr. Tom, a physician but not yet a surgeon, had flown in to assist. Given his desire to serve more effectively, Sister Dede patiently taught him the surgical skills and techniques most needed for missionary work. When he shared his particular desire to minister in the Sudan, Sister connected him with Bishop Gassis of the El Obeid Diocese, who was building a hospital there. As such, Dr. Tom credits Sister for his presence and ministry in the Nuba Mountains to this day.

"If it wasn't for Sister Dede, I wouldn't be here now. Arriving in her white habit from head to toe, she is like an angel from heaven. The staff absolutely love her and always ask when she is coming back. They're happy to see me leave if it means they can see Sister Dede when she comes to relieve me," Dr. Tom laughs.

Bishop Gassis, now deceased, had a real heart for the local people and believed providing exemplary medical care was essential. People walk for days to get to Mother of Mercy, as transportation is scarce. Still others travel by bicycle or donkey. It is considered the medical heart of Sudan and, in particular, of the mid-Nuba Mountains.[38]

Mother of Mercy treats more than 167,000 patients (160,000 outpatients and 7,000 inpatients) and performs 2,100 surgeries each year.[39] Given that Dr. Tom is the only physician providing care for the neighboring one million people, the hospital is always busy, and he

---

[38] "Help Dr. Tom Save Lives in the Nuba Mountains," African Mission Healthcare, https://www.healthfornuba.com.

[39] Francesca Pollio Fenton, "This Catholic Doctor Provides Care for 1 Million People in Sudan, South Sudan," EWTN Great Britain, April 28, 2022, https://ewtn.co.uk/article-this-catholic-doctor-provides-care -for-1-million-people-in-sudan-south-sudan/.

has seen as many as 400 patients in a day.[40] For the patients who travel from the north, almost all of whom are Muslim, the loving care they receive from providers such as Dr. Tom and Sister Dede is often their first encounter with a Christian.[41]

While they received primarily non-trauma patients at this time in 2010, they treated very difficult cases and serious illnesses such as malaria, pneumonia, and enteric disease that led to diarrhea and dehydration. All of this resulted in a significant loss of life — sometimes as many as two or three children a week.[42] Interventions ran the gamut from simple to complex, and patients were incredibly grateful for Sister's care. So indebted was one man that he couldn't stop hugging Sister after she provided surgical relief from his hemorrhoidal affliction.

When serious problems arose, however, they were heartbreaking. The loss of a patient is difficult for any surgeon to endure, and Sister is no exception. Such was the sad case of a five-year-old boy who ingested raw meat, which resulted in a stomach full of worms. So severe was the obstruction that during the nurse anesthetist's procedure for intubating the patient, a worm crawled out of his esophagus, flipped into his trachea, and fully obstructed his airway. Sadly, Sister's rigorous intervention was insufficient for clearing the many long worms, some several feet in length, that eventually suffocated the young boy.

Sister loved ministering to the simple indigenous people, and they quickly grew to know and love her in return. Such was their admiration

---

[40] "Help Dr. Tom."
[41] "A Catholic Doctor Helping a Million People in Sudan and South Sudan," *EWTN News Nightly*, April 27, 2022, YouTube video, https://www.youtube.com/watch?v=HZJrBZr3_yM.
[42] Byrne, "In the Service of Christ," 66.

that when the time for her departure arrived, the workers lined the streets to wave goodbye as her truck drove away.[43]

When Sister returned to Nuba for a second time in 2011, a civil war had broken out that radically changed the dynamic. Many of the Nuba people had fought and long identified with the southern rebels in the Second Sudanese Civil War, which ended in 2005. Now, years later, because of armed conflicts between the Sudanese Army and the Sudan People's Liberation Movement in South Sudan's fight for independence,[44] the hospital was receiving "many penetrating trauma victims as a result of the daily bombings of civilian areas."[45] Sister was left to reconstruct those who arrived with missing limbs or pieces of their face dangling from their heads.

Shrapnel bombs would purposefully be dropped, often on Sunday afternoons. They'd explode a foot above the ground and cause slicing and dicing of faces and hands. Many of the casualties were women and children who were simply walking outside after weekly church services. "Some would carry their severed limbs in their cars or arrive with dangling limbs; we'd have to either repair or remove the piece of body," Sister grimly recounts.

The devastated, bombed areas and additional political tension made traveling very difficult and dangerous. Instead of a direct route to Gidel, Sister was redirected to the Yida refugee camp, which not only meant an additional ten-hour harrowing drive over dangerous roads but also required staying in the rat- and malaria-infested diocesan compound.[46]

---

[43] Byrne, "In the Service of Christ," 67.

[44] Paul Jeffrey, "Church Leaders in Sudan's Nuba Mountains Say They Support the People," *National Catholic Reporter*, July 19, 2018, https://www.ncronline.org/news/church-leaders-sudans-nuba-mountains-say-they-support-people.

[45] Byrne, "In the Service of Christ," 67.

[46] Byrne, "In the Service of Christ," 68, 69.

Given that the north was known for bombing vehicles, Sister was grateful for their "lousy aim."[47]

Spina Bifida Repair for Dummies

Sister Dede's overseas missionary work provided on-the-job training in many specialties, and she was able to see and treat many conditions that she might not have otherwise encountered in the United States. In the heat of battle or an emergency situation in remote areas, she quickly learned that it is God who is really in control. She is simply happy to be an instrument in His hands, as her hero, Mother Teresa, was fond of saying.

One memorable case involved a young man who ran into the hospital holding a tiny bundle wrapped in his arms. When Sister opened the tightly wrapped blanket, spinal fluid squirted out. The poor young child had spina bifida.

"That definitely ruined my morning!" Sister reflects. She was not a neurosurgeon and had to think quickly.

"I got the nurse to admit him onto the ward. I e-mailed a neurosurgeon I knew back in the States, told him I had a big problem, and asked for his help. His response could have essentially been titled 'Spina Bifida Repair for Dummies.' In it, he explained, step by step, what to do. I learned on the spot and ended up doing neurosurgery!"

Physicians in remote missionary places must be prepared to help with whatever situation arises, and specialties are of little consequence. In addition to critical bomb-related injuries, Sister would have faced everything from C-sections to strangulated intestinal hernias, ruptured tubal pregnancies, and other life-threatening cases. Based on the emergent need at that moment, the doctor facing a life-or-death situation automatically becomes the neurologist, the ob-gyn, the orthopedic doctor, or the ENT doctor on call.

---

[47] Byrne, "In the Service of Christ," 68.

I'm Sorry, but You Can't Have Your Blood Back

One real obstacle for providing adequate medical care in the Sudan was responding to cultural beliefs at odds with treatment plans. For example, native women with breast cancer might resist surgery for fear of losing a body part. Similarly, overcoming religious taboos about blood donation left Sister constantly trying to replenish the depleted blood banks. Some believed that giving blood would result in death, others that any forthcoming good luck would be diverted to the new blood recipient. Some donors even later returned to demand their blood back. Sister routinely explained how bone marrow works to replenish blood and how replacing their donated blood was impossible.

A patient who arrived with an open femur fracture was severely anemic and in need of blood and a leg amputation. Not one of the four sons who accompanied him to Mother of Mercy was willing to donate blood, for fear of dying himself, and nothing Sister Dede said could convince them otherwise. The poor man died shortly after his admission.[48]

While there were many devastating experiences in Nuba, there were also beautiful ones. For example, Sister fondly recalls Mass under what the bishop dubbed the "Sudanese cathedral." This was essentially a big outdoor area with a canopy of enormous trees that became the location for celebrating Mass. Sister typically lived in scrubs because of her many surgeries. On Sundays, however, she also wore her white veil while making rounds quickly through the hospital before going to Mass. As for the locals, they donned festive colors and costumes for the tribal dances they added to the celebration.

In sum, Sister made a huge impact on the staff, patients, sisters, and priests in Nuba, and there was an instant bond between all of them.

---

[48] Byrne, "In the Service of Christ," 74.

"Catholics here are very pious and faithfully adhere to the teachings of the Church. There is no funny business or progressivism. Sister Dede is straightforward and disciplined, and people here really love that about her," Dr. Tom confirms.

When asked what most impresses him about Sister, Dr. Tom comments, "She has really bolstered my faith and that of so many others. She's dogmatic, but in the best possible way. I love that she's also the most honest and plainspoken person I know. She knows and believes what is true and is not afraid to proclaim it. There aren't many in the world willing to do that. It's a matter of courage, and I admire that."

Operation Unified Response

The Haiti earthquake of January 12, 2010, was estimated to be the worst modern disaster on record. The impoverished nation is vulnerable to natural disaster, and the 7.0 magnitude earthquake, whose epicenter was just fifteen miles from the densely populated city of Port-au-Prince, took hundreds of thousands of lives and left nearly an equal number of others injured.[49] Sister Dede was among many from all over the world who offered humanitarian aid, and the United States military's response was dubbed Operation Unified Response.

The MCs operate several centers in Haiti, one of which is an orphanage that cares for malnourished children whose parents can no longer afford to care for them. When the MCs called Sister Dede and mentioned the great need for assistance after the disaster, she arranged to connect with a group of medical professionals in Florida for travel to Port-au-Prince.

---

[49] Matthew Keith Charalambos Arnaouti et al., "Medical Disaster Response: A Critical Analysis of the 2010 Haiti Earthquake," *Front Public Health* 10 (November 2022), National Library of Medicine, https://www.ncbi.nlm.nih.gov/pmc/articles/PMC9665839/.

The capital's airport had been transformed into a makeshift receiving area. Cots were set up, and the tented areas were decorated to make them as welcoming as possible for the countless children who were brought for care.

The presence of the medical teams also attracted parents from the mountain areas of Haiti who were desperate for medical attention for their children with chronic health problems. For example, Sister saw severe cases of hydrocephalus, a disease that disproportionately affects children in the developing world.[50]

Officials worked to keep people out of dangerous buildings whose structures had been compromised by large cracks, which, coupled with the hundreds of thousands of already displaced people, added to the large numbers of those wandering the streets. Sister partnered with another physician to assemble a makeshift clinic to assess and prepare patients in need of surgery.

"Countries all over the world were sending entire medical teams of twenty or thirty people at a time," Sister reflects. They erected their nation's flag outside their respective tents, and the outpouring of global humanitarian efforts and camaraderie in the midst of such horrific suffering was moving. Among other things, Sister triaged patients, dressed wounds, and prepared them for a team of surgeons arriving from the Netherlands.

It was at this time that Sister met (then) U.S. Army Captain Andy Coulter. Both graduates of Virginia Tech, they were happy to have made the connection. Andy was a commander of the airborne troops with the Eighty-Second Airborne Division, based out of North Carolina, when the earthquake hit Haiti. Originally scheduled to be

[50] Michael Ragheb et al., "Epidemiology of Pediatric Hydrocephalus in Haiti: Analysis of a Surgical Case Series," *Journal of Neurosurgery* 23, no. 5 (February 2019), https://thejns.org/pediatrics/view/journals/j-neurosurg-pediatr/23/5/article-p568.xml.

deployed to Afghanistan, Andy and his division boarded a C-130, headed for Port-au-Prince airport, and arrived within forty-eight hours of the disaster. This is where he first met Sister. "The hospital ship is coming to provide additional relief," Andy commented to Sister. "But if there is something you can do to help us stabilize patients until we can get them to the ship, we could sure use the help." Sister was eager to assist.

"The suffering in Haiti was the worst human suffering I have ever seen in my life," Andy now reflects. "The state of daily living there, even in areas untouched by the quake, was worse than a war zone." He explains that, even before the disaster, many of the mountainside people were living under nothing more than a tarp held up by four poles. Assigned to cover shelter distribution after the quake, he recalls locals fighting over the tents he was giving away because they were vastly superior to the tarps under which residents had been living.

While Sister found lodging at an MC convent during her missionary stay and provided medical support in the area, Andy relocated to a farm, where he lived in a horse stable for three months and was assigned to logistical assessment, food and shelter distribution, sanitation support, and mapping of displaced people. He crossed paths with Sister several times during Operation Unified Response.

"People were wandering the streets with wound dressings on which a date had been written in marker: it was the last date that their dressing had been changed," Sister recalls. When she encountered a patient in need of a dressing change, she irrigated and cleaned the wound and marked the new date on the fresh dressing. Such was the case of one poor man who came to her with missing digits and whose dressing date revealed he was long overdue for a change.

As for Andy, part of his sanitation tracking responsibilities included following medical waste trucks to a garbage dump outside Port-au-Prince. It wasn't until one of the steel dump-truck baskets hit forty-five degrees upon emptying that he saw children falling out onto the piles of human remains, limbs, hypodermic needles, dirty wound dressings, and the like. He was stunned to learn that local children rode the waste trucks as a form of entertainment.

"When I think of nuns, I think of demure, quiet, reserved women," Andy, now a lieutenant colonel, comments. "But that won't cut it in the army. What struck me immediately was Sister's strong leadership. As a full-bird colonel, she outranked me several times over back then! She was organized and got things done!" He further reflects on Sister's versatility and the many "tools" she had at her disposal. "Her compassion as a sister combined with her leadership and ability to handle things logistically equipped her to adjust to any circumstance, based on the need at the moment. Cool lady!"

6

Final Vows and Continued Mission Work
2011–2019

On August 21, 2011, after a long journey of searching, discerning, and backtracking, Sister made her final vows at the age of forty-five. It was also the feast day of Our Lady of Knock and her parents' wedding anniversary, so the day held further special significance.

She chose the religious name Sister Deirdre of the Most Blessed Sacrament, modeled after the saint she so highly esteemed, Sister Faustina of the Blessed Sacrament. "The name was a natural fit," Sister reflects. "I found that many of my prayers over the years were clarified before the Blessed Sacrament. The Little Workers' founder, Monsignor Francesco Greco, also once stated, 'It was before the most Blessed Sacrament that I found the love of Jesus and the power of that love.' This also influenced my name choice."

A Fourth Vow: Free, Loving
Medical Care for the Poor

While Sister professed the customary formal vows of poverty, chastity, and obedience, she also took a fourth personal vow of free, loving medical care for the poor and the uninsured throughout the world. It was this fourth vow that so beautifully brought to fruition the calling she sensed as a young child while leafing through missionary magazines in her living room more than forty years earlier.

So compelling an example is Sister, however, that others are also frequently drawn into her mission of providing free medical care to the poor. For example, when Mother Teresa needed two knee replacements, the first call Sister Dede made was to her brother John, the orthopedic surgeon. Dr. John not only performed the surgery (and others upon her request) for free, but also recalls her asking other physicians to donate their surgical services to the needy as well. "I've done quite a few freebie surgeries for Dede. You never turn her down when she asks you for something, I'll tell you that!" John reflects. Those who recognize the gift and impact of Sister's continual self-giving are, in turn, inspired to give of themselves. As iron sharpens iron, one person sharpens another (see Prov. 27:17).

Third Tour in Nuba

In 2013, Sister returned, for the third time, to the Nuba Mountains; this tour was a seven-week mission. She was shocked to find more than three hundred patients admitted to the inpatient wards at Mother of Mercy Hospital — four times as many as in 2011.[51] Frequent bombings of civilians continued and resulted in horrific casualties. Sister reflects on the continual devastation:

> There were patients overflowing in the hallways, and the rear of the hospital was arranged to provide chronic care (i.e., patients with chronic wounds, malnutrition and fractures, and who had had one or more of their limbs amputated). The Nuba Mountains were now being attacked, and we felt like an open target.... Civilians continued to be bombed by Antonov bombers and continued to suffer from a dearth of food, thus the hospital was increasingly inundated with new patients.[52]

[51] Byrne, "In the Service of Christ," 71.
[52] Byrne, "In the Service of Christ," 71–72.

It was at this point that she ministered to Imani, the aforementioned mother (see the prologue) who arrived at Mother of Mercy Hospital in critical condition.[53] The mass casualty that brought a dismembered mother, clinging to life, into Sister Dede's operating room is forever burned in her memory. Her face blown away, her leg sheared off above the knee, and her other foot completely missing, combined with the loss of blood from shards of metal throughout her torso were simply too much to sustain. Despite Sister's best efforts, the poor woman died, leaving her children motherless.

As Sister tended to the dying mother on her operating table, the nurses treated the wounds of the orphans in another room. There was so much senseless death and so little means of helping the victims. "No experience — not my days at the Washington, D.C., General Hospital or my three months in Afghanistan during my army days — matched the tragedies that unfolded before me during my seven weeks in the Nuba Mountains," Sister states.[54]

The Nuba people were a source of great inspiration to Sister Dede. Christians lived alongside Muslims in great harmony and peace, and the love and joy they exhibited amid such incredible suffering and loss were inspiring. Not only did her experiences there shape her into the surgeon she is today, but the faith-filled people will always hold a special place in her heart. She recalls one Muslim man on her operating table who, just before undergoing anesthesia, asked, "Doctor, will you please pray with me?"[55] Such is the faith of the Nuba people who openly seek God.

Sister recalls a similar story from 2014 when she traveled to Iraq on a mission trip to serve displaced Muslim and Christian refugees in the

---

[53] Byrne, "In the Service of Christ," 72.
[54] Byrne, "In the Service of Christ," 72.
[55] Byrne, "In the Service of Christ," 74.

camps there. One man, with tears in his eyes and mindful that God's mercy and love would ultimately prevail, cried out to Sister, "They've taken my home. They've killed members of my family. But they cannot take my God away from me." In the midst of real suffering, it is easy to find connection and commonality in our shared humanity.

Ministering to the Kurds

Sister's other mission work includes volunteering with the Global Surgical and Medical Support Group (GSMSG), which was founded by a fellow Georgetown colleague, Dr. Aaron Epstein, in 2015 to provide medical care and training in conflict zones and disaster areas overseas.[56] After the rise of ISIS led to the persecution of millions in Iraq and Syria, people fled to Kurdish areas of Iraq for safety. Many needed cost-prohibitive surgeries, and GSMSG put boots to the ground by sending physicians and surgeons to minister in hospitals on the front lines. In 2016, they provided more advanced surgical care in a two-week period in one region of Iraq than all European governments combined in a year.[57]

Sister Dede's influence on the evolution and impact of GSMSG is noteworthy. Aaron Epstein was originally a volunteer medic with a fire department in Virginia from 2010 to 2014. He met Sister Dede through a fellow medic friend who worked at his station. When Aaron mentioned an interest in overseas humanitarian work, his friend suggested, "There's this wonderful lady in D.C. who does medical mission work all over the world. You need to connect with her."

After one of his mission trips to Cambodia, Aaron contacted Sister Dede about various other possibilities. Not only was she supportive,

---

[56] "Mission," Global Surgical and Medical Support Group, https://www. gsmsg.org/menu.

[57] Aaron Epstein, "Join GSMSG," YouTube video, https://www.youtube. com/watch?v=HemJwg45b9w&t=25s.

but she even encouraged him to apply to medical school so that he would be able to aid those in need more comprehensively. With Sister's mentorship, support, and recommendation, Aaron was admitted to Georgetown Medical School in 2014. When he couldn't find an organization in existence that fit his ethos of training partner populations in war-torn areas of the Middle East, where he eagerly wanted to serve, Sister Dede encouraged him to form his own 501(c)3 and even introduced him to a lawyer friend who could assist.

Given his student status at that time, Aaron found it difficult to recruit seasoned physicians willing to volunteer for mission work in dangerous territories such as Iraq. Disappointed, and thinking he might have to abandon the idea, he decided to call upon Sister Dede one more time.

"Would you be willing to go to Iraq for medical mission work, Sister?" he asked.

"Yes!" she replied without hesitation.

In fact, she was the first surgeon to join his group and fly to Iraq in 2015. "She is completely fearless!" Dr. Aaron states. "When we arrived in Iraq, ISIS was attacking head-on, and there was Sister Dede, unafraid, in full habit, doing surgeries!" While they recommended that Sister "lie low" and out of sight, especially dressed in habit from head to toe, she was concerned only about getting the job done.

Dr. Aaron vividly recalls the medical team working in a clinic in northern Iraq when they spotted a series of trucks with "armed dudes" approaching. "They're going to kill us all!" Dr. Aaron exclaimed. Sister Dede, completely unfazed, stepped up to the caravan to assess the situation.

"We couldn't believe it! We were expecting ISIS to take us out. Instead, the back doors opened, and three Catholic cardinals stepped out — the cardinal of Beirut, the cardinal of Syria, and the cardinal of Iraq!" Dr. Aaron now recalls with a chuckle. "These kinds of things happened when she was around. We were scared to death, and she thought it was 'no big deal.'"

Similarly, when the team told Sister that an ISIS suicide bomber recently blew up a café they had just visited, "she didn't flinch. Her attitude was, 'If it's my time to go, it's my time to go,'" Dr. Aaron states.

GSMSG provides much more than just physical healing. Oftentimes, Iraqis, whose health-care system is in crisis, simply need assurance from an American physician that they will be okay. When Dr. Aaron and Sister Dede arrived at the refugee clinic one day, hundreds were in line. "There is no way everyone in this line is sick," Dr. Aaron commented to Sister. After examining one rough-looking man who limped in, neither Aaron nor Sister could find any real medical concern. "I think you're fine," Dr. Aaron assured the man. "It's a miracle!" the man shouted as he jumped up and ran out the doors. Such patients find mental and spiritual healing in the mere presence of American doctors, whom they esteem so deeply. Dr. Aaron reflects, "This affirmed for me that medicine is one of the best means of serving people."

Sister Dede and the GSMSG group also train women to provide care to those in their communities.[58] Unfortunately, "women in the Middle East are often relegated to the kitchen," Dr. Aaron explains. "Because male physicians aren't even permitted to touch female patients, women are often left without the appropriate medical attention they need."

The training sessions that Sister Dede and other female military veterans conduct empower Iraqi women, who eagerly return year after year to increasingly advance their knowledge base. One young woman who came for training the first year returned the next year to say she was finally trusted to provide basic care to her family members.

[58] "About Us," "Empowering Women," Global Surgical and Medical Support Group, https://www.gsmsg.org/menu.

The following year, she returned and commented that she was now further trusted to provide care to a few of her neighbors. Finally, after several years of training, she shared that she was authorized to provide care within her broader community. This far-reaching ministry thus not only assists medically but, Dr. Aaron hopes, will also eventually elevate the status of Iraqi women. In this way, Sister Dede's strength and service with GSMSG continues to touch the lives of today's women.

When the surgical team returned to the States after their first Iraq mission trip, "nobody listened very much to what I had to say," recalls Dr. Aaron. "But Sister is so well respected and has such standing in the medical community that when she said my organization was legit, everyone wanted to join!" Furthermore, when Aaron mentioned to Sister that they were personally paying out of pocket for the mission trips, Sister connected him with generous donors who were eager to support the worthy initiatives financially.

Dr. Aaron states that, thanks to Sister Dede, GSMSG started from nothing and grew to more than two thousand members and two dozen medical teams that travel to Iraq. Fifty percent of the Iraqi population — essentially, the female population — are also now finally beginning to enjoy the fruits of basic medical care for the first time in their lives, and the organization's original focus of training people in the Middle East has expanded to South America, Africa, and the Ukraine.

"[Sister Dede] brings a credibility to our efforts that only a former U.S. Army surgeon turned sister of the Church can — and I think there is only one person like that in the world. She is unique, and courageous beyond all measure," Dr. Epstein reflects. And what do the people she serves there think of Sister Dede? "The Kurds absolutely love her and always inquire about when she is coming back."[59]

---

[59]   Quoted in Donahoe, "Sister Dede Answers the Call."

Based on the number of people GSMSG has trained and the number of people those physicians have trained in turn, "easily over 100 million people have been positively impacted over the span of the organization's existence as a result of what Sister Dede set into motion," Dr. Aaron estimates. "Fearless people like her who have absolute moral standing, character, and values should be elevated in our world. I'm grateful that she now has a larger voice on a wider platform so that her example can inspire more people."

A Modern-Day Mother Cabrini Witnessing to the Faith

In 2018, Sister was introduced, through a mutual friend, to Father Vincent Woo, now a professor of canon law at Saint Patrick's Seminary and University in Menlo Park, California. At the time, he was pursuing doctoral studies at the Catholic University of America in D.C. and celebrated daily Mass for the Sisters at the convent. He has many fond memories of his interactions with Sister Dede.

Father is particularly impressed with Sister's humble and unmeasured service. Given so many demands on her time, even the amount of sleep she frequently sacrifices is likely formidable. He also comments on how she completes the most menial of tasks with great love. Despite being the house superior, she cooks, mops the floors, mows the lawn, and is willing to do whatever else is necessary for running a household.

"The way Sister opened her own clinic and cares for the sick reminds me of Mother Cabrini," Father Woo states. The comment is noteworthy, especially given that so many others have likened her to saints as well — first to Saint Joan of Arc, then to Mother Teresa, and now to Mother Cabrini.

Father Woo also admires Sister's generous hospitality to visitors, especially pro-life advocates who come to town in association with pro-life cases being tried in court. He specifically recalls her court testimony in support of a Catholic religious who was involved in a 2022 pro-life court case in Pennsylvania. Given Sister's medical expertise and role as a physician, her important testimony indicating that life begins at conception was especially impactful.

Father Woo notes that Sister Dede fights not only for the unborn but for all the economically disadvantaged as well, even once offering to drive food trucks to those in need. "She also has the ability to combine traditional femininity rooted in Eucharistic spirituality in a unique way. She humbly and respectfully combines her work life while still appreciating the traditional family role of women in the Church."

Father Woo also vividly recalls when a politician approached Sister at a public event to request a photo with her. The congresswoman remarked that she thought her mother would enjoy a photo of her standing beside a sister in full habit.

"Oh, you're a congresswoman. Are you pro-life?" Sister asked.

Discovering that the legislator supported abortion, Sister declined to pose for the photo.

"I'm sorry, but I don't want my photo to be used the wrong way. You support the death of babies, and my mission is to support life," Sister responded.

Sister's constant prayer is that all might come to defend prenatal life.

Recognition from the President

In his Salute to America speech at the Lincoln Memorial on July 4, 2019, President Donald J. Trump celebrated past and present American heroes. He honored Sister Dede and thanked her for her many years of military and medical service.

This evening, we are joined by Sister Deirdre Byrne. Sister Byrne is a retired Army surgeon who served for nearly 30 years. On September 11th, 2001 … Sister raced to Ground Zero. Through smoke and debris, she administered first aid and comfort to all. Today, Sister Byrne runs a medical clinic serving the poor in our nation's capital. Sister, thank you for your lifetime of service.[60]

In a subsequent interview about the president's acknowledgment, Sister quickly redirected attention back to those she deemed the real heroes seated next to her at the event — honorees such as a Navy SEAL who rescued an American (Doctors Without Borders) physician and a soldier who received a medal for his heroism during World War II.[61] She was simply honored to sit beside other compatriots who gave so much in defense of their country.

The Vocation of Medicine

In August 2019, a Vermont nurse was allegedly forced to assist in an elective abortion at the hospital where she worked.[62] Sister Dede publicly spoke out in defense of health-care workers' rights to refuse to participate in abortions and indicated that pressure on some medical professionals to violate their beliefs was, unfortunately, becoming more widespread. A hospital in Washington, D.C., had also just expanded their services, under the cloak of "reproductive rights," to

---

[60] Donald J. Trump, "Remarks by President Trump at the 2019 Salute to America," Trump White House Archives, July 4, 2019, para. 26, https://trumpwhitehouse.archives.gov/briefings-statements/remarks-president-trump-salute-america/.

[61] Kathy Schiffer, "Sister Deirdre 'Dede' Byrne — Surgeon, Soldier, Sister, Servant," EWTN Great Britain, August 24, 2020, https://ewtn.co.uk/sister-deirdre-dede-byrne-surgeon-soldier-sister-servant/.

[62] Wilson Ring, "US Agency: Hospital Forced Nurse to Participate in Abortion," Associated Press, August 28, 2019, https://apnews.com/article/b4f4dc46734f49f88198bc31f9013506.

include second-trimester abortions.[63] The Church, however, teaches that abortion is neither health care nor a reproductive right,[64] and medical professionals must not be forced to violate their consciences.

While doctors and nurses are disturbed by recent administrative changes that could potentially undermine their faith, they also know that refusal to cooperate could result in job loss. Sister has helped countless health-care workers over the years with issues related to the intersection of faith and medicine. She encourages them to stand strong in their beliefs, uphold ethics and morals, and never compromise on tenets of their faith.

"The vocation of medicine is under attack and needs to be safe-guarded and nurtured," Sister stated in a recent public appearance. "Our present health-care system is in great need of Our Lord's healing presence through the influence of faithful physicians."

In October of that same year, the Mission Doctors Association recognized Sister Dede at their White Mass — a Mass so named for physician attendees who don white lab coats — at the Cathedral of Our Lady of the Angels in Los Angeles. Annually, the organization honors a Catholic doctor who has responded to Christ's call to heal the sick and who has made a difference in the world.[65] Sister was honored to accept, but in her humble way, directed attention back to God.

---

[63] Dede Byrne, "HHS Says University Hospital Forced Nurse to Assist in Abortions,"interview on *EWTN News Nightly*, YouTube video, August 29, 2019, https://www.youtube.com/watch?v=7eQ0XC yMuQQ.

[64] "We proclaim only that none of these reasons can ever objectively confer the right to dispose of another's life, even when that life is only beginning." Sacred Congregation for the Doctrine of the Faith, *Declaration on Procured Abortion* (November 18, 1974), no. 14.

[65] "Catholic Doctor of the Year," Mission Doctors Association, https://www.missiondoctors.org/catholic-doctor-of-the-year/.

"Well, you know, it's like anything. It's really all God's glory," Sister stated. While she shuns awards for her own sake, she readily welcomes the opportunity to share more about the ministry of the Little Workers of the Sacred Hearts, talk about the issue of life, and shed light on "the work that [God] does through all of us, regardless of how much we may fail Him."[66]

She recounts the story of her father being elbow deep in a patient's chest during surgery one day. There was a call for a vascular surgeon to "OR 11, stat." The lead surgeon accidentally nicked the inferior vena cava, and the patient's abdomen was quickly filling with blood. Bill slipped his size-nine-gloved hand into the man's abdomen and was able to pinch the artery, which allowed the other doctor time to catch up. This helped save the man's life. He came home that day and shared with the family, "God used me this morning." She now relays her father's inspirational message to medical professionals worldwide and reminds them how God, the Divine Physician, uses their hands to facilitate His healing. "[My real vocation] is a healing ministry, and God is the healer. I just try to stay out of His way," Sister states.[67]

[66] Dellinger, "Nun with a Gun," Paragraph 28.
[67] Stacy Rausch, "Soldier, Surgeon, Sister," *Arlington Catholic Herald*, August 12, 2015, https://www.catholicherald.com/article/local/soldier-surgeon-sister/.

7

COVID — The World Closed
2020

In 2020, the world closed. The COVID pandemic indelibly marked this planet, and Sister Dede was at the forefront, fighting to keep patients alive and protect their religious freedoms. She has stacks of medical records of people she has helped since 2020 — not only those who needed medical treatment but also those whose jobs were threatened because they refused to be vaccinated or whose employers refused to honor their religious exemptions.

Sister has treated more than five hundred COVID patients, has offered her expertise worldwide, and continues to treat for active infection as well as adverse effects from vaccine administration. She publicly spoke out about the effectiveness of early treatment as well as the travesty of oppressive governmental restrictions and mandates: "We have lost all common sense, and, as a result, we are losing our religious freedom."[68] Such experimental drugs, in the absence of longitudinal studies related to potential long-term side effects at that time, left her deeply concerned. Several recorded interviews featuring Sister's discussions of these topics were even removed and banned from social media within hours of their posting.

---

[68] Ashley Sadler, "We Have Lost All Common Sense and as a Result We Are Losing Our Religious Freedom," Lifesite News, August 4, 2021, https://www.lifesitenews.com/news/735731/.

She was convinced that the pandemic was not as devastating as the media portrayed it, and she partnered with a popular D.C.-area cardiologist and a privately owned pharmacy to provide care and effective protocols to treat five Missionary of Charity homes with more than sixty religious and laypeople over the course of just one weekend. Every single patient fully recovered with no complications.

Interestingly, the medicinal protocol responsible for Sister's successful patient outcomes was suppressed by mainstream medicine. After filling out a medical history form and completing an assessment, Sister worked with various compounding pharmacies for prescribing ivermectin and hydroxychloroquine. Unfortunately, Sister reflects, her partnering physician was later persecuted and received death threats for his opposition to masking and his assertion that children should be permitted to return to school.

Sister contracted COVID herself in 2022. One night before retiring, she developed a severe, stabbing headache, which was atypical for her. She began the medicinal protocol she had prescribed for so many others and self-quarantined so as not to infect others in the convent. While all in the convent inevitably contracted the virus at one point or another, the timing of the illnesses was such that they were successfully able to stagger care for one another. By God's grace and Sister's attentive care, even Sister Licia and Mary Byrne, then the most elderly and fragile of the group, recovered well and with no adverse outcomes.

During patient assessments, Sister sometimes utilized resources for investigating the number of adverse reactions associated with a vaccination's batch or lot number. She also closely followed the work of Dr. Peter McCullough, who discussed inequity with vaccines, some having stronger dosages of spike proteins than others, as well as Dr. Naomi Wolf, who was deplatformed for publicly outlining adverse side effects of COVID vaccines that she and a team of clinicians allegedly discovered when examining primary-source medical documents.[69]

Sister recounts her offer to assess one eighty-year-old patient who was very active in gardening, involved in many outside activities, and in otherwise good health — until he took the vaccine. After each of his four vaccines, he became more debilitated and too weak even to walk. He had been to countless neurology, orthopedic, and rheumatology specialists, all of whom seemed unable to assist or diagnose the problem. "When you hear doctors say things like, 'I've never seen this before,' investigating for vaccine injury is a good place to start," Sister states.

The man ended up at Sibley Memorial Hospital under the care of a Johns Hopkins gastroenterologist, who diagnosed him with autoimmune hepatitis.

"Have you been vaccinated?" Sister asked the man.

"Yes, of course, Sister. Should I get another?" he replied.

"Absolutely not! I'm sorry to hear you had all the others!"

Sister checked his vaccine lot numbers and found them to be associated with very high numbers of adverse reactions. The man's daughter also developed trigeminal neuralgia immediately after receiving the vaccine.

"We're going to see more and more people injured by this war crime," Sister warns.

COVID Cataracts

The real pandemic, according to Sister Dede, was the "COVID cataracts" that people developed as a result of sacramental withdrawal and government overreach. "The virus is very real — I am not at all

---

[69] Naomi Wolf, "What's in the Pfizer Documents?," Hillsdale College, YouTube video, https://www.youtube.com/watch?v=T9Y_W_30hsM.

discounting it! But the reaction to the virus blinded so many."[70] While illness and mandates might have seemed the worst part of COVID, Catholics everywhere were denied the life-giving Eucharist for so long that they developed a kind of metaphorical blindness that Sister Dede calls "COVID cataracts." Though, postpandemic, she has also characterized the phenomena as "spiritual cataracts," her message is the same: infrequent reception of the sacraments can lead to clouded vision and a dull conscience.

Sister states that COVID "unroofed"[71] a deep abscess in health care and revealed a lack of compassionate care for patients. "An experimental vaccine mandate was shoved down our throats. Thousands developed vaccine-related injuries or diseases; thousands lost their jobs for refusing to be injected with abortion-tainted vaccines; thousands died alone or separated from their families; monasteries were closed; Mass and the Eucharist were withheld. What a physical and spiritual disaster!" she states.

In a June 2024 address to a group of physicians in Mundelein, Illinois, Sister recounted how the Little Workers' founder ministered to those suffering with the plague during the late 1800s. With no concern for his own well-being, Blessed Francisco Maria Greco traveled the streets to administer lifesaving sacraments to his flock. "That's how we Christians must live our lives daily," Sister states. "Our focus should be on eternity with our Lord — not on this temporary world."

Given the importance of our spiritual health over even our physical well-being, she believes that the Eucharistic Lord is our lifesaving answer. She esteems the medical and religious heroes who emerged during the pandemic and who made a return to the sacraments possible. "We could not have done this without our dear priests, who

---

[70] Byrne, "Preparation for Battle," 32:15.
[71] Unroofing is a surgical procedure that includes removing a top layer.

acted '*in persona Christi*,'" Sister states. "Thank you, dear Fathers, for your holy priesthood."

Sister's antidote for spiritual cataracts includes remaining in the state of grace, as this allows us to hear Christ's voice. "Make it your daily mission to be in the state of grace," Sister exhorts. "Prepare yourself and those around you for our ultimate goal: eternity with Our Lord. There is nothing to fear but the loss of Christ."

8

Republican National Convention
2020

Having a love of country, Sister Dede is deeply concerned about the nation she served, religious freedom, and the intersection of faith and the public square. She is saddened by the rhetoric of pro-abortion stances that directly oppose the teachings of the Catholic Faith. Two Catholic religious, Father James Martin and Sister Simone Campbell, offered prayers at the August 17–20, 2020, Democratic National Convention, and she was disturbed that more religious didn't speak out to clarify any potential confusion that might result. She stated:

> There was a lot of talk on the news about the Democratic vote, the Catholic vote and how Joe Biden was a good Catholic, despite his support for legal abortion. Also, the [Democratic National] convention featured a priest and religious sister speaking, and I feared many Catholics would be confused by this support. As a Catholic doctor, sister, and human being, I believe that legalized abortion is the most critical issue for us, and so I was distraught by what I heard. I also reflected on how other issues go hand in hand with our responsibility to defend unborn life, such as respect for religious freedom and freedom of speech.[72]

[72] Joan Frawley Desmond, "The Unconventional Mission of Sister Dede," *National Catholic Register*, September 3, 2020, https://www.ncregister.com/interview/the-unconventional-mission-of-sister-dede.

I'm Your Gal, Lord

During her afternoon holy hour the day after the Democratic National Convention, with a heavy heart and wanting to do more, she begged God, "Lord, use me in whatever way You deem fit for advancing the pro-life message. Let me be Your voice to do more. I'm Your gal, Lord — whatever You will!"

Less than two hours after she prayed this prayer, the telephone rang. It was an aide from the White House asking if she would be willing to speak at the Republican National Convention.

"Can I speak about the sanctity of life?" Sister asked the aide.

"Yes, of course, Sister," she replied.

"Then, yes! I'm interested!"

Sister contacted her mother general in Rome to seek permission. "Mother, the White House has invited me to give a pro-life talk," Sister Dede told her.

"Bella! Brava!" Mother responded in support.

Sister's motive in accepting the invitation was clear: "to do God's will and bring more souls to Christ for eternity." In her humility, she recognized her "littleness," knew that this request was a calling from God, and felt an obligation to make this public statement in support of the unborn. "Like anyone else, I just wanted to do God's will and would have felt worse if I had ignored His invitation. As a doctor, I had given many pro-life talks at smaller venues before, and this was just one more opportunity to share the message."

The Republican National Convention, something she previously knew very little about, wasn't even on her radar. "To be honest, I didn't even exactly know the extent of what I was getting into," she reflects. "I only knew one thing — that I was going to speak about pro-life! People need to understand that prenatal life makes all the other life issues possible. It is the cement that holds all the other issues together; and without it, everything else, planted in sand, will crumble. This moral and human issue supersedes politics. So, I didn't see myself as a political speaker, but as one just representing the Church's teaching on life. God also answered my heart's desire to clarify the issue of when life begins."

Sister was honored to use the platform as an opportunity to state what she knew to be true: "Human life must be respected and protected absolutely from the moment of conception. From the first moment of his existence, a human being must be recognized as having the rights of a person — among which is the inviolable right of every innocent being to life" (*CCC* 2270).

The Four Minutes That Changed My World

Given COVID restrictions at the time, most of the 2020 Republican National Convention speeches were pre-taped in an empty auditorium at the Reagan Building in Washington, D.C. It was a grace-filled experience being on stage, and Sister recalls that all the American flags were inspirational. As a retired military colonel, the mere sight of a flag and the personal sacrifice so many have offered in response still evoke a sense of pride and love of country. She comments that the evening even had hints of a Catholic revival of sorts — strong messages in support of life, a sister with rosary in hand, and the playing of the Ave Maria at the end. She wanted to be a voice for the unborn, and this platform provided the opportunity to share that message with an entire nation. The words were all Sister's, but they were finessed a bit with the assistance of her friend Dorinda — a professional writer and "aggregata" (coworker) of the Little Workers — and a White House speechwriter.[73]

---

[73] See "Full Text: Sister Dede Byrne's Speech at the 2020 Republican National Convention," Catholic News Agency, August 26, 2020,

The pre-recorded format allowed for Sister to watch the televised broadcast with her mom, who was then living in McLean. After Mass the next morning at Saint Luke's, parishioners were approaching to say they saw her on TV the night before. Simply blessed to have shared the pro-life message, she was unprepared for the storm that would hit upon her return to the convent. Dorinda was there visiting at the time.

"I can't keep up with all these calls!" Dorinda exclaimed, pointing to the string of paper towels on which she had logged the countless messages. "And I'm sorry to say, it is clear that you don't have very many friends right now."

"Well, I have you, don't I?" Sister teased.

"Well, yeah, you have me. But that's about it!"

One call Dorinda answered was from a woman who shouted, "How *dare* Sister Dede speak at the Republican National Convention. Nuns have *no* business being in politics!"

Dorinda tried reasoning that Sister's intent was simply to defend life and share facts. "Well, ma'am, she would have also happily spoken at the Democratic National Convention if they would have called to ask her. But they didn't. And by the way, if they had invited her, she would have delivered the same message — that killing an unborn baby is not what God wants."

It Wasn't about Politics;
It Was Just about the Truth

With so many incoming calls, Evelyn, a convent health-care aide, inquired, "What's happening? Why does the phone keep ringing?" While Sister was accused of being political, Evelyn's subsequent assessment

https://www.catholicnewsagency.com/news/45617/full-text-sister-dede-byrnes-speech-at-the-2020-republican-national-convention.

was insightful: "This had nothing to do with politics. Sister was just telling the truth about what is happening in the world and was being a witness to Christ's truth. She just also happens to be a sister, so that drew attention. But not all people love or recognize the truth. Sister is a soldier for the Lord."

Sister's ever-calm, ever-steady repeated response was simply to state the truth: abortion is not a political issue but a moral one. "It was three or four full days of answering calls from irate Catholics who went absolutely nuts when they saw me on that convention stage," Sister recounts. "I had people calling from all over the world. One man from Belgium called demanding, 'I want to speak with the nun who spoke at the convention! She needs to know the full scope of what is going on in the world! She obviously doesn't know!'"

Sister knew that, in defending the sanctity of life, she was doing God's will. She prayed for those who called, and she offered up the verbal persecution as a sacrifice for the unborn. Drawing an analogy to pilots under fire during World War II, Gloria reassured, "Well, Dede, if you aren't feeling the bullets, you're going the wrong way." But as an army veteran who had seen several war fronts, Sister was steady under pressure.

Trying to be a good friend, Dorinda lent support as they shared conversation during the tumultuous seventy-two hours.

"People are being conned and swindled into thinking that what they are voting for is a noble thing — even some religious are now voting for an agenda that is anti-life," Dorinda aptly affirms. "They are willing to sacrifice the right of a person to live in order to pass what they deem an economically equitable agenda for feeding the poor. We believe in a God who took the womb as His entry port into time, and here we are saying that the womb isn't sacrosanct? And further, that we are going to slay people because we have to feed the poor? People say, 'Oh, yes, abortion is a very bad thing, we know, but we must tolerate it because we will then be able to better feed the poor.' It doesn't make sense!"

Interestingly, the irate calls Sister received were not limited to those on just one side of the aisle. Many daily-Rosary-saying Catholics called to object as well. "How dare Sister call our beloved Rosary a weapon!" they criticized.[74]

But Sister's analogy was a sound one. Father Calloway, in his book *Champions of the Rosary*,[75] refers to the Rosary as a spiritual weapon and highlights the many miracles attributed to its recitation.[76] In fact, when Father learned about the persecution Sister was enduring, he mailed her a big box of rosaries as a show of support.

Bishop Coffey, auxiliary bishop for the Military Archdiocese and retired navy captain, stated that her appearance on the convention stage was "electrifying" and that he actually cheered when she held up her rosary and declared herself to be "not only pro-life but pro–eternal life." The two have since become good friends. Other shows of support included a call from a former Trappist monk who made it a point to research and call the convent number just to share how proud he was of Sister Dede and how proud he was to be a Catholic; a message from an esteemed cardinal to his good friend Bishop Byrne, that read, "Bravo, bravo, Bill!"; and even international support from a bishop in Iraq.

[74] During her 2020 Republican National Convention speech, Sister pulled out her rosary, held it high for everyone to see, and referred to it as her "weapon of choice." See Catholic News Agency, "Byrne's Full Speech."

[75] Donald Calloway, *Champions of the Rosary* (Stockbridge, MA: Marian Press, 2016).

[76] See also Donald Calloway, "The Rosary: The Spiritual Sword of Mary," *Catholic Exchange*, December 19, 2022, https://catholicexchange.com/rosary-spiritual-sword-mary/.

The Womb Is Ground Zero

Sister remained firm amid the tumult and subsequently stated, "The unborn are under attack, and everything flows from it — issues regarding marriage, transgenderism, fatherless families, and many other societal ills.... All these things flow out of a lack of respect for the dignity of God's design for life. When you take a stone and drop it into the water, it has a ripple effect — just as abortion has a ripple effect that causes confusion and destruction in society."

Her reference to the womb as a place of life but also potential death echoes Pope Benedict XVI, who stated, "How can it be that the most wondrous and sacred human space, the womb, has become a place of unutterable violence?"[77] In this regard, and as one of the few people on earth able to speak from firsthand experience, Sister chillingly refers to a mother's womb as Ground Zero.

My Life Took a 180-Degree Turn

After the initial storm, things began to quiet down at the convent. As a welcome change of events, Sister eventually began receiving thank-you letters and donations to the Little Workers from supporters who discovered that she performs surgery internationally for the poor and that her order is also dedicated to serving the marginalized in Washington, D.C.

The calls of gratitude forged many new friendships and opportunities. The fiat she offered in allowing God to use her for advancing the pro-life message has provided her with a louder voice on a wider stage. Sister shares, "My life has dramatically changed 180 degrees since the RNC speech. I refer to it as the four minutes that changed my world."

---

[77] Address in Barangaroo, Sydney Harbour, Australia, July 17, 2008, https://www.vatican.va/content/benedict-xvi/en/speeches/2008/july/documents/hf_ben-xvi_spe_20080717_barangaroo.html.

Sister, Soldier, Surgeon

A Battle Cry for Christians Worldwide

While Sister's address changed life as she knew it, it changed others' lives as well. Sam Lee, a nondenominational Christian millennial living in New York at the time, stumbled upon Sister's RNC speech online. Sam confesses that, like many of his friends, he had no moral objections to abortion under certain circumstances. Nonetheless, Sister's willingness to state boldly what she believed, without apology, elicited his respect. In his mind, her experiences as a physician, a colonel, a religious, and one devoted to caring for the marginalized and the vulnerable lent credibility to her claims about the unborn.

"She seemed to be one of the most qualified people I could have imagined to be speaking on the matter, and her experiences on multiple battle fronts — as a colonel in the army and as a physician on the front lines of the pro-life movement — meant she was living what she believed; they weren't just empty words. Even though I wasn't Catholic, I could see that she embodied Christ's command to live biblical principles and a Christlike life."

From Sister's address, Sam intuited only words of conviction, not words in support of a political party. "It seemed to me she was speaking about the Lord's issue, not a Republican or a Democratic issue," he now reflects. Sister's statements challenged him to reexamine the moment at which human life begins, and her simplicity inspired him. "She is like any one of us. While we have all failed in some way, she demonstrates that it is possible for simple, ordinary people to live the light of Christ by fighting for others."

Sam continues: "We live in a demonic age when Satan uses ignorance as a tool to lead people to think abortion is acceptable. I was one of them. So many well-meaning people are just like me; they just need to be exposed to the truth. After more closely examining science and the issue of abortion, I eventually determined my thinking on the matter was wrong. But Sister reminded me that God's mercy and forgiveness are always available. I now see how abortion is always an act of evil and a rebellion against the ultimate sacrifice of Our Lord on the Cross."

Upon the invitation of a mutual friend, Sam eventually met Sister in person and even attended Mass at her D.C. convent. Though he still comments on the delicious breakfast she served him that memorable Sunday morning, he also admits that attending Mass for the first time in his life inspired him to learn more about the Mass as the sacrifice of Christ and how it likewise encompasses the Lord's Last Supper, Passion, death, and Resurrection. He is now a strong advocate for life from the moment of conception and is grateful to Sister for her part in the freedom and peace this has brought him. Today, Sam is never without the patriotic rosary that Sister gave him. Furthermore, thanks to her four-minute address that changed *his* world, he now attends Catholic Mass, almost daily.

"Out of the ashes comes a new beginning, and Sister's words are light in a darkened world," Sam summarizes. "The Church is in a state of disunity and disarray, and strong, fearless voices willing to correct the confusion have been sorely missing. Sister reminds us that the issue of life is what unites us, regardless of religion or creed. For me, her RNC address was like a spark that ignited a fire — a fire that is now rumbling across the globe — to highlight this critical issue. Her clear and courageous voice is a battle cry for Christians worldwide, and she is an inspiration for the Church of our times."

Waking the Faithful

In addition to her other ministries, Sister Dede now juggles a busy international travel schedule for sharing her messages. In this respect, God has tapped her on the shoulder to awaken His faithful who have fallen asleep. "Of course, I always talk about the evils of abortion, but I have also been given opportunities to spread the most important message of all: that we need to be in the state of grace. That's my modus operandi, to just encourage people to always be in the state of grace."

Sister also uses her new platform to talk about the Eucharist, her parents, and how faithful parents can have an enormous influence in the lives of their children. She reminds us that the cultural battle in which we currently find ourselves is really a battle between our Lord and the devil — and we are now called to choose sides.

Dorinda is fond of saying that Sister is using her new stage to evangelize, one person at a time, and to remind people what a priority looks like when it's God-given. "Protecting prenatal life is not the only concern for consideration when casting a vote or formulating laws. But it is the single issue that must be prioritized above all others, and one that is foundational for our very civilization," Dorinda comments. "Our thinking and decision-making on the issue of abortion define how we see our humanity and inform the laws we make. Without proper prioritization, we demean our own personhood and make of it a utilitarian function, exactly as the Marxists would have us do."

Sister's continued exhortations have impacted lives, not only as evidenced by the conversions set into motion because of her influence, and the ripple effect of so many who are then impacted as a result, but also because of the way her words stir the hearts of the faithful to permeate the culture with God's truth. Sister's strong witness at the RNC even prompted one woman to register to vote: "My Catholic neighbor, who had never registered to vote, saw your speech at the RNC, and [now] she is registered and voting for life! Thank you," a woman posted during one of Sister's online interviews.[78]

Dr. Stewart, Sister's childhood neighbor, further comments: "I admired her courage and fortitude. She spoke truth even though she knew she would be criticized for it. But the thing with Sister Dede is

---

[78] Quoted in "My LIVE Interview" (comment section), 15:52.

that she speaks the truth with love. It's not human judgment or using God or religion for political gain. It's just all about love. Even as a young boy I recognized that. In some respects, she imprinted on me what womanhood should be. It's Sister's love that is remarkable: her love for the kids in our neighborhood growing up, her love for the animals and people she brought home, her love for everyone she encounters."

9

The Feminine Genius and Continued Impact

From rising to retiring, Sister Dede's days are spent in service to others. Just as Dr. Stewart, based on the young Dede's influence in his life, better understood what womanhood should be, this continual self-giving, in combination with her strength and leadership, exemplify not only authentic feminism but also what Saint John Paul II characterized as the feminine genius.[79]

In keeping with her fourth personal vow, of free and loving medical care for the poor, Sister's vocation today is manifested through her medicine as well as her simple daily service to others. She sees with her heart, acknowledges each patient's dignity, and reveals God's plan working in the world and in her patients' lives.[80] Sister encourages all women to embrace their God-given identity and special gifts, not only to nurture life but also to imitate the Blessed Mother by the selfless rendering of their fiats. Like our spiritual mother, Sister now runs to her children who have fallen, physically and spiritually tends

[79] "Necessary emphasis should be placed on the '*genius of women*,' not only by considering great and famous women of the past or present, but also those *ordinary* women who reveal the gift of their womanhood by placing themselves at the service of others in their everyday lives. For in giving themselves to others each day women fulfil their deepest vocation." Pope John Paul II, *Letter to Women* (June 25, 1995), no. 12.

[80] Pope John Paul II, *Letter to Women*, no. 12.

to their wounds, and helps them learn from their mistakes so that they won't get hurt again.

The Vocation of Motherhood

Reflecting on her family life and the incredible example set by her mother, Sister further affirms the special calling and critical impact of mothers on the lives of their children. "I'm grateful for those mothers who can afford to stay at home with their children." She sometimes refers to mothers who sacrifice so much for their families as front-line heroes.

Furthermore, she recalls how her mother's daily reception of Holy Communion brought blessings to her children and into the home. The grace, peace, joy, and love that this inevitably manifests in family life cannot be underestimated. "Faithful mothers and frequent Mass water the garden of vocations," Sister adds.

The great dignity of motherhood and the calling of women to embrace their femininity is manifested in Sister Dede's example. John Paul II beautifully referenced the manifestation of such selfless and beautiful love by stating, "The basic plan of the Creator takes flesh in the history of humanity.... [In this way, we give thanks to the Creator] for the gift of *this great treasure* which is womanhood."[81]

The Influence of Strong Women

Sister often references not only Joan of Arc but other strong women, such as Dr. Mildred Jefferson (1926–2010), a prominent pro-life African American physician, also from the D.C. area.

"I became a physician in order to help save lives," said Dr. Jefferson. "I am at once a physician, a citizen, and a woman, and I am not willing to stand aside and allow the concept of expendable human lives to turn this great land of ours into just another exclusive

---

[81] *Letter to Women*, no. 12.

reservation where only the perfect, the privileged, and the planned have the right to live."[82]

In a very tangible way, Sister Dr. Dede echoes the same message and continues that lifesaving work by ministering to women in the D.C. area. In fact, her abortion pill reversal procedures have resulted in the delivery of many healthy babies.

Her strength and fortitude are also evidenced in lifesaving work of the soul. Such was the case with Dr. Marcarelli, a surgeon at Sibley Hospital who was shocked when she entered the female changing area one day and found Sister's habit hanging on the door.

Approaching the lead nurse on duty, Dr. Marcarelli inquired, "Janet, why in the world is there a nun's habit hanging in the changing room?"

"Oh, that's Dr. Byrne's! She is a surgeon here, but she is also a nun!" the nurse replied.

"Well, I definitely need to meet this woman!" Dr. Marcarelli replied.

Dr. Marcarelli met Sister and eventually shared that she was no longer practicing her Catholic Faith.

"Well, you need to start!" Sister Dede encouraged.

Weeks later, Jennifer, Sister's former college roommate, was at the convent for Evening Prayer and dinner, when Sister Dede and Dr. Marcarelli passed through the receiving area.

"This is Dr. Marcarelli," Sister Dede said as they walked by.

"Pray for me!" the nervous doctor replied, as she continued through the room and out the other door.

Perplexed, Jennifer later inquired, "Where is she going?"

"She is going to Confession with Sister Dede's confessor," one of the convent Sisters replied.

---

[82] "Mildred Jefferson — Trailblazer for Justice," Radiance Foundation, https://radiancefoundation.org/trailblazer/.

In just several short weeks, not only was Sister Dede instrumental in Dr. Marcarelli's reversion to the faith, but she also subsequently arranged to have a priest administer the last rites to Dr. Marcarelli's dying mother, secured a priest to hold a private funeral Mass for the deceased woman, helped choose Mass readings and a cemetery plot, and even further guided Dr. Marcarelli on how to properly inter her late brother's cremated remains at the same time.

"You're not like some of the other Catholics and nuns I've met," Dr. Marcarelli later shared. Sister Dede's approachable and welcoming demeanor, paired with her authentic and radical witness to Christ's love, elicit almost immediate trust and openness from many who meet her. This is precisely what it means to encounter Christ in others.

"Sister Dede is a kind of Renaissance woman," notes Father Ed Meeks, a retired priest from Towson, Maryland. "Her personality and approach to life are a compelling witness to what the world needs right now. Most importantly, her authentic femininity is an example of what a strong woman of God should look like."

Our Feminine Cry and Maternal Hearts

On March 9, 2021, when COVID was still plaguing the globe and the vaccine mandates were in full swing, Sister Dede joined eighty-five other strong women in the Lord, including physicians, bioethicists, religious, and other leaders from four continents, in signing a statement opposing the use of abortion-tainted COVID-19 vaccines.[83]

Despite a statement published in 2020 by the (then) Congregation for the Doctrine of the Faith indicating that the use of the vaccines was

---

[83] "The Voice of Women in Support of Unborn Babies and in Opposition to Abortion-Tainted Vaccines," Edward Pentin, March 8, 2021, https://edwardpentin.co.uk/wp-content/uploads/2021/03/STATEMENT-The-Voice-of-Women-in-Defense-of-Unborn-Babies-and-in-Opposition-to-Abortion-tainted-Vaccines-WORD-DOC.pdf.

morally licit under the circumstances and "[did] not constitute formal cooperation with the abortion from which the cells used in production of the vaccines derive,"[84] the opposing signatories implored: "We humbly suggest that such statements, including some official ones issued by bishops and even the Vatican, are based on an incomplete assessment of the science of vaccination and immunology, and beg such proponents to reevaluate their statements in light of the following facts."[85]

The women went on to cite evidence for their opposition, including one peer-reviewed study by the World Health Organization that found a 98.3 percent survival rate for those who contracted the virus that causes COVID-19.[86] Sister Dede felt called to be a voice in defense of the unborn, refused to "be complicit in the modern-day Massacre of the Holy Innocents,"[87] and pleaded that leaders, including Vatican officials, reconsider. "We, as women, wish our feminine cry to be heard round the world. This declaration comes from the depths of our maternal hearts, which are devoted to defending the cause of life and combating the culture of death."[88]

Helping Overseas from Her Convent

Sister's many varied experiences and travels have resulted in friendships and connections around the globe. With her former military deployments now a distant memory, however, she was not prepared to intercept the call she received later that year, in December 2021.

---

[84] "Catholic Women Issue Statement Opposing Use of 'Abortion-Tainted Vaccines,'" Catholic News Agency, https://www.catholicnewsagency.com/news/246797/catholic-women-issue-statement-opposing-use-of-abortion-tainted-vaccines.

[85] "Catholic Women Issue Statement."

[86] "Catholic Women Issue Statement."

[87] "The Voice of Women," 1.

[88] "The Voice of Women," 1.

"Sister, can you please help rescue my mother? You knew her and worked with her in 2008 at Camp Salerno near the Pakistani border. She is now in hiding after her capture and release from the Taliban. She is fearing for her life and needs help," stated the young man on the other end of the phone.

Skeptical at first, Sister requested verification of her identity. Weeks later, she received an e-mail from the doctor with proof of her identity and the following plea in broken English, "I am lefted behind and facing deadly situation. Please do something for me and my family and get us out from Afghanistan. I need urgent evacuation."[89]

Not sure how to assist, Sister called her friend Piero Tozzi, the staff director of the Congressional-Executive Commission on China and former senior foreign policy adviser and counsel to Representative Chris Smith (R-NJ), who subsequently connected her with Jason Jones and Prince Wafa of the Vulnerable People's Project.[90] Given the organization's dedication to assisting Christians who converted from Islam and are still living in fear for their lives after the Taliban seized control, they seemed the right people to assist.

In the short term, Prince Wafa was able to get an aid package of food and coal delivered to the physician and her twelve family members within hours of the initial outreach. Plans were then made for getting them visas and evacuating them safely across the border in February 2022. Along the harrowing journey, Jason called to provide regular updates: "Sister, please pray. We finally got the family to a lily

---

[89] Jonah McKeown, "A Doctor Begged a Religious Sister for Help. Last Week, She and Her Family Escaped Afghanistan," Catholic News Agency, February 17, 2022, https://www.catholicnewsagency.com/news/250418/a-doctor-begged-a-religious-sister-for-help-last-week-she-and-her-family-escaped-afghanistan.

[90] "About," Vulnerable People Project, https://vulnerablepeopleproject.com.

pad."[91] Sister quickly credits the rescue to the Holy Spirit's interven-tion.[92] "The Holy Spirit used me, in a small way, to get the rescue going. I was like the center who hiked the ball, and I just passed it to the quarterback and let him run with it."[93]

[91] A U.S. military term for a host nation facility.
[92] McKeown, "A Doctor Begged."
[93] McKeown, "A Doctor Begged."

10

Medical License Revoked and Lawsuit against D.C.

2021–2022

Washington, D.C., began requiring vaccinations for health-care work-ers in August 2021. Some people, including Sister Dede, opposed the mandate and submitted religious exemption requests. "I just knew I wasn't going to have anything to do with vaccines that were developed from or tested on fetal cell lines," Sister states. "In the fight against abor-tion, we must stand firm in our protection of the unborn."

By that time, she had treated hundreds of COVID patients and kept them out of the hospital. In the absence of feedback about the exemp-tion, Sister assumed that no news was good news. Sibley Memorial, a public hospital, required only submission of a religious exemption. Sister was able to maintain her schedule of surgeries and only had to provide proof of COVID negativity via weekly sputum tests. Con-versely, a Catholic-based health-care system where she also ministered did not readily accept her exemption.

Many months passed after filing her exemption, and all seemed quiet. One night in late February 2022, however, when Sister was tending to Sister Licia's needs, she glanced down at her phone and saw an e-mail from the D.C. Health Department. It was a form letter, not a personal one, that denied her exemption and required vaccination within five days, or she would lose her medical license.

Interestingly, the form letter listed a host of reasons for exemption denials and included check boxes next to each reason. This allowed the person completing the form simply to check the appropriate reason for the denial. But not one of the boxes was checked! In short, it appeared that Sister Dede didn't meet any of the government's preexisting reasons for denial. Instead, in the margins of the form letter, someone had handwritten, "To grant this religious exemption would be an undue hardship on D.C. health."[94]

Nun Sues D.C.

The next morning, Sister welcomed several well-connected people for breakfast at the convent, including attorney Piero Tozzi. "Can you believe that I'm going to lose my medical license in five days if I don't get vaccinated?" Sister shared. "I've been taking care of patients all this time and now, in February of 2022, after we have all contracted COVID and are part of the 'antibody club,' this happens!" Frustrated, Sister sought the advice of her friends.

All agreed that attorneys at the Thomas More Society would be well equipped to assist. Thus, on Saturday, March 9, 2022, a lawsuit on the basis of the Religious Freedom Restoration Act of 1993 and the First Amendment of the United States Constitution was filed in the U.S. District Court for the District of Columbia for denying Sister a religious exemption from the COVID vaccination mandate.[95]

The day after the suit was filed, she received requests from Fox News and EWTN to appear on Laura Ingraham's *The Ingraham Angle* and Raymond Arroyo's *The World Over* TV shows.

[94] "Nun Sues DC over Being Denied 'Vax Mandate' Religious Exemption," Fox News, YouTube video, 3:23, https://www.youtube.com/watch?v=tXZNiI0bE3I.

[95] Shannon Mullen, "If This Nun-Doctor Can't Get a Vaccine Religious Exemption, Who Can?" Catholic News Agency, March 11, 2022, https://www.catholicnewsagency.com/news/250642/catholic-nun-doctor-deirdre-byrne-vaccine-mandate.

Attorney Chris Ferrara, who joined Sister for one of the interviews, referred to her as the Mother Teresa of D.C. and stated, "This represents yet another example of the intersection of politics and bureaucratic intransigence, and religious liberty. The result is a constitutional train wreck."[96] Laura Ingraham thanked Sister for her service and applauded her efforts: "Sister Dede ... we need you out there serving this community! ... More now than ever."[97]

When Raymond Arroyo asked Sister why she decided to speak out in opposition to the vaccine mandate, she stated that she was "just the tip of a little arrow of so many others being forced to take the vaccine" and "had to fight for so many others who [were] in the same boat."[98]

During the three-week period of Sister's medical-license suspension, however, she had to close her clinic and couldn't see patients. Two abortion-reversal procedures had to be canceled, and she was even prohibited from administering a simple IV to Sister Licia, who was very ill at the time.

Countless people offered prayers of support, including parishioners at Christ the King parish in Towson, Maryland, many of whom Sister had treated for COVID. When the pastor at the time, Father Ed Meeks, was preparing for Mass one Sunday, parishioner Trish Palumbo informed him of the bad news. Everyone in the sacristy gasped.

When Father Ed made the announcement from the pulpit, he was in tears, and the parishioners were stunned. "How many people in this congregation have been helped by Sister Dede?" Dozens of

---

[96] "Nun Sues DC," 2:30.

[97] "Nun Sues DC," 3:50.

[98] EWTN, "Suing District of Columbia: Sr. Deirdre Byrne," *The World Over*, March 10, 2022, YouTube video, 7:43, https://www.youtube.com/watch?v=uPbFbQqM468.

people raised their hands. "Please keep her in your prayers because her medical license has been suspended," Father said.

As a show of support, members of the parish held a fundraiser for Sister Dede to assist with needed legal fees. The building was filled to capacity, and they had to turn people away. Father Ed, a former Protestant pastor who brought his entire Anglican congregation with him into the Catholic Faith after his own conversion, retired from Christ the King parish on July 1, 2023, at the age of seventy-five and will be forever grateful to Sister for her impact on the community and his parish.

Like many others, Father Meeks first learned about Sister Dede when he saw her on the RNC stage in 2020. Shortly thereafter, he and Bishop Coffey led a prayer service for a twenty-five-week-old aborted baby. Father Meeks was moved by Sister Dede's attendance at the service.

Thus, when Father contracted COVID on Christmas Eve 2021 and was instructed by his primary care physician just to keep an eye on things and go to the ER if he had trouble breathing, he decided to contact Sister Dede for help instead. She offered much more extensive care and immediately made sure Father had an effective treatment plan in place. "Her careful attention and care, even on an evening as busy as Christmas Eve, definitely kept me out of the hospital. She followed up until I had fully recovered and couldn't have been more caring. This was the case for dozens of my parishioners as well. She did everything in her power to help and minister to us all," Father reflects.

License Restored

Shortly after attorneys filed the lawsuit, the defendants responded by indicating that they reevaluated the situation, decided to accept her religious exemption, and would allow Sister to continue practicing medicine.

"I suspect why I was being targeted," Sister shares. "I support the unborn and I make no bones about it. While this is not a political issue at all, I can still clearly spell out the facts. And we must do this, because there are nonnegotiables in our Faith that we must never be afraid to speak the truth about."

Sister's hope and prayer were that her case might help others exercise their First Amendment rights to religious freedom and that it potentially brought the pro-life issue to light.

Every religious exemption Sister wrote for employees in the Washington, D.C., area was accepted by their employers. Random strangers approached her in hospitals, hugged her, and thanked her for making it possible for them to keep their jobs. "In the case of my license, I had nothing to lose by fighting back," Sister says. "I don't receive any salary for caring for the poor. The only ones who would have lost out would have been the poor and the immigrants — the very people that D.C. says they want to support!"

Today, more people are standing strong in their beliefs, and employers are a little more supportive. Sister has spoken with many people about their medical exemptions — people all over the world. When some bishops instructed their priests to refuse support to anyone seeking a religious exemption, Sister encouraged laypeople to speak for themselves and write their own. She also wrote an exemption for a Jewish woman — an out-of-state physical therapist who feared losing her job because she couldn't find a rabbi willing to write her an exemption. The one Sister Dede provided was accepted by the woman's employer and she was able to keep her position.

Defending What Is Right

The case to restore her medical license was not the first time Sister was involved with the law, however. In one tragic instance years ago, a mother threatened to sue Sister for reversing her daughter's chemical abortion. The mother wanted her daughter to have the abortion and argued that her daughter, as a minor, shouldn't have been treated without parental consent. "You didn't mind that she had an abortion as a minor, but you have a problem with the reversal because she is a minor?" Sister questioned. Unable to reason with the woman, Sister continued, "I am very sorry you feel that way. But your daughter came to our clinic seeking our help, and I gave it."

In search of a good lawyer, Sister called the same legal firm that had just won a case for the Little Sisters of the Poor. Thanks to Becket legal representation, the Little Sisters were finally granted an exemption from the mandate that would have forced them to provide contraceptive coverage to their employees. The ruling was an important step in the fight for religious liberty, so Sister Dede knew she was in good hands.

Becket attorneys convincingly made the case that because it is legal in D.C. for a minor to seek an abortion without parental consent, it is also legal for a minor to seek a reversal. "Don't worry, Sister Dede. We have your back!" her lawyers assured her.

Sister is saddened that while telemedicine abortion pill services are available in many places, physicians who would like to treat patients seeking to *reverse* their chemical abortions risk losing their medical licenses in some states. She calls this "malpractice" and cites the irony of those who believe that "it's okay to kill the baby, but not okay to try to save the baby's life."[99] She further illustrates the contradiction of surgeons who may work vigorously "to save the life of a child needing surgical correction of a congenital anomaly, and yet, in the same hospital, a perfectly healthy baby's life is being ended

---

[99] Sister Dede's address to the Arlington Advisory Forum, March 2024, 4.

by abortion."[100] In her many addresses to physicians nationwide, Sister continues her plea for compassionate health care that honors the dignity of each human life from conception until natural death.

[100] Address to the Arlington Advisory Forum, 4, referencing a comment attributed to C. Everett Koop, the surgeon general under Ronald Reagan in 1981.

Part 2

A Week in the Life of Sister Dede Byrne

11

The Convent (Setting the Stage)

The convent of the Little Workers of the Sacred Hearts of Jesus and Mary is in Northeast D.C., about a five-minute drive from the Catholic University of America (CUA) and the Basilica of the National Shrine of the Immaculate Conception. The humble convent buildings and associated casa — a small white residential home for religious or guests — take up one small D.C. city block. The large sign on the corner displays the order's name and indicates they have been "Serving [the] Brookland [neighborhood] since 1955 and Serving the World since 1894." Approaching the front of the unassuming buildings, one sees a sign in the front window that simply reads "PRAY."

Immediately inside the front door is a small table on the left filled with reading materials, such as abortion-pill-reversal brochures, a police officer's devotional book, copies of the Emancipation Proclamation, and countless prayer cards and devotionals.

Just beyond the small table is the humble chapel. The sisters have morning Mass daily and adoration three times daily — morning, noon, and evening. The chapel seats ten to twelve comfortably, and the small tabernacle window allows Sister Dede to expose Our Lord for adoration by simply opening and closing the window shutters. The oval wooden plaque beneath the altar includes the Sacred Heart, the Immaculate Heart pierced with a sword, and an Italian inscription: *Venga il Regno Tuo* (Thy Kingdom Come). The image was designed by the Little

Workers' founder, Blessed Francesco Maria Greco (1857–1931), in the late 1800s.

The kneeler on the right side of the chapel is used by attendees, all of whom kneel, one after the other, for reception of Holy Communion. The sanctuary is a semicircle, and wooden statues of the Blessed Mother and Saint Joseph are displayed on wall shelves. Handbells on the small table beside the altar are rung during the Consecration. On the left side of the wall is a photo and first-class relic of Blessed Greco.

An Interesting Library

One point of interest for the many convent visitors are the diverse reading materials throughout, which provide a glimpse into who Sister Dede is — her ministry, charisms, personality, and interests. The pew area in the chapel is stuffed with devotionals and other reading materials, such as *Fatima Priest*, a manual for home enthronement of the Sacred Hearts, Latin Mass compendiums, the Way of the Cross, and a guide for saying the Patriotic Rosary to invoke God's blessing on our nation.

To the right of the front door is a small reception area to receive and visit with guests. The room includes simple glass cabinets with many relics and a commemoration plaque in honor of Mother Teresa's June 3, 1997, Congressional Gold Medal Ceremony in which Sister Dede was excited to play a supporting role. The Infant of Prague statue sits atop the fireplace mantle, and next to it is displayed a varied set of books: *The Basilica of the National Shrine of the Immaculate Conception*, *A Treasury of Irish Art* (Sister is *very* Irish), *The Olympic Spirit* (she is also an avid sports enthusiast), *Notre Dame Cathedral*, and, finally, a 3.5-inch-thick *Illustrated History of Surgery*. Sitting on a table by the front window is a book titled *EKG Interpretation*.

Though there are, of course, the typical reading materials one would expect to find in a convent — books such as Fulton Sheen's *Life of Christ*, Pope Benedict's encyclical letter *Deus Caritas Est*, *Slaying*

Dragons: What Exorcist Priests See and What We Should Know, Saints who Saw Hell, and the like — there are as many surprising books as well. Examples include *The Truth about COVID-19* by Drs. Mercola and Cummins; *Sudan's Nuba Mountains People Under Siege,* which features Sister as a contributor and highlights her surgical experiences there; and a Xeroxed article about a film that explores the controversy of vaccinations. Also interesting is a book about abortion that contains research, key elements of which were said to have been given to the attorneys in preparation for the Mississippi case *Dobbs v. Jackson* — the very case that led to the overturning of *Roe v. Wade.*

In the room behind the chapel is a sacristy, which includes another tabernacle, vestments for visiting priests, altar vessels, kneelers, and beautiful icons of the Divine Mercy and Our Lady. Gloria, Sister Dede's sister, often wheels Mrs. Byrne (now 101 years old and living at the convent) out the sacristy door and onto the porch for sunlight and fresh air during her visits. There, Mrs. Byrne can watch the neighborhood children who frequent the sisters' backyard, which has been converted into a playground. The area includes a padded playscape with monkey bars, slides, swings, and small ride-on toys.

The Clinic Area

The convent basement has been converted into a medical clinic and has large windows with ample natural light. Sister alternates her schedule by running an eye clinic on certain days of the month and a physical therapy clinic on others. Medical students from the Physical Therapy Departments at Howard University and George Washington University help manage the clinic, and Sister sees approximately fifteen patients each clinic day. She receives patient referrals from several clinics throughout the city that serve the poor.

There was previously a music room equipped with classroom desks, white boards, small electric keyboards, and music education materials for use by children during lessons. Given that the eye clinic currently shares space with the physical therapy area, renovations are now underway to transform the music room into a dedicated eye clinic where Sister Dede and other doctors will be able to serve countless poor and uninsured patients.

A local renowned ophthalmologist at George Washington University screens diabetic patients in the clinic who may be at risk of complications, including ocular vascular problems, hemorrhaging, and even blindness. Early detection of those with leaky retinal membranes can lead to subsequent laser treatments and potentially save a patient's eyesight. The clinic is named after Dr. Finkelstein, who was an ophthalmologist from Johns Hopkins and a Catholic convert from Judaism. Sister Dede and Dr. Finkelstein started the eye clinic together after they met on a pilgrimage to Lourdes. During one visit to the convent, college students were volunteering their time to help with physical labor related to the expansion improvements.

There is one room specifically dedicated to receiving pregnant women and providing ultrasounds. This is particularly helpful for monitoring women's status and gestation related to the abortion-pill-reversal procedures. The room is warm and inviting, with live plants, feminine artwork, floral pillowcases, cozy blankets, and a tall cabinet that serves as a small food pantry. Women are given a shopping bag after their appointments and encouraged to take home all the food they need.

Women lying on the exam table are able to view a large monitor that displays their sonogram images. Beside this is a large copy of Michelangelo's *Creation of Adam*, representing God's divine breath of life. The sonographer, Jackie, strategically placed this image in direct patient view, as she references it during appointments, to teach expectant mothers how God breathed life into their babies at the moment of conception.

The physical therapy (PT) room includes a therapy table with a huge crucifix mounted above it, a stationary bike, blood pressure machines, an entire wall full of PT equipment, medical photos, and all the other things one would expect to see in a PT clinic. There is no mistaking the Catholic identity, however, as it also includes church-sized statues of Saint Joseph and Baby Jesus, and a large picture of Our Lady of Guadalupe.

Faith-Based Health Care: From Managing Diabetes to Praying the Rosary

Mounted on the wall is a patient education center that contains flyers and brochures on diabetes, asthma, high blood pressure, cancer screening, ADHD, and allergies. Nestled in between brochures on high cholesterol and insulin therapy is a stack of holy cards on the Eucharist and the Mass. Under the wall display is a table with a CD player and a selection of sacred music sometimes played during clinic hours to create a peaceful atmosphere for patients. Leaning against a bottle of hand sanitizer — and beside a stack of brochures on managing cholesterol — is a beautiful picture of the Blessed Mother. And under the instructions in Spanish for those with diabetes are instructions for praying the Rosary. It is a beautiful combination for truly holistic care — body, mind, and soul.

Additional Ministries

Around the corner are two other buildings the sisters own. One is an additional small convent for Indian sisters who are in the United States, and the building next door is a large boardinghouse. There is currently a waiting list for rooms at the boardinghouse, as its location in the area makes it conveniently situated. The cost of maintaining the many buildings is a financial burden, and the sisters are losing money on the boarding home. But despite having more than two hundred thousand dollars in needed repairs, the sisters are grateful to be able to provide temporary housing for those in need, particularly religious and students pursuing graduate studies at the Catholic University of America.

Next to the main convent is a white residential home that the sisters own and that they lovingly call the Gesu Bambino House. In the past, it has housed expectant mothers who chose life or reversed their abortions and had no place to go. Currently, two laywomen are living a community-type life there with hopes of eventually receiving permission to begin a new religious order dedicated to serving abortion-minded women. They have already helped nearly a dozen expectant women and also helped secure money for the ultrasound machine used in Sister's clinic.

The clinic maintains a modest reserve fund to assist with things such as the ministry at the casa, providing rides for women to and from their abortion-reversal appointments, taking them to lunch after their appointments, and providing any other needed TLC. And sometimes donations come from the most unexpected places. When people hear about Sister's work, they want to help.

Sister was invited to speak at a meeting for Legatus, an international organization of Catholic business professionals dedicated to witnessing to the love of Christ both personally and in the workplace. She laughingly shares that when she attended the hosting chapter's meeting and was seated at the head table next to a priest who had never heard of her, she immediately felt at ease. She disdains attention for her own sake but docilely allows God to use her for His glory or to advance His truth.

After the meeting, a couple approached and asked Sister with what needs they might assist. They admired her courage and wanted to help advance her ministry. The couple donated enough monthly to cover utilities, casa repairs, and other expenses that allowed for the sisters to house a mother and her baby for more than a year. One talk resulted in advancing the pro-life cause. "That's just how God works," Sister states. As for any needed repairs, Sister dives right in to assist and is no stranger to manual labor. During one visit to the convent, she was supervising the casa renovations and was up and down the ladder as frequently as the workmen!

Grandma's House Times Ten

When Sister Licia's health took a turn for the worse in 2017, Sister Dede needed additional assistance at the convent to help care for her. A Filipino nun by the name of Sister Helen recommended two faithful Catholic laywomen, Evelyn and Lea, as caregivers. Evelyn recalls hearing of Sister Dede for the first time and wondering, "So is she a doctor or a sister? Or a sister and a colonel?" — as well as her resultant delight in learning that Sister was all three! The loving and tender care these women provided for Sister Licia before her death, as well as the care they now provide for Mrs. Byrne (who is lovingly called "Mama") is beautiful to witness. Another caretaker, Melani, recently came to assist. "Sister Dede has helped all three of us, personally and in our families. We are so grateful!" Evelyn, Lea, and Melani lovingly reflect.

The number of long- and short-term patients continually varies at the convent, as does the number of sisters. Depending on availability and patients at the time, the sisters also occasionally host attorneys in town for pro-life cases or business on Capitol Hill. Sister Pamela, who served as an intake nurse at the Catholic Charities clinic, was recently sent on assignment to Rome, and both Sister Licia and Martha (a terminal lung cancer patient) recently passed on to their eternal rewards. In fact, Sister met Martha's son when he flew in from France to attend her funeral, and the two have had many subsequent visits. During one discussion en route back to the convent from Reagan

International Airport, Sister shared, "John, you know your mother very much wanted you to be baptized. Although she's gone now, you really need to consider what God is calling you to do." Little did she know that the occasion would present itself so quickly. "Sister, I'm ready now; I want to be baptized," John excitedly shared during his last visit. By God's grace and Sister's influence, John was baptized and welcomed into God's family.

Bishop Billy sometimes offers Mass at the convent and enjoys his visits with Mrs. Byrne. "Mama, how are you?" Evelyn recalls his asking her as he prepared to take her outside for some fresh air. "Mama, I think you need a little color," the good bishop commented as he searched for her lipstick.

During a visit to the convent in 2020, Sister Licia was still able to walk. The two entered the guest area singing an excerpt from an Italian song together. The loving joy was moving. Twice during subsequent visits, Mrs. Byrne could be heard singing "Walkin' My Baby Back Home" and other Sinatra songs in her bedroom. Howard Walsh, special counsel for the Thomas More Society, calls the convent "Grandma's house times ten," as those who visit sense the love, warmth, and joy manifested by the sisters, who so beautifully witness to the love of Christ.

Taking Christ to the Streets

On nice days during the warmer weather, Sister Dede sometimes arranges for outside Rosary walks as part of Afternoon Prayer. Aides, sisters, volunteers, and anyone staying at the casa meet outside to walk through the neighborhood for fresh air while praying the Rosary aloud. Everyone takes turns pushing those in wheelchairs up the steep neighborhood sidewalks and uses translation cards to recite each decade of the Rosary in a different language. It's charming to witness the reactions of neighborhood children who stop to watch the small parade of sisters walking down the D.C. sidewalks and praying aloud.

On one walk, we were accompanied by a young Hispanic woman who, after Sister's assistance, had chosen life and was now the proud mother of a beautiful eight-month-old boy. Those who frequent the convent commented how beautiful it is to see the boy — once in danger of abortion — now crawling around on the chapel floor.

The Patriotic Rosary

Given Sister's great devotion to the Rosary and mindful of its power to bring about great miracles, it is not surprising that the Little Workers begin each morning praying for our Church and our nation's leaders by recitation of the patriotic Rosary. They ask that the precious blood of Jesus cover each state (one Hail Mary for each of the fifty states) and dedicate the Rosary for the conversion of our country. The first decade is devoted to the presidency, the second to the Supreme Court, the third to the Senate and the House of Representatives, the fourth to the nation's governors, and the fifth to county and municipal offices. They also pray for certain Church leaders by name, asking that God guide and strengthen them in their ministry of speaking truth to a world much in need.

The Rosary Is Our Weapon of Love

During one of my visits to see Sister, she was preparing her address for the National Rosary Rally held in D.C. on Sunday, October 9, 2022. She was to be a featured guest among an esteemed group including Bishop Coffey, Monsignor Charles Pope, Father Richard Heilman, and Doug Barry.

She spoke of how supplication via fervent prayer and recitation of the Rosary, our weapon of love, has been responsible for winning many wars and conflicts. In a huge crowd assembled in front of the

United States Senate, she explained how, in April 2014, Boko Haram kidnapped two hundred young girls in Nigeria. Our Lord appeared in a vision to Nigerian bishop Doeme, held out a sword, and said thrice, "Boko Haram is gone!" When the bishop reached out to take the sword, it turned into a rosary. This prompted him to plead with all of Nigeria to pray the Rosary for the oppression levied by Boko Haram. She explained how the Rosary was thus responsible for the eventual release of the girls and the surrender of seven hundred Boko Haram members.[101]

Sister went on to say that while the victims of Boko Haram escaped decapitation, babies are still being decapitated daily here in the United States through abortion. She exhorted attendees to pray fervently for lawmakers and summarized, "All this craziness in the world will be over if we continue to unite and pray as one family with the most powerful, yet sweet, and loving weapon that has ever existed — the Rosary!"[102]

Sister also suggests that the need for the Patriotic Rosary is more urgent now, post-Dobbs, than ever before. On June 24, 2022, in *Dobbs v. Jackson Women's Health Organization,* the Supreme Court ruling to overturn *Roe v. Wade* returned the authority to regulate abortion to the people and their elected representatives in individual states. When the sitting president at the time, a Catholic, stated that the decision marked "a sad day for the Court and for the country,"[103] Sister Dede commented, "[The] president is saying that it's a sad day in America

---

[101] "2022 National Rosary Rally and National Eucharistic Procession," Rosary Coast to Coast, October 9, 2022, YouTube video, https:// www.youtube.com/watch?v=0MrUNud3Rbc.

[102] "2022 National Rosary Rally."

[103] "Remarks by President Biden on the Supreme Court Decision to Overturn Roe v. Wade," White House, June 24, 2022, https://www .whitehouse.gov/briefing-room/speeches-remarks/2022/06/24 /remarks-by-president-biden-on-the-supreme-court-decision-to -overturn-roe-v-wade/.

now that *Roe v. Wade* has been overturned, but what Catholic would say that?"[104]

Sister believes the current battle for the rights of the unborn is a quickly escalating battle of good versus evil between Our Lord and the devil. While Our Lord was victorious in the overturning of *Roe v. Wade*, "that vote seemed to ramp up the devil's anger," Sister continues. As the legal battles continue at the state level, she reiterates the powerful efficacy of the Rosary as a remedy for overcoming evil and confusion in the world.

* * *

Much has been written in the media about Sister Dede since she first garnered attention nationwide in 2020. But reading about her inspirational life pales in comparison to an eyewitness account. What follows is a first-person narrative account that reflects Sister's life, impact, love, and courage in a seven-day period. I found the experience to be an incredible blessing in my life.

All patient names and identifying characteristics have been changed.

---

[104] Zelda Caldwell, " 'Rosary Rally' outside U.S. Capitol to Unleash Prayers for a 'World Gone Mad,' " *Catholic World Report*, October 7, 2022, https://www.catholicworldreport.com/2022/10/07/rosary-rally -outside-u-s-capitol-to-unleash-prayers-for-a-world-gone-mad/.

12

Day 1: Clinic Day

Sister Dede wears many hats, and keeping her medical and surgical skills honed is important. She alternates her clinic schedule at Catholic Charities and surgery days at Sibley Hospital as a means of engaging in outside medical work at least weekly. This outside work, when added to the continuous stream of patients she sees at her convent clinic, keeps Sister incredibly busy. Every other Tuesday, she sees patients at the Spanish Catholic Center, and every other Friday, she volunteers at a nonprofit hospital managed by Johns Hopkins.

D.C. law requires that area hospitals perform a certain number of free surgeries for the uninsured. By offering free or low-cost services at various clinics in more-impoverished areas of D.C., Sister is able to perform any needed surgeries at Sibley Memorial.[105] She was once the director of the medical clinic where she now serves, and her leadership is still valued and evident. She sees first-time or returning patients as well as pre- and post-op surgical patients, many of whom are referred from Mary's Clinic, another local health-care provider.

On the day of my visit, I drove through city streets and arrived at the Catholic Charities clinic, otherwise known as the Spanish Catholic Center, in the Palisades neighborhood of D.C. — the very place Sister Dede's father volunteered his services so many years earlier. This clinic serves D.C. as well as Maryland's Montgomery and Prince George

---

[105] Schiffer, "Sister Deirdre."

Counties. Clinic services include medical and dental care, English as a Second Language classes, job training programs, a food pantry, and other family support services, such as assistance with clothing, shelter, medication, and publicly funded insurance.[106]

When I entered, there were seven people of differing ages in the small waiting room. Sister texted to say she was running late and was bringing a fifteen-year-old homeschooled girl named Maria who was visiting from out of state. Maria was considering following in her father's footsteps as a physician and was also considering the possibility of a religious vocation. Hoping to cultivate both her spiritual and academic growth, her parents arranged for her to shadow Sister shortly after they met her last year. Sister Pamela, who had recently graduated with an RN degree from the Catholic University of America and passed her board exams, also came to serve as Sister's intake nurse.

Before rounds, Sister introduced us to various clinic employees and volunteers in the large, multilevel clinic. Physician and employee responses and deference to Sister clearly reflected their respect and admiration.

Not atypical, Sister had a full schedule of fifteen patients, most of whom were native Spanish speakers. She reviewed charts as Sister Pamela completed preliminary intake, updated histories, and logged patient symptoms. Sister Dede's basic Spanish skills facilitated initial patient interactions, while Joseph (a clinic volunteer) and Sister Pamela, both proficient speakers, were able to assist with more advanced translation needs. Each patient was treated with incredible dignity and respect, and Sister's warm bedside manner and sense of humor immediately put them at ease.

[106] "Spanish Catholic Center," Catholic Charities, https://www.catholic charitiesdc.org/about-us/our-locations/spanish-catholic-center/.

Day 1: Clinic Day

You Can Thank Me by Sending Us
Your First-Born Daughter

Patient 1 was a young tattooed woman with a ten-centimeter lipoma. Joseph was present to facilitate translation as Sister measured the mass. The patient was concerned she might have a tumor, but Sister reassured her that it was nothing serious and could be removed with minor outpatient surgery there in the clinic. Sister completed the necessary paperwork for a follow-up appointment and jested that, as compensation, the woman could send her first-born daughter to join the Little Workers of the Sacred Hearts.

Patient 2 was a middle-aged woman who was in excruciating pain and referred from a local clinic for potential gallbladder problems. She ranked her pain level as ten out of ten and was desperate for relief. Sister Pamela, in her typical joyful manner, completed the intake and medical history and also engaged her in more personal conversation. When Sister Dede entered the room, both she and Sister Pamela helped the patient onto the exam table as she moaned in pain.

"Have you had an H. pylori test?" Sister asked.

"No, Sister," responded the patient.

Sister's thorough examination and probing questions revealed that the patient's diffuse pain and other symptoms were not consistent with gallbladder pathology but, instead, raised concerns about a more serious diagnosis. Sister instructed her to go immediately to the ER for a CT scan to rule out the possibility of a burst appendix.

Patient 3 was a middle-aged woman with a history of uterine fibroids, hemorrhaging, anemia, esophageal reflux, bloating, and upper GI discomfort. She had just received a blood transfusion to treat hemorrhaging and presyncope, and also tested negative for H. pylori, a useful test for ruling out gastritis-related illness.

"Joseph, please ask her if she remembers what the results of her recent ultrasound showed," Sister instructed.

"The ultrasound you received at Mary's Clinic — do you remember if it showed anything?" Joseph inquired.

"Inflammation," the patient responded.

"Please tell her that it is risky for her to keep getting transfusions like this. Has she had a gynecological exam recently?" Sister asked.

"Yes, just last month," Joseph translated.

"Good, tell her she will need to be careful to have her gynecologist closely monitor this." And then, privately to Joseph, Sister continued:

"Sometime in serious situations like this, a hysterectomy or ablation are required. On the other hand, at only forty-one years old, it's important to weigh everything very carefully before considering a hysterectomy. After all, my mother had Bishop Billy at the age of forty-two!"

Of course, Sister was referring to her own brother, who was recently elevated to the bishopric in Springfield, Massachusetts. Had her own mother had a hysterectomy at forty-one, the Church would be missing a shepherd.

In the end, the woman did not require surgery and was to return after her next gynecological visit if her GI symptoms persisted. Meanwhile, elevating the head of her bed and refraining from meals immediately before lying down could assist with her gastroesophageal reflux disease (GERD).

Patient 4 was a middle-aged male who was referred for left quadrant pain. He was accompanied by his twenty-year-old daughter. A keychain with an image of Our Lady of Guadalupe hung from his belt, and his daughter sported a glitter iPhone case, also with a large image of Our Lady. The patient had fatty liver disease and elevated liver enzymes. Though he also had a history of gallstones and was being referred for potential hernia, Sister was more concerned about the possibility of hepatitis. His recent H. pylori test was negative.

"On a scale of one to ten, how bad is your pain?" Sister asked.

"Five out of ten," he replied.

"Okay, hop up here, and let's have a look. Bend your legs, please. That relaxes the abdomen. Well, I feel something here, but it's not a hernia."

Sister went to the computer, pulled up a medical image online, and asked him to have a look. "You have diastasis recti," she said as she pointed out the area of abdominal musculature. "The vertical bulge I feel between your abdominal walls is not a hernia but the fascia here in the center of your abdomen. In the case of a hernia, there is a tear in the fascia, while with diastasis, there is only a stretching of it."

The patient seemed relieved, and his daughter commented how "cool" it was to have a "nun doctor" tending to her father. It was the first time she had ever seen such a thing.

Patient 5 was a male whose ultrasound revealed a half-centimeter polyp in his gallbladder wall. Sister explained that it wasn't a gallstone, as he had originally thought. She suggested a yearly exam to monitor things.

Patient 6 was a middle-aged man who was accompanied by his two young boys. They played videos and games on an iPhone while their father spoke to Sister to discuss pre-op concerns for his upcoming hernia surgery scheduled for that Friday.

Patient 7 was a young woman who was recovering from gallbladder surgery and had come for suture removal. She had apparently been very scared to have surgery and was now very grateful and relieved. She hugged Sister before she left.

Patient 8 was an older man who had a history of hernia difficulties and was there for additional assessment. Sister's questions and physical examination revealed nothing abnormal. He had a hepatitis screen and fortunately tested negative. All seemed well, and he was told to return for a pre-op exam.

Patient 9 was a middle-aged woman with a hernia, and though there was some improvement since her previous exam, she needed to be scheduled for surgery. Joseph assisted, and she was added to Sister's surgical schedule at Sibley Memorial Hospital.

Patient 10 was there for a pre-op appointment. Sister Pamela went over all the required instructions with her.

Patient 11 was referred for a small lipoma. Sister reassured her it was nothing of concern and that she could follow up for minor surgery.

Patient 12 had a six-month history of fasciitis, pain, and foot swelling. Though he had already seen three doctors, nobody was able to provide relief. He had faithfully maintained his prescribed exercises, but nothing worked to alleviate his pain. Sister examined him.

"Well, we can try an injection of corticosteroids, but I can't promise that it will help."

"Please try," he begged.

As she was administering the injection in the side of his foot, Sister instructed him to offer up his pain as a sacrifice. As the man grimaced, she lovingly comforted, "Just think of Jesus on the Cross."

Patient 13 was a last-minute addition to Sister's patient schedule — someone she squeezed in as a personal favor to a man she had met in Sudan and who was now living in the United States. The patient was his sister-in-law who was visiting from overseas. The young woman was in D.C. to visit her family. She typically walks three and a half miles a day but now had a swollen leg and ankle. She had recent scans to rule out deep vein thrombosis. Sister requested copies of her medical records and MRI results from Germany and asked her to come back for a follow-up appointment at the convent that Saturday.

Patient 14 was a pre-op appointment. Sister Pamela visited with the patient to review instructions for her upcoming surgery with Sister Dede.

Patient 15, the last patient of the day, was a beautiful young woman who was accompanied by her young daughter. She was coming in for the removal of her contraceptive implant. When reading the notes before entering the exam room, Sister explained that it is not unusual for some doctors to press young female patients to agree to birth control implants. Removing these implants is among Sister's favorite things to do at the clinic. She finds it very rewarding, uses it as an opportunity to catechize patients, and celebrates with them their openness to life.

Sister asked Joseph to translate.

"Do you have any allergies? Or maybe just to doctors, huh?" Sister teased. It immediately put the woman at ease, and they both laughed.

"Did your doctor in El Salvador pressure you into getting this implant?" Sister asked.

"I miscarried five years ago, and my doctor told me I needed it to let my uterus heal. He said the implant would help," she responded.

Sister put on her size-6.5 gloves, searched through medical supplies, and draped the woman's arm for minor surgery and removal of the implant.

"I'm very happy you are getting this out! It's very good to be open to life."

"How long do I have to wait before I can get pregnant?" the woman anxiously asked.

She shared that she wanted at least four more children and had already chosen a name for her next girl: Maria. As Sister finished dressing her arm, the grateful woman commented that she couldn't believe a nun was removing her birth control implant. She left elated and with great hope for her future and family.

Sister Dede's Loving Care for All

The clinic day was winding down at about 3:30 p.m., but Sister still had many notes to enter. She had seen fifteen patients in five and a half hours. As she was finishing, I spoke with various clinic employees.

"Do I understand correctly that you came out of retirement to volunteer here?" I asked Joseph, who had accompanied us much of the day. After his retirement, he returned to school for additional training that would equip him to assist Sister in her ministry.

"I was so inspired by Sister's love and treatment of people that I wanted to help her in any way I could," he stated.

Walking down the hall, I encountered Dr. Jones, who was also happy to share his insights.

"Sister has such a big heart and loves all people. It doesn't matter what color, what religion, what background, she loves everyone and treats them with great respect."

"Do the other physicians feel the same?" I asked.

"Absolutely. Do you remember that man that Sister saw with the fasciitis? He has previously seen three other doctors and has received no relief. Sister Dede is his fourth doctor. All the doctors in the area know that if they've tried everything and don't know how to help a patient — if they don't know what else to do — they say, 'Send them to Sister Dede. She'll find a way to help.'"

Another worker at the clinic has been employed there for more than fifteen years and loves Sister very much. When asked if it was typical for Sister to see fifteen patients in a day, she responded, "Oh, there were only so many because Sister Dede never refuses anyone. She will see any number of people. She is very special and helps so many people — Spanish, African American, everyone — they are all special to her."

It was also Sister's beautiful influence that persuaded Dr. James, a general surgeon whom Sister Dede first met at Sibley Memorial in the early 2000s, to volunteer his services at the clinic. When he announced his retirement from Sibley many years earlier, Sister already had plans for him.

"Congratulations, Dr. James! What will you do with your free time?" Sister asked.

"Well, I'm gonna play golf, go fly-fishing, and travel," he responded.

"You should come volunteer at Catholic Charities. It will be good for your soul!"

Unable to refuse the invitation — he jokes that Sister's requests are like "bear traps" — Dr. James agreed to volunteer and has many fond memories of his years caring for patients together with Sister at the clinic. In particular, he notes that her good sense of humor was a blessing for everyone involved.

"Surgery was started by barbers in the Middle Ages. You remember that, don't you, Dr. James?" Sister once teased.

"Yeah, yeah, I heard that!" the good doctor responded with a smile.

The two worked well together, and he distinctly recalls her down-to-earth manner, which immediately put patients at ease. When there was a female patient in need of additional support or counsel about a personal or pro-life matter, Dr. James covered the other clinic patients to provide Sister extra needed time for the consultation. He counts his years with Sister as some of the most rewarding of his career and finally "retired from retirement" in 2018. "While many people just wear their beliefs on their sleeves, Sister Dede lives them," he remarks, "and every action and interaction is an outpouring of her love. I am proud to know her."

13

Day 2: Abortion Clinic Day

Schedule permitting, Sister Dede frequently travels with another sister to pray outside a clinic that provides abortions. They silently pray for those entering and exiting the clinic, with the hope that they might be able to witness to Christ's love or offer assistance to those in need. Sister is also sometimes able to speak outside with women who may have begun a chemical abortion and share with them that an abortion pill reversal procedure exists. Never judgment, always love.

Sister's hope is that the regular presence of the Little Workers at the clinic will touch a patient's or employee's heart. The abortion clinic escorts and visitors don't typically make eye contact with her, but on one occasion, a man waiting outside did. He was wearing a sweatshirt that read, "I support women." Sister Dede approached and gently asked, "Do you know that they are taking the lives of babies in there?" The man offered no response, and Sister prayed that the Holy Spirit might open his heart to hear her words.

Sister tried showing him an ultrasound video of an expectant mother in hopes that the active baby in utero might prove impactful. The man's heart was unmoved, however.

Given the close proximity of the clinic's front doors to the sidewalk and street, our small group of five — Sister Dede, Sister Pamela, Sister Elias, Maria, and I — were positioned close enough to the escorts to hear personal conversations about their dinner and weekend plans.

When a lunch delivery man arrived to take food inside, Sister asked, "Are you aware that they do abortions in there?" She later explained that educating third-party delivery people about what is going on at abortion clinics can sometimes be enough to prompt their refusal to do future business there.

I Can Reverse Your Abortion

Sister spoke with women coming out of the clinic, one of whom was a beautiful young woman wearing gym pants, a sweatshirt, tennis shoes, a baseball cap, and large sunglasses. Sister followed her down the sidewalk. "If you just took a pill for a chemical abortion, it can often be reversed. I'm a physician, and if you google 'abortion reversal,' you can be connected with a person who will help you. If you visit my clinic within seventy-two hours of taking the abortion pill, we can begin the reversal process, which poses no harm to you or the baby. I'm asking you to please consider the life of your baby."

Stunned, the woman stopped and responded, "Huh. I appreciate you," and walked away.

Have Altar, Will Travel

Sister approached other women exiting the clinic in this same manner. Though it's possible to track the number of women who call the Abortion Pill Reversal hotline in a specific geographical area, it is impossible to know just how many expectant mothers may have stopped to reconsider or had eventual conversions of heart after their interactions with Sister outside the abortion clinic. The sisters believe that prayer and a steady presence help, however.

Trish Palumbo recalls bringing friends from Baltimore to pray with Sister Dede at this very clinic in 2021. It was a sunny Sunday morning in March, and they all drove to the clinic to pray. "It was eighty degrees, and people were peeling off their coats," Trish remembers. "A big white van rounded the corner and stopped directly in front of the clinic's front door, which is only feet from the street. The van doors slid open to reveal an altar set up for Mass." It was Bishop Coffey and Father Peter Ryan, S.J. — have altar, will travel!

And thus, the good bishop and Father Peter celebrated Sunday Mass just feet from the front doors of the abortion clinic. Random passersby stopped to participate in the Mass — men, women, children, babies crying and playing on the sidewalks — right in front of the abortion clinic!

Bishop Coffey asked someone to use an iPhone to bring up the names of all the abortion clinic doctors who worked at that location. One by one, he called out the names of each clinic doctor, asking that God's enlightenment, healing, and mercy be drawn down upon them. He prayed for the women who entered the clinic and asked that the Holy Spirit descend on that location. "It was an incredible and moving experience," Trish now fondly recalls.

Supporting Pro-Life Colleagues

After praying the Rosary at the clinic for hours, we needed to get back to the convent for Afternoon Prayer. As we rushed back to the car, we came upon a woman sitting in front of a grocery store who asked for money.

"Let me buy you lunch. What kind of sandwich would you like? Turkey? How about chips?" Sister asked.

The woman eagerly agreed. Sister bought her lunch, took it back out to the grateful woman, and told her that Jesus loves her. When traveling with Sister, these sorts of interactions are common experiences and ones that her travel companions have come to expect.

On the way back to the convent, Sister explained that attorney Howard Walsh and several others were in town to defend a high-profile case involving pro-life advocates who were being tried for their involvement in a 2020 rescue at a local abortion clinic. Sister hoped to make it downtown to the courthouse to listen to the hearings.

After prayer and lunch, we took the Metro to Judiciary Square and walked to Constitution Avenue, where the U.S. District Court for the District of Columbia is located. Sister Dede was immediately recognized by many in the gallery who waved or quietly greeted her. In fact, it quickly became evident during the break that most in the courtroom — lawyers, defendants, and gallery attendees — knew and loved Sister. Her courageous witness has made her a strong advocate in pro-life circles. The defendants and lawyers were grateful for her presence and commented that her prayers on their behalf provided comfort and much needed support.

The defendants and witnesses were offering weighty testimony related to the matter at hand, and things were heated and contentious. After listening to testimony and speaking with defendants and attorneys during breaks, Sister needed to get back to the convent for Evening Prayer and adoration. We decided we would return the next day for continued testimony.

Exiting the courthouse, Sister called for an Uber ride back to the convent. She immediately engaged the driver in conversation and shared that we had just heard testimony related to a pro-life case. The man shared that he was from Ethiopia, and Sister asked what religion he was.

"I'm an Evangelical Christian," he replied.

"Do you see that tree over there?" Sister asked, pointing to the side of the road. "The trunk is like the Catholic Church. And those branches represent the various religions that broke off the trunk. Do you know who started your Evangelical church?"

He didn't know.

"Wouldn't you rather belong to a church started by Jesus Christ Himself?"

"Well, yes, I guess I would," the humble driver replied.

Day 2: Abortion Clinic Day

"Welcome home!" Sister exclaimed.

Shortly after returning to my hotel room for the evening, I received a text from Sister with the next day's schedule. "Tomorrow after Mass, prayer, & breakfast, I will take Maria to the airport then run a few errands. At 12:30 (hopefully) APR [abortion pill reversal] mom is coming, followed by midday prayer, feeding mom and Sister Licia for lunch, then I would love to head back to court."

Sister had apparently received a text from her colleague that evening indicating that a woman had just phoned the Abortion Pill Reversal hotline. "I was told it might be possible to reverse my abortion. Is this true?" the nervous woman asked.

The nurse who intercepted the call connected her with a physician who assessed the situation and explained how the reversal works. The doctor prescribed the reversal medication and, since the woman was calling from the D.C. area, referred her to Sister Dede for follow up care the next day.

Not having a clue at that time what Sister meant by "APR," I simply replied to her text by indicating I would be there to pick her up after morning Mass in time to take her and Maria to the airport. Little did I know that the next day would prove to be one of the most memorable of my life.

14

Day 3: Abortion Pill Reversal

On Thursday morning, we had many errands to run. Sister mentioned that she couldn't understand my interest in accompanying her for simple errands around the city. What history has revealed, however, is that Sister's gifts and impact are often manifested in the smallest of daily tasks. While she is certainly known for her courage and testimony on a larger stage, her strength is drawn from daily Mass and Eucharistic adoration, a steady diet of prayer and spiritual reading, and in doing small things with great love. Her practice of employing mundane, daily duties as opportunities to evangelize and witness to Christ's love is precisely what nurtures sanctity and makes her so inspiring.

Our last stop that morning was to be to the military commissary to pick up a few groceries. Her military benefits afford her a 30 percent savings on groceries compared with civilian stores. Not unusual for the D.C. area, traffic was heavy.

"Oh boy, we are running late. I think we need to abort mission. We need to be sure we are back for the 1:00 p.m. APR."

"I meant to ask what that acronym stands for, Sister," I replied.

"APR? Abortion pill reversal," Sister answered.

"Abortion pill reversal? Are you kidding me?" I exclaimed.

Since Sister had been praying in the chapel when the original call came in the night before, her colleague, a physician from Charlottesville, Virginia, took the call and contacted Sister with an update. The good news was that the girl was within the seventy-two-hour window of having taken the RU-486 abortion pill, which meant better odds of saving the baby.

The bad news was the woman was only five weeks pregnant. This was bad for two reasons. First, when a woman is only five weeks along, the images on the ultrasound are not easily identifiable as a baby. This can, sadly, sometimes result in their refusal to believe they are ending a human life. Second, the abortion pill is more highly toxic to smaller embryos than to more developed infants. Thus, the further along mothers are in their first trimester, the higher the chance the abortion-reversal process will work.

While statistics indicate that administration of oral progesterone averages a 64 to 68 percent success rate nationwide,[107] Sister Dede currently averages a success rate greater than 76 percent at her clinic. Since she first began the abortion-pill-reversal procedures in 2021, thirteen healthy babies have survived as a result.

"Women seeking chemical abortions are instructed to first take the RU-486 pill. If they don't have a miscarriage within twenty-four hours, they are told to take the second pill. This causes horrible contractions, which aborts the baby," Sister explains.

The following is taken from the Charlotte Lozier Institute:

The Abortion Pill Reversal protocol is started within 72 hours after taking the first abortion drug, mifepristone, and before the second drug, misoprostol, is taken. The medical provider will prescribe bioidentical progesterone to outnumber and outcompete the mifepristone in order to reverse the effects of the mifepristone. An ultrasound is performed as soon as possible to confirm heart rate, placement, and dating of the pregnancy. The progesterone treatment will usually continue through the

---

[107] "Can the Abortion Pill Be Reversed?" Abortion Pill Reversal, https://abortionpillreversal.com/abortion-pill-reversal/overview.

first trimester of pregnancy in an attempt to reverse the effects of the mifepristone.[108]

God Will Forgive You. . . . Will You Forgive Yourself?

We arrived back at the convent at 12:45. Sister Elias and Sister Pamela were getting Mrs. Byrne and Sister Licia ready for Afternoon Prayer, and we headed to the clinic. Walking down a narrow staircase at the back of the convent, the door on the left at the bottom of the stairs leads into the clinic. The cozy room is equipped with a quaint seating area, an exam table, an ultrasound machine, and a large monitor for patients to view the ultrasound images.

Jackie, the sonographer, was seated on the left with a computer, and on the right sat a beautiful young woman, slender and fit, with the eyes and facial features of a model. Her straight, shoulder-length hair was draped over her pale floral sundress, and she wore designer sandals that were apparent primarily because of the way she was so nervously swinging her crossed legs. Jackie introduced the young woman as Emma.

"Hi, I'm Sister Dede. We'll take good care of you. Thank you for doing this," Sister comforted as she placed her hand on the young woman's shoulder.

Tears immediately welled up in Emma's huge eyes, and she nervously wiped them away. Sister asked Jackie to continue the intake questions and said she'd return in fifteen minutes for the exam.

"They want to be sure she 'does the deed,' so they often make the woman take the pill while she is at the clinic," Sister later explained. They were going to let her see the ultrasound at the abortion clinic, but Emma declined.

[108] "Abortion Pill Reversal," Charlotte Lozier Institute, September 24, 2021, https://lozierinstitute.org/abortion-pill-reversal-a-record-of-safety-and-efficacy/.

The sonographer completed an ultrasound and confirmed what Sister thought to be true: the baby was just five weeks old.

"Is the baby okay?" Emma nervously asked.

"It looks like it's just a little too early to tell. You'll need to come back on Sunday, and we can tell more then. If the reversal worked, we may be able to see a heartbeat at that point," Jackie responded.

During the course of the exam, Emma shared with Sister that she was Catholic.

"Oh, so you are Catholic, huh?" Sister asked.

"Yes, and I've always been pro-life. I even *voted* and canvassed for pro-life candidates," she responded.

"Ah, I like you already!" Sister replied smiling.

Emma has a secure and rewarding job. She was involved in a confusing situation with her boyfriend, didn't know what to do, and panicked.

"Will God forgive me?" Emma asked.

"Absolutely. But the question is, will you forgive yourself?" Sister responded. "One of the ways you can help with that process is to go to Confession."

"But I haven't been to Confession since I was nine years old."

"That's okay. I've got people who can help with that!" Sister reassured.

Sister also went on to tell Emma about the conversion of Saint Paul and the conversion of abortionist Dr. Bernard Nathanson. She explained how Dr. Nathanson was the father of abortion clinics and even aborted his own child. "You've got to read his book. It's a long story, but he had a change of heart and became very pro-life," Sister recounted. "But remember, Emma, no matter what happens — whether your baby dies or whether he survives — Christ is pleased with your attempt to save your baby."

During the appointment, I had stepped into the chapel to join the Afternoon Prayer in progress. Who was this courageous woman who had made the brave decision to save her baby? How strong she must be amid her pain and confusion to have recognized her mistake and to have shown up here today. As moved as I was at that moment, however, I was unprepared for the blessing that followed.

"Well, we are done, and now we pray," Sister stated. By God's providence, Emma was the woman who had been at the abortion clinic the day before and whom Sister had approached and pleaded with to reverse her abortion — the woman who had responded, "Hmm, I appreciate you." Sister Dede's words had tugged at Emma's heart, and she began questioning her decision. Frightened, she went for a two-hour walk to reflect further on Sister's plea. By the time she arrived home, she realized she had made a terrible mistake and called the reversal hotline.

We couldn't believe it! *This* was the very young woman we were praying for less than twenty-four hours before as she walked by us after taking her first dose of Mifepristone. None of us had recognized her, as yesterday she had her hair pulled back and was wearing sunglasses and a hat. As if all that weren't dramatic enough, Sister added, "She said she'd like to go to lunch, but first she'd like to go to Confession. Would you mind taking her to the basilica for Confession, please?"

We Flood These Moms with TLC

"Are you kidding? Of course!" I answered, stunned.

"We like to flood these beautiful moms with all the TLC they need during this traumatic time," Sister said. "They just need to be loved."

I was overcome with gratitude and joy, mindful of the impact Sister's intercession had made. When I asked Sister Elias later about Sister Dede's ever-calm, ever-composed demeanor in the face of such situations, she commented that Sister has "seen so much over the years." While Sister is tenderhearted, part of the training that prepares military and surgical personnel for dealing with devastating traumas in combat includes the requirement, at times, for some level of emotional detachment. The calm and steady presence so necessary in the operating room or the heat of battle is the same quality that her anxious patients have come to appreciate and love in Sister.

Twice now, in just forty-eight hours, Sister's actions facilitated life — first in the removal of the progesterone implant at the clinic and a second time by the administration of the abortion-reversal protocol. Little did I know that two more abortion reversal patients were yet to come that week.

Sister Elias kindly offered to join us and secure a priest at the basilica in the event that confessions were not taking place when we arrived. Emma seemed eager to talk and engage during the car ride. She has an impressive educational background and shared more about her quickly advancing career, which she finds rewarding and exciting.

We arrived at the basilica at about two o'clock but discovered that confessions would not begin for another hour. We sat in a pew, side by side. I held her hand, and she cried in my arms.

"I haven't been to Confession since I was nine years old, and I don't remember what to do," she said.

Sister Elias pulled up an examination of conscience and an act of contrition on her phone.

"Can we light a candle?" Emma asked.

We prayed for her and her baby, and we prayed in thanksgiving for her heroic choice.

"I'm so proud of you, Emma! Thank you for your courage and strength."

"I don't feel strong," she replied. "I feel weak and awful. I was just promoted at work, and my career was really on track. I got confused about my situation. I didn't know if wanted to marry the guy I was with, and I didn't think I could raise a child on my own. I was so scared and didn't know what to do."

"What made you change your mind?" I asked.

"I knew what I did was wrong. For the first two hours after I got home, I kept thinking of what Sister said to me when I came out of the abortion clinic. When I called the number she told me about, the doctor explained that there was a two-thirds chance that the reversal would work. The way I figured it, even if I did lose the baby, I would at least know I tried to reverse it. I figured I'd try and then let God decide. As soon as I made the decision to reverse the abortion and picked up the reversal pills, I immediately felt peace," she said with a sigh.

Emma wanted to tour the shrine and take photos of her favorite altars and images. She has traveled the world, including Mexico, and Our Lady of Guadalupe now held a special place in her heart.

It was certainly no coincidence that she was first in line for Confession at three p.m. — the hour of Divine Mercy. While she entered with anxiety and despair, she exited with grace, gratitude, and hope. "Begin anew!" we shared with a hug. We visited the shrine gift shop, where she picked out a medal. Then we went to lunch and drove Emma home. It wouldn't be until Sunday's follow-up ultrasound appointment that we would learn the fate of her baby. Until then, we could only pray.

15

Days 4 and 5: Maintenance Days

On Friday, in addition to her daily duties, Sister spent much of the day at her computer, preparing for her various upcoming talks. She now manages a tightly booked speaking schedule, as she travels the nation addressing groups and churches about the need to be in the state of grace, receive the Eucharist, pray, and defend life from conception until natural death. As such, I next arrived to pick her up on Saturday morning, a day often devoted to tending to matters around the convent.

I was greeted at the door by Gloria, who comes every Saturday to visit and help care for her mother, Mrs. Byrne. Two years younger than Dede, she was sharing wonderful childhood memories of young Dede when Sister entered the reception area where we were sitting.

"It was a rather rough night," Sister shared. "We ended up tending to Sister Licia, who needed to be catheterized. She was in such incredible pain from everything she has going on that she was up most of the evening. This morning, I also saw two MC sisters who had bronchitis and needed medical attention."

Sister Elias wheeled Mrs. Byrne into the room to greet us.

"Hi, Mrs. Byrne. It's so nice to see you again," I commented. "You look wonderful!"

"Oh, I'm so fortunate that I always get such good care here," Mrs. Byrne commented with her typical optimism and cheerful smile.

Several years ago, Mrs. Byrne took a fall, which resulted in a C2 and L1 fracture, a left hip fracture, and a subarachnoid bleed. She was ninety-nine years old at the time, and the children were finally able to convince her that it was time to sell her condominium and move into the convent, where aides could provide her with continual care. Under Sister's loving care and vigilant medical attention, Mrs. Byrne recovered nicely. Because she is fragile, however, it is imperative to prevent additional falls.

Given that Mrs. Byrne is able to use her heels as leverage to pull the wheelchair forward, Sister Dede suggested that Sister Elias simply let her wheel about the convent and ensure her safety along the way. As she joyfully scooted away, she launched into another verse of "Walkin' My Baby Back Home."

Finally, Someone We Can Be Proud Of

Sister Elias is from Long Island originally, but she became a Carmelite in New Jersey. Previously working for attorney Howard Walsh and helping care for a quadriplegic, Sister has been assisting at the Little Workers' convent since July 2023. She was so moved by Sister Dede's example of charity that she changed the spelling of Sister Dede's name in her cell phone to read "Dēdi" because of its Latin meaning: "I have given." "Sister Dede has 'given' herself to others in every respect," she fondly offers. Sister Elias also distinctly recalls learning more about Sister Dede after her RNC speech, and thinking, *"Finally!* Finally, someone we can be proud of! We need women like her in leadership positions!"

Sister Elias is honored to be able to care for Sister Dede's mother: "It's clear the apple doesn't fall far from the tree," she reflects. "One of the healthiest signs of a good spiritual life is a good sense of humor, and Sister Dede has that in spades. As Mother Teresa said, 'I don't want any somber saints.' To have humor amid all the things she is juggling is a grace and a virtue that is given by God."

It's Who She Points to That Really Makes Me Pay Attention

Sister Elias shares charming stories of Sister Dede's evangelization of everyone she meets. "She's not afraid to engage people in grocery store lines in discussions about the Faith and even explained to the men coming to clean the convent dumpsters why they needed to vote pro-life."

"When I see how many times and how many people Sister Dede evangelizes in one day, it makes me ask myself, 'How many opportunities have *I* missed?'" Sister Elias reflects. "Sister has authentic simplicity and simple honesty. There is no pretense. She also has the grace of living the gift of the present moment, no matter where she is — even when she has to tend to a sister during the middle of holy hour. How could it ever take away from God when she is tending to Christ in another person?"

Sister Elias states that while Sister Dede has many gifts, "it's who she points to that really makes me pay attention." And it's Christ to whom Sister points. Her actions and interactions are all intended to lead others to Christ. Her many gifts and wide appeal mean she is different things to different people. When mentioning Sister Dede's name to various people she meets, Sister Elias recalls people's differing reactions: "Oh, Sister Dede, the retired colonel who is a nun!"; "Oh, the nun doctor!"; "Oh, you mean the pro-life warrior!" Everyone seems to find something in Sister Dede with which to connect.

Jesus' Donkey

As Saint Alphonsus Maria de Liguori stated, "The truly humble reject all praise for themselves and refer it all to God."[109] Despite impressive credentials, accomplishments, and nationwide impact of which few can boast, Sister Dede exudes simplicity and humility. From Jack

---

[109] Quoted in "He Must Increase, I Must Decrease," Diocesan, January 12, 2019, https://diocesan.com/he-must-increase-i-must-decrease/.

Cheasty, who remarked that Sister was a truly gifted physician, "without an ounce of ego," to Lisa and Dorinda, who reflected on Sister's continual deference to others, everyone who meets Sister is struck by her humility.

In imitation of the Blessed Mother, she seeks only to reflect the love of the Son. Amid acclaim, she diverts honor and glory immediately back to Christ and is quick to admit her own weaknesses by referencing Saint Philip Neri, to whom is attributed this prayer: "Watch me, O Lord, this day; for, abandoned to myself, I shall surely betray Thee."

"We are all special in God's eyes. Each of us is like His only child. I have nothing more special to offer than each of you does," states Sister. When delivering an address to a Catholic group on the feast of Saint Thérèse, the Little Flower, she teased that while she was born on the feast of the Little Flower, she deems herself a "big weed."[110]

Even in the penning of this book, Sister frequently advised that I should instead be writing about this or that other contemporary person, as such lives would prove far more noteworthy than hers. Just as she redirected attention at the July 4 Salute to America speech to those she deemed the "real heroes," she frequently shares credit with others for her own accomplishments.

"She always says 'we,' never 'I,'" Joseph from Catholic Charities shares. "Whenever there is a good outcome for a patient or initiative she has led, she credits Christ. For her, it's always a team effort and a success for Jesus and the Kingdom."

While many speak of Sister's courage, strength, and virtues, she is the first to admit her own weaknesses. At a September 2023 fundraiser for a Catholic medical clinic in Detroit, where Sister was a keynote

---

[110] Address to the Catholic Evidence League, Baltimore, Maryland, October 21, 2023, 1.

speaker, the sold-out crowd rose in ovation when she took the stage. With a dismissive wave of her hand, she deflected attention, indicating people should sit back down.

"Thank you for standing up for Jesus; I'm just His donkey," she stated.

She recounted the words of Cardinal Sin from the Philippines, who told a story about how the donkey carrying Our Lord on Palm Sunday — tempted to pride for all the attention — quickly realized that "it was not *he* that was 'the big deal' but the guy on his back." Like Cardinal Sin, Sister jokes that she is only the "simple ass carrying Our Lord's message."

When I mentioned to Sister Elias how many greatly admired Sister Dede, she agreed but added, "Ah, yes, but don't bring it up too much in front of her, because it hurts to hear it when you are trying to be little. Even so, Sister Dede is called to share the grace of God. God gives us these people as beacons of hope. And because He continues to give us gifts like Sister Dede Byrne, we know He hasn't abandoned us."

Speaking the Truth in Love

Among the faithful laity, there is a rising tide of frustration over Catholic public officials who advance anti-Catholic agendas. Amid the confusion, Sister clarifies Church teaching by speaking the truth in love. She has been blessed with a tender heart for the suffering and is saddened to see how those with such clouded vision are risking the possibility of eternal separation from God. "Hell is very real. Anyone who knowingly does things contrary to Church teaching yet still receives Our Lord in Holy Communion and remains unrepentant has chosen a path of separation from God. The loving and merciful response is to speak God's truth and pray for them." In an interview during the Forty-Eighth March for Life in D.C., Sister expressed dismay over a self-proclaimed Catholic president reversing nearly all the pro-life gains made during the previous four years. "That's not a Catholic movement to me; that's anti-Catholic."[111]

"If we promote a culture of death our souls are in jeopardy," Sister states. "I don't want to speak with any judgment.... I'm the worst sinner of all, and we are all on this journey together."[112] Sister describes Christ as the North Star on our compass of life. Love obliges us to help any members of the Body of Christ who veer off track to convert and return to that North Star.

Sister is straightforward with her patients as well. Mindful that many of those whom she sees in her clinic are cohabitating and contracepting, she desires to give them what is needed not only for their physical well-being but also for their spiritual health. Preparing for eternity means following Christ's teachings. Sister desires her patients' happiness in Heaven and loves them enough to give them "the straight talk." Because she sprinkles the truth with her wonderful sense of humor, patients openly and humbly receive her counsel, even though it sometimes challenges them to honestly reevaluate their sinful habits. "I do this because no one else has or will do it," Sister continues. "And if I don't, I will have to answer to the Lord, who will ask me, 'Why didn't you do more?'"[113]

---

[111] Sister Dede Byrne, "Sister Deirdre Byrne Shares Her Thoughts on the March for Life," *EWTN News Nightly*, January 29, 2021, https://www.youtube.com/watch?v=U5ilmgpYamg.

[112] Deacon Geoff Bennett, "Catholics, Hear Sister Dede Byrne on Life, Then Vote Your Conscience," Catholic Charities Archdiocese of Denver Respect Life Radio, 5:20, https://respectliferadio.podbean.com/e/catholics-hear-sister-dede-byrne-on-life-then-vote-your-well-formed-conscience/.

[113] Desmond, "Unconventional Mission."

16

Day 6: Abortion-Pill-Reversal Follow-Ups

Late the night before, I texted Emma to ask how she was feeling and to convey that I had offered that day's Mass for her. She was grateful for the prayers but was "nervous about the upcoming ultrasound and also feeling nauseated." I told her I would be there to support her, and she was grateful.

That morning, Sister hosted a small breakfast for a group of visitors after Sunday Mass. "Breakfast is a well-oiled machine around here, so we'd love to have you join us," Sister commented to the people she invited. Also joining were Piero Tozzi and a priest visiting from California.

Sister rises at 5:00 each morning, and Sunday breakfasts include a much larger offering than is typical during the week. She served homemade waffles, bacon, eggs, fruit cups, yogurt, and coffee, some of which she had prepared in advance and simply reheated after Mass. After all the sisters and guests were served, she finally sat down with a cup of yogurt for herself. She wore a white apron with "Sister DD" on the front and participated in the spirited conversation unfolding at our table.

And What's Wrong with the Valley, Father?

During a discussion about the Eucharist and Communion rails, the visiting priest mentioned the persecution he would surely encounter if he tried placing kneelers at the front of his church for use by communicants.

"I'd love to do it, but I'd immediately get pushback, get reported to the bishop, and be asked to leave," Father stated.

"And where would you go, Father?" Sister asked.

"A priest who tried that would get exiled to the valley for sure."

"And what's wrong with the valley, Father?" Sister asked. The conversation was interrupted as an aide walked in to get Mrs. Byrne.

Sitting at the table, Sister recounted an experience she once had at Mass. She was last in line for Holy Communion and desired to receive Our Lord on her knees, just as she does at her convent. As she approached, she felt someone press her shoulder down and heard an inner voice say, "Adore me." Consoled, she knelt to receive Our Lord. As she walked back to her pew, she turned around, but there was nobody behind her. She believes this was a heavenly intervention affirming her inclination that reception of Holy Communion on one's knees gives God great glory.

Emma's Follow-Up

Shortly after a lively discussion with Piero, the visiting padre, and Sister Elias, Emma arrived for her follow-up ultrasound appointment. Just a few days earlier, she had begun the abortion pill reversal procedure, and at just five weeks, the previous ultrasound did not yet show a heartbeat. Only time would tell if her baby had survived the attempted abortion — and today was to be the first important step in assessing that status. I couldn't believe that just a matter of a few days was enough to show a beating heart, but Jackie confirmed that this is possible to predict with a great deal of reliability.

When I entered the clinic, the exam in progress had just begun. I held Emma's hand as Jackie passed the transducer probe back and forth over her abdomen.

"How are you doing, Emma?" I asked.

"Okay ... but I'm scared. I'm afraid there won't be a heartbeat, but I'm also afraid there *will* be a heartbeat."

"You can do this," we all encouraged.

The silence was deafening as we awaited the results. And then, finally, Jackie's verdict:

"And there it is — your baby's heartbeat!"

Tears welled up, and Emma wiped them away to examine the monitor closely. We watched that beautiful, strong, beating heart for many minutes.

Jackie calculated Emma's due date.

"Hmmm. That's a week after my birthday," she said, smiling.

"This is great news, but you're not out of the woods yet," Sister cautioned. "As I mentioned, we are able to save about two-thirds of these babies. Once you reach the threshold of your second trimester, we can be much more certain that all is well."

She was elated and relieved. Just days before, she indicated that she would get the reversal and "let God decide." She stepped out in trust.

After the exam, Jackie called for Uber to send a driver to take Emma home. The new mother left excited and hopeful. From death and despair just days ago, to life and hope — what a difference a few days, the intercession of Sister Dede, a good confession, and Our Lord, the Divine Physician, can make!

Congratulations! You're Expecting a Hamburger!

The second appointment that day was a twenty-six-weeks pregnant young woman accompanied by one of the missionary laywomen living in the casa next door. They had originally met Ayana when she was coming out of an abortion clinic after having just taken the RU-486 pill. They shared that Sister Dede could help her reverse the abortion and suggested that she could put the baby up for adoption.

Their words made an impact. Though scared, Ayana decided to try to reverse the abortion and took the reversal pills prescribed for her. Her mother had flown in from her village to join her the previous

Tuesday and was present for the follow-up exam. The baby was very well developed, and Jackie spent twenty to thirty minutes showing Ayana all the features of the baby's body and capturing memorable shots on ultrasound film. And then, the gender reveal!

"We look for what is called either a hamburger sign or a turtle sign," Jackie explained. "A hamburger sign means it's a girl and a turtle sign means it's a boy. And you have … a hamburger!"

Everyone laughed as Jackie continued to explain the images on the film. She outlined the "ring of fire," also known as the ring of vascularity, associated with the working ovary. The baby girl was very active, and we had the pleasure of watching her antics for another twenty to thirty minutes. She was standing up, yawning, sticking her tongue out, spreading her fingers, and sucking her fist.

Sister and Jackie had a very open and frank discussion with Ayana about what delivery day would look like and how hard it might be to give the baby up for adoption. "When the baby comes, I will have my mind made up. Maybe that will make it easier," Ayana nervously responded.

The missionary women provided the young expectant mother with financial assistance for her housing needs and continued to be a means of great support.

Preserving Purity

The third appointment that Sunday was a young woman named Sarai from Nigeria. Her previous ultrasound at Mary's Center confirmed she was pregnant.

"Is this good news?" the Mary's Center physician had asked.

"Yes!" she excitedly exclaimed.

Sarai is a single woman who had been with her boyfriend for more than five years. Unfortunately, when she told him about her pregnancy, he was not supportive.

"You have to get an abortion. We can't afford this," he told her.

"No! God condemns abortion. He will provide for us. I am not going to kill my baby!" Sarai exclaimed.

Her boyfriend's intimidation made her feel as if she had no voice in the matter, and he drove her to the abortion clinic for an early-morning appointment. Sarai held the RU-486 pill in her hand.

"I stared at it for a long time. I couldn't take it. My boyfriend kept pressuring me, 'Take the pill. Take it.' But I kept trying to think of ways I could back out. Maybe I could pack the pill in my cheek and spit it out after the nurse left the room!" Sarai reasoned.

Eventually, Sarai succumbed to her boyfriend's coercion and she ingested the pill.

"I immediately knew it was wrong! I went home and searched the Internet for ways to stop an abortion," Sarai shared. "I found the number to call to have it reversed and was so happy! In the meantime, my boyfriend kept calling to be sure I had taken the other abortion pills."

"You took the other pills, didn't you?" her boyfriend pressed.

But instead of ingesting the abortion drugs, Sarai texted her boyfriend a photo of powdered sugar she had put under her tongue instead.

"See, there is the crushed pill! Yes, I took it," she assured.

"What he doesn't know is that I flushed the abortion pills down the toilet and took the pills to *reverse* the abortion instead!" Sarai admitted with a smile.

When she woke up from a nap later that afternoon, she was startled by what she saw:

"I went to the bathroom shortly after I woke up, and I saw a huge blood clot and panicked! I called my boyfriend at work and even sent him a picture. But he wouldn't even come home. I thought to myself, 'So I'm going through this all alone. He made me do this, and now he won't even help in an emergency?'"

She immediately sent the photo to Sister Dede, who advised her to go to the ER. Sister was concerned. Such a large clot could be a sign that Sarai was losing the baby. Nervously, the young mother showed up for her appointment, anxious for answers about the status of her pregnancy.

"When you went to the ER last night, did they do an ultrasound?" Sister asked.

"Yes. They said they thought the baby was okay!" Sarai responded.

"Oh, that's great news! After you texted me that picture of the large clot last night, I was afraid we might be consoling you today rather than celebrating with you. So, remember, if the reversal is about two-thirds effective, that means there is a one-third chance you could still possibly miscarry. We'll have to watch carefully. When you get to the thirteenth week, you'll be more in the clear. After that first trimester, you should be in good shape. But keep in mind, we are only emergency triage here, so you need to follow up with your regular doctor and carefully follow his instructions."

"Last night, they said the baby wasn't harmed, so why was there so much blood?" she probed.

"It's from the first abortion pill you took," Sister explained. "We will just have to pray that the bleeding stops."

Jackie completed the ultrasound, measured the baby, confirmed that Sarai was just over eight weeks pregnant, and shared the calculated due date. The ultrasound showed a strong heartbeat of 182 beats per minute, and Sarai was delighted that her due date was just one day after her dad's birthday.

"Your right ovary is working very hard and has a good blood supply," Jackie assured as she showed Sarai her ovarian ring of fire.

"You'll need to continue the progesterone, keep your weight steady, take your prenatal vitamins, eat well, and remember, no drugs or alcohol," Sister added.

Sarai shared that she considers herself to have two close supporters, her mother and the aunt who raised her. Her mother would be flying in from Africa in a couple of days to share the joy of her pregnancy and offer support that the boyfriend never provided.

"Now, Sarai, you know I'm a Catholic sister, and it was you who sought me out. So, you won't be surprised when I tell you that God says you have to be married first before any hanky-panky."

"Yes, I know, I know," agreed Sarai, smiling.

Let Me Tell You How to Find a Good Man

Sister took the opportunity to speak further with Sarai about a woman's dignity and about God's design for marriage.

"A husband will be much more supportive as a partner than a boyfriend. Marriage is a bond and a contract with God at the center. If you have relations outside marriage, it's like saying, 'Hey, God, I love You in every instance except this one.'"

Sarai nodded in agreement.

"So let me tell you how to find a good man. When you meet a guy, tell him that you intend to save yourself for marriage and see how long he sticks around. If he wants to keep dating, that's at least one good sign."

"Yes, yes," Sarai agreed again.

"Now, we have a whole network of people who donate food. Let me get you a bag. Come over here and fill it up with groceries to take home."

When Sarai only filled the bag halfway, Sister added more items. While waiting for her Uber ride after the appointment, Sarai admitted, "I never thought I'd be coming to see a nun for this!"

While penning this account, I learned that Sarai gave birth, prematurely, at thirty-two weeks, to a healthy baby boy, whom she tenderly refers to as "Baby Love." Both mother and son are healthy and well.

I'm Not Judging Them; I'm Loving Them

Sister Dede believes love and mercy mean never withholding the truth. She speaks openly and honestly with those who are cohabiting or contracepting. She counsels them that undergoing anesthesia for surgery always carries with it some degree of risk, and they should reconsider their lives and habits, lest they find themselves before God. Given the great love with which the message is delivered, patients readily accept her counsel.

"I'm not saying these things because I'm judging them," Sister explains. "I am saying them because I love them."

Jackie is fond of saying that Sister ministers in a "four-M" fashion — medically, morally, militarily, and motherly. While she provides superb medical care, she loves her patients enough to explain the moral implications associated with their actions, and she does so in a straightforward manner. Her experiences as a surgeon and a colonel in the army prepared her to deal with life-threatening trauma in a quick, effective manner, just as loving intervention is needed for those practicing lifestyles unbefitting their dignity as sons and daughters of the King. Like a good mother, she will not rest until she has fed her children. In the case of her patients, this means making sandwiches for them or filling their bags with food to take home. She also gives them instructions that, while sometimes hard to hear, are needed for their well-being.

It was an extraordinarily moving day. Three abortion-reversal patients in one week is not the norm, but it was certainly a blessing.

17

Day 7: Sister's Faith in the Public Square

Sister wanted to go back to the courthouse to support her pro-life colleagues. When I arrived at the convent, she asked, "Would you mind picking up Father Francline? His church is only about five minutes away. He'd like to go with us to the courthouse today. Oh, and he has quite a story, so be sure to ask him about it."

The number of remarkable people in Sister Dede's circle of friends is noteworthy. Father Francline Javlon is originally from Cameroon, Africa. On his way to celebrate Mass in a neighboring city on August 14, 2019, he was kidnapped by terrorists and held captive for six days. "Beaten like an animal and fed only twice in six days," he describes them as the worst days of his life. Area Christians who heard about his kidnapping came to help and were also taken hostage. After many prayers, they were miraculously released. Father is now stationed at Saint Francis de Sales Church in D.C., studies at the Catholic University of America, and celebrates daily Mass for the Little Workers at their convent. Sister Dede has become a friend and guiding light for him.

"With the passing of every day, I realize more and more the blessing and goodness of Sister Dede," Father states. He believes that three things likely shaped the woman she has become — her faith-filled upbringing, her military formation, and her religious formation. "It impresses me that she never wastes time and is busy from rising to retiring. When she meets you, she has business, and that business is Christ!" Father also comments that Sister proposes Christ to everyone she encounters. When the two shared an Uber ride en route to the March for Life, Sister greeted the driver, introduced herself, and asked if he minded if she and Father prayed the Rosary together aloud.

Living so close to the convent and celebrating Mass for the sisters daily affords Father many opportunities to see Sister's interactions with others. "She treats everyone with such dignity. Everyone is comfortable with her — whether Christian or not. If I came to this country and never met another American person, having met Sister Dede would be enough. This is how much she means to me."

Witness to Love

Strongly pro-life, Father Francline was eager to accompany us to the court hearings. He, Sister Dede, Sister Elias, and I all went to the courthouse for another day of testimony in the *United States v. Handy* trial. Needless to say, when three habited religious enter a courtroom, it draws attention.[114]

The prosecution brought to the stand a witness using the alias Tina Smith. An abortion clinic worker since 1988, Smith claimed she tried to appease the pro-life rescuers on the 2020 day in question by pulling out her rosary and exclaiming, "I have been raised Catholic my entire life."[115]

Sister Dede, sitting among many in the gallery of the packed courtroom, made the Sign of the Cross and prayed to herself, "Jesus, Mary, and Joseph" in reparation for the seeming contradiction and scandal of a Catholic working at an abortion clinic. A defense attorney who was also struck by the incongruity of the woman's statement and her

---

[114] The conversations in the courtroom as noted on this day are taken from August 21, 2023, court transcripts (a.m. session), pp. 64–85.

[115] August 21, 2023, court transcripts (a.m. session), 64.

employment status objected that this was a "mischaracterization of the [Catholic] faith."[116]

During the ten-minute break outside the courtroom, Sister paused an impromptu interview she had granted to a reporter in the hall, prayed the Hail Mary aloud as Tina passed by, and then continued the interview: "It's so disturbing for misguided souls who think that they can stand for the mutilation of babies in the womb and go home in the evening and feel that they have done their work as a Catholic."[117]

When we returned to the courtroom after the break, the prosecuting attorney addressed the judge and indicated that a member of the clergy in the gallery had not only made the Sign of the Cross during Ms. Smith's testimony but also "started reciting the Hail Mary in her presence"[118] as she walked by in the hallway.

"Which clergy is it? Is it one of the nuns or the priest?" the judge questioned.

"One of the nuns, Judge," the attorney replied, referencing Sister Dede.

While a defense attorney submitted that "everybody is entitled to pray," the judge eventually closed the discussion by insisting that Sister's prayer was directed "*at* the witness," and, as such, was impermissible.

While my subsequent joke to Sister outside the courthouse — "Sister, I can't take you anywhere!" — was meant to tease, the irony of the truth of the matter later struck me. Whether it be the Uber driver with whom she spoke about the Catholic Faith, a woman who had just begun a chemical abortion, the people in the grocery line, or the men coming to empty the convent trash bins, you truly can't take Sister Dede Byrne anywhere without her witnessing to the truth and love of Christ.

---

[116] August 21, 2023, court transcripts (a.m. session), 65.

[117] Hale, "Abortion Worker Claims."

[118] Court transcripts, August 21, 2023 (a.m. session), 84.

After the hearing, we ran into one of the defense attorneys, Howard Walsh, on the sidewalk. Like many Catholics, he first saw Sister on the RNC stage in 2020 and was immediately impressed with her. A year and a half later, lead counsel Chris Ferrara from the Chicago-based Thomas More Society called to ask if Howard would join as local counsel in the case filed against the D.C. government when they failed to honor Sister's religious exemption and revoked her medical license.

Howard accepted the invitation, not only because he had come to esteem Sister Dede but also because he welcomed the opportunity to defend a nun who had been denied a religious exemption.

Howard is also grateful to Sister for having been such a strong advocate and resource when his father was dying of cancer in January 2022. He was caring for his father in New Jersey when he mentioned to Sister that his father couldn't keep down liquids and was quickly losing his appetite.

"How far are you from Newark?" Sister asked.

Sister was on her way to the Holy Land for her annual pilgrimage and had a layover in Newark. She hauled a fifteen-pound bag of fluids and supplements to New Jersey, where Howard met her in between flights to accept the supplies so that a nurse friend could minister and offer relief to his suffering father.

"She is an example of real womanhood," Howard remarks. "In a world that is so materialistic, it's so easy to respect someone like her who has given everything up for love and service to Christ. For her, prayer and her vocation are first. She and other faithful religious like her make it easy for me to know that I'm on the right path."

Euthanasia Prevention — The Other End of the Pro-Life Issue

In *Living the Gospel of Life,* the U.S. Bishops state, "Euthanasia and assisted suicide are *never* acceptable acts of mercy. They *always* gravely exploit the suffering and desperate, extinguishing life in the name of the 'quality of life' itself."[119] In support of Church teaching, Sister Dede strongly advocates for the rights of patients until natural death and is engaged on several public fronts to oppose assisted suicide and euthanasia.

In an address to attendees at a Catholic Medical Association conference, she explained that there is "insidious activity behind the walls of some hospitals and nursing homes [to hasten] the death of those with no voice using a stealthy technique I call the 'unholy trinity'—starvation, dehydration, and oversedation."[120]

Sister is even currently collaborating with a film producer to produce a short documentary exposing the euthanizing of her beloved spiritual mentor. Though chronically but not terminally ill, her devastating death deeply impacted Sister Dede.

In response to her recent anti-euthanasia initiatives, Sister has received calls and e-mails from others concerned about their loved ones. "We cannot forget our elderly murdered by euthanasia.... We need to do more about fighting this other end of the pro-life issue."

Sister implores and empowers physicians to stand strong in a health-care culture drowning in a sea of confusion regarding life and the dignity of the human person. She speaks frequently at medical conferences in support of adherence to Church teaching in Catholic health care, and on November 11, 2023, in National Harbor, Maryland, she testified before the American Medical Association (AMA) against a resolution supporting physician-assisted suicide. If passed, the resolution would have changed the AMA's former opposition to assisted suicide to a neutral position. Thankfully, after Sister's testimony, as well

---

[119] United States Conference of Catholic Bishops (USCCB), *Living the Gospel of Life: A Challenge to American Catholics* (1998), no. 20, https://www.usccb.org/issues-and-action/human-life-and-dignity/abortion/living-the-gospel-of-life.

[120] Address to the Catholic Medical Association in Illinois, June 15, 2024.

as that of her colleagues at the Catholic Medical Association and the Christian Medical and Dental Associations, the AMA voted against the proposal and currently maintains its opposition to physician-assisted suicide.[121]

---

[121] Jonah McKeown. "American Medical Association Retains Opposition to Assisted Suicide," Catholic News Agency, November 14, 2023, https://www.catholicnewsagency.com/news/256012/american-medical-association-retains-opposition-to-assisted-suicide-amid-catholic-doctors-advocacy.

Part 3

Living Our Faith in the Public Square

18

The Problem That Ails Us

Both the world and the Church are crying, and the two are inextricably linked.[122] Sister Dede similarly reflected on this sentiment when, in a talk she gave to a group of Arlington Healthcare professionals, she stated, "The decline of compassionate health care, I believe, goes hand in hand with the rise of secularization in society and, sadly, the decline of faith in our Church." As examples, she sometimes comments on how it saddens her to see Catholic public officials advance anti-Catholic legislation and to see the number of Catholics who do not believe in various Church teachings such as the Real Presence of Christ in the Eucharist. The strength of our nation is a reflection of the strength of our Church.

Cardinal Sarah recently stated that "since the 1960s, Catholics have increasingly lost their Catholic identity."[123] Quoting Saint Paul, who stated, "The time will come when people will not tolerate sound doctrine but will follow their own desires … and will stop listening to the truth" (see 2 Tim. 4:3–4), he noted that a temptation to "practical atheism" is evidenced by a vast number of Catholics whose beliefs do not differ from that of the general public, as well as self-identified

---

[122] "About Us" section, ACTS XXIX, https://www.actsxxix.org/how-we-think.

[123] Robert Cardinal Sarah, "The Catholic Church's Enduring Answer to the Practical Atheism of Our Age," Napa Institute, June 14, 2024, https://napa-institute.org/cardinal-sarah/.

Catholic public officials who pick and choose which Church teachings they will accept and which they will discard.[124]

The *Code of Canon Law*, however, indicates that Catholics are not free to choose which teachings on faith and morals to obey (see canon 752). Furthermore, specifically as regards the preeminent issue of life, the Church's teaching has remained constant: "Since the first century the Church has affirmed the moral evil of every procured abortion. This teaching has not changed and remains unchangeable."[125]

In a document issued by the Congregation for the Doctrine of the Faith about the participation of Catholics in public life, Cardinal Ratzinger articulated: "Those who are directly involved in lawmaking bodies have a grave and clear obligation to oppose any law that attacks human life. For them, as for every Catholic, it is impossible to promote such laws or to vote for them."[126]

The *Catechism of the Catholic Church* identifies other problems by stating, "Ignorance of Christ and his Gospel, bad example given by others, enslavement to one's passions, assertion of a mistaken notion of autonomy of conscience, rejection of the Church's authority and her teaching, lack of conversion and of charity: these can be at the source of errors of judgment in moral conduct" (no. 1792). Further adding to the confusion, erroneous definitions of freedom, rights, and truth, and other factors such as indifference, news narratives, sound bites, and powerful groups who use the media to coerce people to violate their beliefs,[127] have resulted in dull consciences that lead people to

---

[124] Sarah, "Church's Enduring Answer."

[125] *Catechism of the Catholic Church* (CCC), no. 2271.

[126] Congregation for the Doctrine of the Faith, "Doctrinal Note on Some Questions Regarding the Participation of Catholics in Public Life" (November 24, 2002), no. 4.

[127] See "Two Challenges," in USCCB, *Understanding Conscience* (2017), https://www.usccb.org/prolife/understanding-conscience.

believe they may behave as they choose rather than as they ought. This is evidenced by the many patients Sister Dede sees who are unaware that the behaviors in which they engage undermine the happiness they so desperately seek.

As regards the intersection of faith with the public square, the late beloved Catholic evangelist Al Kresta aptly articulated that one reason Christian activism has failed to be as effective as we had hoped in permeating culture and government is that "American Christians don't have believable churches."[128]

Ineffective evangelization and poor catechesis in the years following Vatican II disastrously impacted our churches, liturgy, catechesis, seminaries, and schools[129] and resulted in generations of confused Catholics, many of whom may be unaware of Church teaching and the corresponding obligation to witness to it in the public square. Catholics who may have poorly formed consciences are not only ill-equipped to realize their eternal end but also unprepared to influence society, build the Kingdom of God, and cast informed votes that would bless our nation.[130]

Sister Dede's friend and colleague Bishop Joseph Coffey, auxiliary bishop for the Military Archdiocese, commented on the Church's obligation to help form faithful citizens in this regard and stated, "Part of faithful citizenship includes having a well-formed conscience that equips one to assess issues and candidates in light of Church teaching."

---

[128] "Al Kresta: Build the Church; Bless the Nation," YouTube video, 2:08 and 2:40; https://www.youtube.com/watch?v=Y5pUhjLOG4A.

[129] Pope Benedict, in a February 14, 2013, address to bishops and priests, stated that the "Council of the media" (also dubbed the "virtual" Council), which hijacked the Council's intent for its own purpose, was, sadly, initially more effective than the real Council.

[130] Catholic evangelist Al Kresta launched a campaign and coined the phrase "Build the Church; Bless the Nation."

Furthermore, such a well-formed conscience "does not permit one to vote for a political program or an individual law which contradicts the fundamental contents of faith and morals."[131]

Despite this, it is not uncommon for Catholics to cast votes in support of candidates who support legislation at odds with Church teaching. For example, November 2020 Edison exit polls estimated that 52 percent of Catholics voted for the abortion-supporting presidential candidate (up over five points from the previous race), while 47 percent voted for the pro-life-supporting candidate (down three points from the previous race.[132] Also disturbing was CatholicVote's analysis that, on average, one-third of practicing Catholics in key states did not vote in the presidential race in 2016[133] and, further, that 25 to 30 percent of American Catholics refused to vote in 2020.[134] These analyses signal a twofold problem: first, the need for catechesis and evangelization to equip the laity to develop well-formed consciences, and second, the need for laity to take seriously their obligation to advance the common good by engaging in the voting process thereafter. "This is a tragedy for America and for the entire Catholic Church," stated the Honorable Tim

---

[131] USCCB, *Forming Consciences for Faithful Citizenship — Part I — The U.S. Bishops' Reflection on Catholic Teaching and Political Life* (2019), no. 30, https://www.usccb.org/issues-and-action/faithful-citizenship /forming-consciences-for-faithful-citizenship-part-one.

[132] Frank Newport, "Religious Group Voting and the 2020 Election," Gallup, November 13, 2020, https://news.gallup.com/opinion/polling -matters/324410/religious-group-voting-2020-election.aspx.

[133] E-mail exchange between the author and Tommy Valentine of CatholicVote.

[134] Per the Honorable Tim Huelskamp, "Poll Shows Large Percentage of Catholics Did Not Vote in 2020," Catholic Vote, May 14, 2024, https://catholicvote.org/poll-shows-large-percentage-of-catholics -did-not-vote-in-2020/.

Huelskamp. "I call upon all laity, priests and bishops to work together to inspire all Catholics to become responsible citizens and vote."[135]

While charity and mercy require that both the laity and Church leaders speak clearly about the nonnegotiable moral issues that intersect with the public square, Sister states that some people are still afraid to speak out against the evils that are unfolding in today's world — especially things related to pro-life, pro-family, and pro–religious freedom. She exhorts us to pray for those who actively support the destruction of children in the womb, especially public officials working to make abortion accessible, even through the third trimester.

Mindful that one of the roles of a disciple is to speak truth, Sister states, "We religious are particularly responsible. We must speak out [with love and compassion] even when the words might be difficult [for others] to hear."[136]

Specifically related to her address at the RNC, Sister states, "Many Catholics are confused. And because some bishops aren't able to speak out, for whatever reason, I felt someone had to say something.... [The laity] aren't seeing many [religious] who speak out on the prolife issue."[137] Sister wasn't thinking about the Republican National Convention or such a public venue when she went into the chapel that August day. She was simply praying in reparation for not doing enough and was renewing her commitment to do more. "But while we limit ourselves, God always has a bigger plan for us," Sister reflects. While she deemed herself "the most unworthy person to do so," she allowed God to use her voice nonetheless.

This is precisely why the nation gasped when Sister Dede Byrne took the 2020 stage. While the faithful have been crying out for more

---

[135] Quoted in "Poll Shows Large Percentage."
[136] Bennett, "Hear Sister Dede," 9:30.
[137] Bennett, "Hear Sister Dede," 8:00.

religious leaders willing to speak the truth and correct the confusion, Sister charged the front line, without fear or hesitation, like the good colonel that she is.

As Father Meeks beautifully summarizes, "The culture is in desperate need of God. But sadly, people don't even realize what or whom they are desperate for! What Sister Dede brings is the presence of God to our world and culture. The infusion of Christ into our culture is the answer, and Christ is exactly who Sister Dede brings to everyone she meets. She is a selfless, modern-day Mother Teresa."

19

The Remedy That Heals Us

Sister Dede's call to conversion in every aspect of our lives exemplifies that of a modern-day Joan of Arc. Not surprisingly, the saint's image is displayed in the convent and often visible during her virtual meetings and interview broadcasts. Saint Joan implored the army she led to be prepared to meet God in the state of grace, and Sister Dede implores today's faithful to do the same. She reminds us to seek holiness with humility, as it is only in the state of grace that we will we be able to rise above our natural inclinations.

"I'm imploring you that we first need to work on ourselves and be in the state of grace. It's akin to being on a plane when the oxygen mask drops," Sister states. "You are told to first put the mask on your own face before trying to help the person next to you. You can't give what you don't have. Make it your daily mission to be in the state of grace so that you can hear Christ more clearly."

Her prescriptions for remaining strong and fighting against temptations include drawing closer to our Lord in the Eucharist, prayer, continually exercising trust in God, and abandonment to God's will rather than her own.

Speak the Truth Even When It's Difficult

Sister states that in a complicated world, life is much simpler than we think. We have only two goals: "to do all we can to stay in the state of grace — as Catholics, that means participating in Confession,

Holy Communion, and adoration — and to bring as many with [us to Heaven] as [we] can. That means telling the truth to people, even when it's difficult."[138]

Frequently citing 1 Corinthians 11:27–28, which references the spiritual harm a person brings upon himself by unworthy reception of Holy Communion, Sister suggests: "It is so important that our bishops, who are our beloved shepherds, lovingly correct Catholic public figures, such as politicians, sports figures, and celebrities who are habitually living in opposition to Church teaching yet still receiving Our Lord in Holy Communion."

Competent physicians would never ignore a patient's cancerous tumor. Likewise, it is never loving or merciful to ignore spiritual illness, particularly of those public figures whose words and actions might scandalize and confuse other members of the Body of Christ. Overlooking malignancy — whether bodily or spiritual — only leads to metastasis and death. Furthermore, once malignancy is diagnosed, lifesaving treatments must be administered. Dr. Dede continues, "Just as chemotherapy is necessary for cancer treatment — even though it may cause painful side effects in the short term — such correction by strong bishops is not a punishment but a loving and life-giving response for a soul potentially in mortal danger."

Sister also expresses gratitude and prays for those faithful bishops who speak truth in difficult situations, some of whom have suffered greatly for the concern they have shown for their flock. Echoing the words of Saint John Paul II, she knows that "Jesus Christ is the answer to the question posed by every human life, and the love of Christ compels us to share that great good news with everyone."[139]

---

[138] Schiffer, "Sister Deirdre."

[139] Pope Saint John Paul II, homily, Oriole Park at Camden Yards, Baltimore, Maryland, October 8, 1995, no. 6.

In his 2019 book, Cardinal Sarah aptly laments, "The West no longer knows who it is, because it no longer knows and does not want to know who made it [or] who established it."[140] But Sister Dede knows that God's faithful *have* the answer and are called to share it. The Church teaches that we are children of God, made in His image and likeness. We were made for eternity — to know Him, to love Him, and to serve Him in this world so we can be happy with Him in Heaven.

Herein lies the identity and worth that humanity still struggles and clamors to find. While many are seduced by or tolerate sinful abominations and ideologies under the guise of intellectual positions and a false notion of freedom, we know that our dignity and worth are rooted in being sons and daughters of the King. Yes, the simple answer to the *Baltimore Catechism* lesson we learned in first grade, "Why did God make me?," is the very answer for which the world and all its "learned" men still so desperately yearn.

Sister Dede Byrne now brings a simple message of conversion and healing to an afflicted world. She entered the chapel that fateful day in August 2020 before her RNC speech as a physician who brought physical healing, but she emerged with a commission to help diagnose and treat spiritual and cultural wounds as well. With the skilled hands of a surgeon, she lovingly works to excise disease that afflicts the Body of Christ and sutures painful wounds via a call to seek God's restorative, healing, and life-giving grace.

Just as Mother Teresa spoke truth to those in power when she stood before President Clinton and Vice President Gore at the 1994 National Prayer Breakfast in Washington, D.C., and identified abortion as "a direct killing of the innocent child — murder,"[141] Sister Dede was

---

[140] Sarah, *The Day*, 270.
[141] "Mother Teresa at the National Prayer Breakfast," EWTN, February 3, 1994, https://www.ewtn.com/catholicism/library/mother-teresa-at-the-national-prayer-breakfast-2714.

called to speak the same truth. Responding to an interviewer about the *Dobbs* decision and the travesty of a Catholic president deeming the overturn of *Roe* a "sad day," Sister shared her simple desire that all of us end up in Heaven together someday and, further, that the best means of acheiving that goal is to pray that all God's faithful will abide by Church teaching and support life from the moment of conception until natural death.[142]

As the apostles traveled from village to village, Sister now travels from parish to parish planting the seeds of Christ's truth wherever she goes. "The devil is very real, and there is a spiritual battle now underway," Sister warns. "We must all pray very hard. Prayer and the Rosary are our only means of overcoming this present evil and winning this battle."

[142] Caldwell, "Rosary Rally."

20

Dr. Dede's Prescriptions

Sister Dede ministered to countless hundreds during the COVID pandemic using a medicinal protocol that was effective. She kept people out of the hospital, prevented further injuries, and saved lives via strategies shunned by mainstream medicine and by using medications that have been around for decades.

Similarly, the moral prescription she offers for an ailing nation is entirely countercultural and yet has been around for millennia. She laughingly comments, "I hope nobody attends more than one of my talks, because I continually repeat the same message about remaining in the state of grace." Her moral regimen, many elements of which have been routinely prescribed by spiritual directors, has a historical record of success.

Prescription 1: Holy Mass:
Take One Eucharist and Call Me in the Morning
Just as Sister's parents prioritized daily Eucharist and brought grace back into their home, Sister stresses the importance of likewise nourishing our souls so that we may strengthen and love those around us. "My parents' actions instilled in me the premise that the Holy Eucharist is the 'source and summit' of our Catholic Faith and a wellspring of miracles," Sister stated during a talk to Legatus members in Oklahoma City.[143]

---

[143] Address to the Legatus chapter in Oklahoma City, June 2024 (taken from her notes).

Even during the years of her rigorous surgical residency schedule, if attending Holy Mass was impossible, she arranged for the Eucharistic minister to bring her communion in a side room in the hospital ward. "The devil particularly hates those who adore God," she states, and this demonstrates the power of the Eucharist and adoration. "During these challenging times, we must flee to the Holy Eucharist, for it is the greatest guardian of our souls against the evil one."[144]

Our hope lies in knowing that when governmental restrictions limited access to the sacraments, faithful shepherds and laity found creative means to overcome the obstacles. Priests at places such as Our Lady of Good Counsel in Plymouth, Michigan, celebrated Masses from two-story parapets, and parishioners listened on low-powered radio stations from their cars.[145] Drive-through Penance was also made available by priests who sat outside to hear the confessions of those who drove up in their cars. Also hopeful are recent statistics revealing upward trends in Mass attendance in various places around the nation, such as in Seattle and Saint Louis.[146]

Prescription 2: Eucharistic Adoration

Before accepting her mission assignments to the Sudan and Kenya, Sister ensured that daily Mass and adoration would be available to her there. "Adoration allows you to immerse your gratitude, needs, and

[144] Address to Legatus.
[145] Dan Meloy, "Drive-In Masses Offer Creative Solution for COVID-Conscious Faithful," *Detroit Catholic*, July 14, 2020, https://www.detroitcatholic.com/news/drive-in-masses-offer-creative-solution-for-covid-conscious-faithful-video.
[146] Kate McEntee Deweese, "Mass Attendance Rising in Archdiocese of Seattle," *Northwest Catholic*, February 13, 2024, https://nwcatholic.org/news/kate-mcentee-deweese/mass-attendance-rising-in-archdiocese-of-seattle; Laura Kosta, "Mass Counts Show Slight Increase in Attendance in 2023," *St. Louis Review*, December 2023, https://www.archstl.org/mass-counts-show-slight-increase-in-attendance-in-2023-9226.

concerns in the Eucharistic Heart of Jesus in a profound way," Sister states. "The heart is the one muscle that never stops working; it never fatigues.... That is how Our Lord is with us. He never stops working; He never fatigues. In fact, at times we are not even aware, He is always at our side comforting us."[147]

Sister was drawn to the Little Workers specifically because of their devotion to the Eucharist. She was rooted in the words of their founder, Blessed Greco: "It was before the most Blessed Sacrament that I found the love of Jesus and the power of that love." Sister Faustina's example also influenced the choice of Sister's religious name: Sister Deirdre of the Most Blessed Sacrament.

While Sister recognizes adoration as a necessity in the life of the Little Workers, even increasing it to thrice daily, our hope lies in the realization that churches in some places are also experiencing increases in Eucharistic adoration. A priest from Sister's neighboring Arlington Diocese stated that he "saw adoration grow from once a month before COVID to twice weekly. [Adoration] began as a necessity in lieu of public Masses ... [and] developed a larger presence in parish life.... Culturally, there is a greater desire for silence. As the culture has gotten noisier, people have sought out silence and found it in adoration."[148] By God's grace, more and more people recognize that Christ is the answer and are now seeking Him out.

Prescription 3: Frequent Confession

When Saint Joan of Arc was interrogated and asked if she was in the state of grace, she answered, "If I am not, may God put me there; and if I

---

[147] Address to Legatus.

[148] Quoted in Kevin Schweers, "Eucharistic Adoration Is on the Rise Locally with a USCCB Campaign Underway," *Arlington Catholic Herald*, October 15, 2023, https://www.catholicherald.com/article/local/eucharistic-adoration-is-on-the-rise-locally-with-a-usccb-campaign-underway/.

am, may God so keep me." During her many talks, Sister often recounts this story and encourages frequent Confession — weekly, if possible: "God wants us to be holy. We ... must be in the state of grace to enter Heaven, and the sacrament of Reconciliation gives us a chance to hear clearly God's voice, reflect on the times we have failed to love well, and change our behavior." Just as Saint Joan implored her soldiers to remain pure and to confess regularly, lest they be spiritually unprepared to meet God upon their demise, and just as sanctifying grace sustained her in the face of torture and death, Sister similarly urges us *always* to be in the state of grace. She is grateful for the Eucharistic revival that has emerged, and she states the need for a Reconciliation revival as well.[149]

Times of crisis, whether COVID or otherwise, seem to lead people to God. Herein is found hope. While some speculate that the spike in church attendance immediately following the 9/11 attacks was the result of people seeking comfort during a turbulent time,[150] another reason might have been a frightened laity shocked out of complacency and honestly facing their mortality. Father Louis Guardiola, C.P.M., then ministering at Sacred Heart Catholic Church in Russellville, Kentucky, recalls that the post-9/11 Confession lines were longer than he had ever before encountered. "People were frantic and wanted to be sure they were in the state of grace," Father reflects. Just as staring death in the face on 9/11 moved believers, the crisis of the COVID pandemic opened the eyes of many and awakened a sleeping laity. "God uses crises, difficulties, and tragedies as *wake-up calls* to jolt people out of their own self-sufficiency and awaken them to their desperate need for Him."[151]

---

[149] Address to Catholic Medical Association, 6.

[150] Eric Ferreri, "After 9/11, a Short-Lived Rush to Church," *Duke Today*, August 19, 2016, https://today.duke.edu/2016/08/after-911-short -lived-rush-church.

[151] Craig Etheredge, "The Pull of Compassion God Can Use to Bring People to Christ," *Discipleship* (blog), https://discipleship.org

Prescription 4: Listen to Your Mother (Praying the Rosary)

In addition to the Eucharist, Sister Dede finds strength for her three-fold mission by invoking the assistance of the Blessed Mother, who always guides the faithful to her Son. "As [the Blessed Mother] said at the wedding Feast of Cana, 'Do whatever He tells you' [see John 2:5]," Sister states. "In my simpleminded way of thinking, God is our door to pure love, and the Blessed Mother is the doorknob."[152] Sister echoes the words of the Blessed Mother, who, at Fátima, Lourdes, and elsewhere, has encouraged daily recitation of the Rosary. As Father Donald Calloway is fond of saying, the Rosary is a portable "Bible on beads"[153] and is a powerful means of overcoming evil in the world. This is precisely why Sister held her rosary high for the entire nation to see during her RNC speech and why she calls it our weapon of love.

Our hope lies in knowing that the intercession of our Blessed Mother has a long history of success: the victory at Muret, when Christians defeated the Albigensians in 1213; the victory of the Christians against the Turks in the 1571 Battle of Lepanto; the victory against the Turks in the 1716 Battle of Peterwardein, Hungary; and modern instances in which the Rosary warded off communism.[154] Pope Leo III stated, "It can be said without exaggeration that for those persons, families, and nations for whom the Rosary retains its ancient honor,

---

/blog/the-pull-of-compassion-god-can-use-a-crisis-to-bring-people-to-christ/.

[152] Address to Legatus.

[153] Donald Calloway, "Champions of the Rosary and St. Joseph," Parousia Media, YouTube video, 4:24, September 2020, https://www.youtube.com/watch?v=xQ1I8Lab8_M.

[154] "Victory through the Rosary," America Needs Fatima, December 11, 2013, https://americaneedsfatima.org/blog/victory-through-the-rosary.

the loss of faith through ignorance and vicious errors need not be feared."[155]

Prescription 5: Catechize Children Well
(Parents as Primary Educators of Their Children)

Sister believes that transmission of the Faith is the critical responsibility of parents and that the best religious instruction and formation begin in the home. Children continually watch and imitate the adults around them, thus making the family an ideal classroom. Sister reflects, "Parents are the best catechists. They bring faith into the family, which is why it is critical that the family be protected at every stage of life, medically and spiritually, from the womb to the tomb."[156]

Mary and Bill Byrne created a family culture that nurtured their children's spiritual lives and ensured that they knew the tenets of their Faith. "My parents taught me . . . the importance of prayer as the foundation of all we do to not only save lives but to encourage others to defend those who cannot defend themselves — the unborn and our elderly."[157] Via daily family prayer, the example of daily Mass, edifying conversations at the family table, involvement in faith-based organizations, the permeation of faith in their daily duties and workplaces, and the many inspiring books they provided, Mary and Bill educated and equipped their children to take Christ into the world.

Our hope lies in knowing that while COVID led to plummeting enrollment in public schools, Catholic school enrollment increased nationwide by about 4 percent;[158] places, such as the Diocese of Venice,

---

[155] Leo XIII, encyclical *Magnae Dei Matris* (September 8, 1892), no. 18.

[156] Address at the Basilica of the National Shrine of the Immaculate Conception, Washington, D.C., October 28, 2023, 3.

[157] Address to Catholic Evidence League, 1.

[158] Susan Klemond, "Catholic Schools Held Steady during Heights of COVID, Relying on Faith and Fundamentals," *National Catholic*

Florida, had upwards of a 39 percent increase, with an average of 25 percent at parish schools. They now have waitlists at every school in the diocese.[159] Homeschooling is also on the rise, with some states showing growth of more than 100 percent.[160] More children equipped with sound education and catechesis will, with God's grace, be better prepared to attain their eternal ends and bless the nation.

Prescription 6: Strengthen Family Life and Nurture Vocations

Sister frequently states that the family is the garden where vocations take root, are fertilized, and grow. Her parents had a strong marriage that was grounded in Christ. They were living witnesses to their Catholic Faith and created a rich, fertile soil for vocations to take root. The sacrifices they made to live, not just preach, their Faith nurtured Sister's and her brother's vocations and echo the sentiment of Pope Paul VI, who stated, "Modern man listens more willingly to witnesses than to teachers, and if he does listen to teachers, it is because they are witnesses."[161]

Sister is saddened that the family is under great spiritual attack from practices such as abortion, contraception, sex transitioning, same-sex unions, and euthanasia,[162] and she encourages strong family life by highlighting the fruit it can bear for the Church and culture. "The nuclear

Register, October 31, 2022, https://www.ncregister.com/news/catholic-schools-held-steady-during-height-of-covid-relying-on-faith-and-fundamentals.

[159] Bob Reddy, "Catholic School Numbers Skyrocket," Diocese of Venice in Florida, August 4, 2022, https://dioceseofvenice.org/catholic-school-numbers-skyrocket/.

[160] Emma Camp, "Homeschooling Has Increased by Over 50 Percent since 2018," *Reason*, November 1, 2023, https://reason.com/2023/11/01/homeschooling-has-increased-by-over-50-percent-since-2018/.

[161] Paul VI, apostolic exhortation *Evangelii Nuntiandi* (December 8, 1975), no. 41.

[162] Address at the National Shrine, 3–4.

family is the heart of this country. Without the Father as the spiritual leader, the heart is weakened and the family less apt to stay together as a sacred unit," Sister states.[163] Just as priestly vocations are positively correlated with a stable family life,[164] the strong faith and marriage of Bill and Mary Byrne rooted their children in beauty, truth, and goodness and nurtured two religious vocations. Likely reflecting on his father's influence, Bishop Byrne recently stated that men who begin their day with the Eucharist set a very strong example.[165] Such is the impact of faithful parents and their valiant efforts to safeguard their children from the cultural forces that threaten to obscure their path to Heaven.

Fortunately, parental rights are now front and center. The pandemic and resultant homeschooling opened the eyes of parents and challenged them to examine school curricula and library materials more closely. Parents nationwide are now making their voices heard at school board meetings to protest politicized and sexualized books and agendas that undermine their rights and threaten their children. Rapidly gaining momentum, the parental rights movement is now also shaping political platforms, incentivizing voters, and empowering parents to reclaim their authority. This is consonant with the Church's perennial teaching that "parents have been appointed by God Himself as the first and principal educators of their children and that their right

---

[163] Address to the Catholic Medical Association.

[164] Kevin J. Jones, "Survey of New Priests: Most Pray Rosary, Go to Eucharistic Adoration, Parents Stay Married," Catholic News Agency, April 26, 2023, https://www.catholicnewsagency.com/news/254179/survey-of-new-priests-most-pray-rosary-go-to-eucharistic-adoration-parents-stayed-married.

[165] Joe Bukuras, "Brother and Sister Who Are Bishop and Nun Say Faithful Parents Helped Foster Vocations," Catholic News Agency, February 9, 2024, https://www.catholicnewsagency.com/news/256788/brother-and-sister-who-are-bishop-and-nun-say-faithful-parents-helped-foster-vocations.

is completely inalienable,"[166] and, further, that students "have a right to be educated in authentic moral values rooted in the dignity of the human person."[167]

Prescription 7: Take Christ into the Public Square

"Love compels us to 'go into all the world and proclaim the good news to the whole creation' (Mk 16:15).... This mandate," our bishops state, "includes our engagement in political life."[168]

Mindful that faith is not only a private matter,[169] Sister Dede courageously takes Christ and her faith to the streets every day — whether she is encouraging her patients to be open to life, explaining the dignity of the human person to pre-med students under her tutelage, inviting an Uber driver to consider Catholicism, or encouraging strangers to vote pro-life.

Sister annually attends the March for Life in D.C., and in annual Rosary rallies, she leads public prayer near the U.S. Capitol to invoke God's intercession for respect for life at all stages, the sanctity of marriage and families, constitutionally protected freedoms, and the return of our nation to God and holiness.

---

[166] John Paul II, apostolic exhortation *Familiaris Consortio* (November 22, 1981), no. 40.

[167] "You [parents of Ireland] have been deeply shocked to learn of the terrible things that took place in what ought to be the safest and most secure environment of all [schools].' [Children] have a right to be educated in authentic moral values rooted in the dignity of the human person, to be inspired by the truth of our Catholic faith.... This noble but demanding task is entrusted in the first place to you, their parents." Benedict XVI, pastoral letter to the Catholics of Ireland (March 19, 2010), no. 8.

[168] USCCB, *Forming Consciences*, quoting *Evangelii Gaudium*, no. 181.

[169] See Pope Francis, 2013, https://www.vatican.va/content/francesco/en/cotidie/2013/documents/papa-francesco-cotidie_20131128_faith-never-private.html.

Our hope lies in knowing that priests and bishops nationwide are now also more frequently taking Our Eucharistic Lord to the streets — and even to the sky — and just letting Him work. For example, on March 21, 2020, Father Mark Rutherford chartered a Cessna 182 from Livingston County Airport in Howell, Michigan, exposed Our Lord in the Blessed Sacrament, and led a three-hour Eucharistic air procession by flying over ten counties in his diocese to pray for healing from the COVID virus.[170]

Similarly, in November 2023, following a standing-room-only Mass at St. Patrick's Cathedral, Bishop Whalen, Father Mike Schmitz, and dozens of priests from across the nation took Our Eucharistic Lord in procession through the streets of Manhattan.[171] The busy streets were filled with astonished passersby, some of whom knelt to adore Our Lord and some of whom, having never experienced such a sight, were intrigued by the fervor. Father commented on his hope that bringing Christ to the streets would shower His hurting people with mercy and love.

"And maybe someone will look up," said Father Schmitz. "Maybe someone will glance over; maybe someone will see the friends of Jesus and ask the question, 'Who is that? What are they doing? Can it be true that God loves me that much? That rather than waiting for me to come to His Church, He leaves His Church to come to me?' "[172]

Finally, in July of 2024 and as part of the Church's three-year Eucharistic revival, the first Eucharistic Congress in over eighty-three

---

[170] "The Eucharistic Procession at 10,000 Feet," Diocese of Lansing, YouTube video, March 23, 2020, https://www.youtube.com/watch?v=jMp9aCQZP2A.

[171] "Eucharistic Procession through New York City," Napa Institute, YouTube video, November 29, 2023, https://www.youtube.com/watch?v=5R-wCd4VSZs.

[172] "Eucharistic Procession," 1:30.

years brought tens of thousands of Catholics together in celebration of the Eucharist, many of whom took to the streets of Indianapolis during a mile-long procession and public exposition and adoration of the Blessed Sacrament.

Prescription 8: Be a Voice for the Voiceless

Sister Dede is a voice for the voiceless every time she speaks with women exiting abortion clinics and exhorts them to reconsider the lives of their babies and choose life. She was a voice for the unborn when she took the RNC stage in 2020, and she continues to defend life from conception until natural death.

Sister is mindful that "in our democratic republic, one of the important ways in which we fulfill our civic responsibility for the common good is by electing government leaders who respect and uphold the moral law."[173] She further advocates for the unborn and the dying every time she testifies in opposition to abortion and euthanasia before the American Medical Association, public policy leaders, or the many groups she now addresses nationwide. She repeatedly shares that the most effective means of opposing the backlash of abortion supporters is the use of love and compassion. "That's the only way we are going to convert hearts — through God working through us," she states.[174] Furthermore, it is by our remaining in the state of grace that God is best able to use us to accompany those in need and witness to His love and mercy.

Inspired by Sister's example, we, too, are called to take our faith unapologetically into our families and neighborhoods, into our nation's schools, into the workplace, and into the voting booth. Recalling John Paul II's word that "the common outcry, which is justly made on behalf of [other] human rights … is false and illusory if the right to life, the most

[173] Burke, *On Our Civic Responsibility*, no. 45.
[174] Byrne, "My LIVE Interview," 11:20.

basic and fundamental right and the condition for all other personal rights, is not defended with the maximum determination,"[175] we can exercise the moral obligation of participation in public life by voting for those whose policies will most effectively limit the undermining of human dignity, including abortion and euthanasia. Specifically as regards limiting evil, Cardinal Burke, in applying an example cited in St. Pope John Paul II's *Evangelium Vitae* (see no. 73), explains, "A Catholic who is clear in his or her opposition to the moral evil of procured abortion could vote for a candidate who supports the limitation of the legality of procured abortion, even though the candidate does not oppose all use of procured abortion, if the other candidate(s) do not support the limitation of the evil of procured abortion."[176] He further states that "the Catholic who chooses not to vote at all when there is a viable candidate who will advance the common good, although not perfectly, fails to fulfill his or her moral duty, at least, in the limitation of a grave evil in society."[177]

Eighteen- to thirty-four-year-olds now make up one of the largest voting blocs in the country. Survey results from Students for Life's Demetree Institute indicating that "3 out of 4 Millennials and [Gen Zers] want limits [on abortion]"[178] is at least a starting point and a reason to hope.

[175] John Paul II, post-synodal apostolic exhortation *Christifideles Laici* (December 30, 1988), no. 38.

[176] "Of course, the end in view for the Catholic must always be the total conformity of the civil law with the moral law, that is, ultimately the total elimination of the evil of procured abortion." Burke, *On Our Civic Responsibility*, no. 42.

[177] Burke, *On Our Civic Responsibility*, no. 43.

[178] "New Poll Finds that Millennials & Gen Z — Now about One-Third of the Electorate — Don't Hold Extremist Abortion Views, Embrace Limits," Demetree Institute for Prolife Advancement, https://www. instituteforprolifeadvancement.org/new-poll-finds-that-millennials

Prescription 9: Be a Fifth Gospel: Speak the Truth in Love

Sister believes her mission is to bring as many people to Christ as possible. Modeling Ephesians 4:15, her unapologetic defense of the truth is always rooted in the forgiving love of Christ, as well as in the hope, freedom, and peace that that truth and love bring. When needed, she diagnoses her patients with "spiritual deprivation" and writes them a prescription for Confession. The call to conversion may be difficult for some to hear, but "if the message is truth, and if it is given with love, then we have done our part. We may leave the rest to the action of the Holy Spirit working through us," she explains.

Sister takes this obligation very seriously and shares that while God is the only one who can save, she is still called to do her part in guiding others to His truth. She frequently references Luke 12:48 which warns that much will be required of those to whom much has been given.

As Dr. Tom Catena and Father Meeks both reflect, there are very few people in the world willing to proclaim their Faith courageously and without apology, and Sister Dede Byrne is one of them. It is never loving or merciful to withhold the life-giving truth of Christ, as loving one's neighbor includes desiring his eternal good.

Just as God instructed Jonah to take Him to the people He loved and allow Him to work — the same people who clearly didn't understand or accept God, the people who even sometimes hated Him — so, too, Sister Dede takes God, His mercy, and His teachings to the people He loves — to those who do not understand the rights of the unborn, to those who do not accept their identities as sons and daughters of the King, to those who may misunderstand God's commandments as restrictions of their freedom rather than a light to their path, and to those who hate Him and His Church.

-gen-z-now-about-one-third-of-the-electorate-dont-hold-extremist
-abortion-views-embrace-limits/.

Prescription 10: Love and Serve Others; Put Faith into Action

Referencing James 2:26 ("faith apart from works is dead"), Sister Dede spends her life in service to others. She characterizes her ministry to the poor and the uninsured as well as her overseas ministry in Haiti, Sudan, and Iraq as "full-time refugee medicine."[179] Her travels have helped her realize how blessed we are, as so many others live in sheer poverty, and how spiritually rich the impoverished are, as they rely entirely on God's providence. "[The suffering and needy] give me much more than I could give them," Sister states. "And I believe it is much easier for them to see the hand and heart of God in their own lives because they have [fewer] material distractions."[180]

Sister explains that in serving others via corporal and spiritual works of mercy, we imitate Mother Teresa, who frequently referenced Matthew 25:40: "As you did it to one of the least of these my brethren, you did it to me." The opportunity to serve the less fortunate is an opportunity to serve and encounter Christ in others.

While the *Catechism* teaches that "charitable actions" include the corporal works of mercy (2447) — things such as tending to the sick, feeding the hungry, and sheltering the homeless, all of which Sister so beautifully practices — she believes spiritual health that readies the soul for union with God in Heaven is essential. As such, she takes seriously the call to practice spiritual works of mercy as well, which include instructing, advising, and counseling. Whether to an unknown teenage girl or to prominent leaders, she loves them all enough to share with them those things that lead to eternal life. As she proposes Christ to every person she meets, her disarming love opens and readies the heart

---

[179] Address to college students at the University of Florida, April 23, 2023, 6.
[180] Address at the University of Florida, 6–7.

for the gospel and Christ's truth — something she is never ashamed to share (see Rom. 1:16).

In sum, a physician's patient care plan and prescriptions are only effective for compliant patients. Sister explains that in any moral regimen, humility is an important element for growth in holiness. Just as Sister Dede writes prescriptions for lifesaving medications, we aspire to be joyfully compliant patients by adhering to the prescriptions that lead to eternal life.

A Call from the Upper Room

In 1974, when Senator Mark Hatfield asked Mother Teresa how she could bear the load of such a suffering world, she replied that she was called not to be successful but to be faithful.[181] Recalling that faith without works is dead (see James 2:17), Sister Dede accepted the commission to advance Christ's truth with the hope that we will all attain Heaven someday. While we may never be sisters, colonels, or surgeons — while we may never play such interesting or prominent roles in life as Sister Dede Byrne does — let us "do small things with great love,"[182] as her hero Mother Teresa advises.

For people like Sister and those she inspires, it is not enough only to pray; we are also called to be leaven for transformation. "The way I figure it, we can either cower or we can stand with Our Lord," she states. "It's time to choose Christ." Like Sister, let us "find the courage to proclaim Christ … and the unchanging truths which have their foundation in Him. These are the truths that set us free."[183]

---

[181] Quoted in Peter Kennedy, "I Am Called to Be Faithful," Sermon Illustrator, https://www.sermonillustrator.org/illustrator/sermon3a/i_am_called_to_be_faithful.htm.

[182] Quoted in Marki Tauceda, "Doing Small Things with Great Love," Missionaries of the Poor, https://missionariesofthepoor.org/doing-small-things-with-great-love2/.

[183] Pope Benedict then continued, "They are the truths which alone can guarantee respect for the inalienable dignity and rights of each man,

Unwilling to accept, as so many others are prone to do, that her one small voice could never make a difference in such a huge sea of cultural confusion, Sister speaks truth with the conviction of Saint Catherine of Siena, who stated, "Be silent no more. Cry out with one hundred thousand tongues. I see that, because of this silence, the world is in ruins."[184]

Our Inspiration and Sister Dede's Place in History

Mindful of the necessary intersection of faith with the public square, we are inspired by Sister Dede as well as by our brothers and sisters of previous generations who courageously "spoke truth to power" (see John 19:10–11). Tradition has it that Matthew was martyred for questioning the morals of a king; Saint Thomas More publicly defended the sanctity of marriage and held King Henry VIII accountable for his lack of adherence to Church teaching; Thomas Becket defended the rights of the Church from encroachment by King Henry II; Blessed Miguel Pro chose death over denying his Faith amid the persecution of Mexico's Cristero War; Father Jerzy Popiełuszko gave his life in standing firm against the Soviet occupation of Poland and encouraged peaceful resistance to communism in the 1980s; John Paul II inspired the members of Solidarity and "contributed to the collapse of communism";[185] and Sister Dede Byrne now defends truth on the

---

woman and child in our world — including the most defenseless of all human beings, the unborn child in the mother's womb." Homily at Yankee Stadium, April 20, 2008.

[184] Saint Catherine of Siena, letter 16, to a "great prelate," cited in Father Horton, "St. Catherine of Siena: The World Is Rotten Because of Silence," Fauxtations, September 4, 2018, https://fauxtations.wordpress.com/2018/09/04/st-catherine-of-siena-the-world-is-rotten-because-of-silence/.

[185] "The Pope Who Changed Poland," Poland.pl, https://polska.pl/history/historical-figures/pope-changed-poland/.

front lines and inspires believers to stand strong in defense of religious freedom and the dignity of the human person.

Saint John Henry Newman commented that we are persuaded of religious truths via the heart: "The heart is commonly reached, not through the reason, but through the imagination, by means of direct impressions, by the testimony of facts and events, by history, by description. Persons influence us, voices melt us, looks subdue us, deeds inflame us. Many a man will live and die upon a dogma: no man will be a martyr for a conclusion."[186] While the unique life and exciting stories of Sister Dede's threefold calling as sister, soldier, and surgeon certainly stir our imaginations, it is her boundless love and her courageous defense of beauty, truth, and goodness that influence, melt, subdue, and inflame us.

Christ's truths are immutable. As such, Sister's exhortations for defending those truths also remain constant. In a nation plagued by relativism and apathy, people of faith hold fast to those absolute truths that lead to authentic freedom — "the freedom to do what we *ought* as human beings created by God according to His plan."[187]

As we recall Sister's impactful address that held our 2020 presidential candidates accountable, we embrace her evergreen exhortations, regardless of year or political candidate.

As followers of Christ, we are called to stand up for life against the politically correct or fashionable of today. We must fight against a legislative agenda that supports and even celebrates

[186] David Deavel, "Discovering the Truth through Holiness and Beauty," *Imaginative Conservative*, October 4, 2023, https://theimaginative conservative.org/2023/10/discovering-truth-holiness-beauty-david -deavel.html; John Henry Cardinal Newman, *An Essay in Aid of a Grammar of Assent* (London: Longmans, Green, 1903), 92–93.

[187] John Paul II, meeting with President Ronald Reagan, Vizcaya Museum, Miami, September 10, 1987, no. 3.

destroying life in the womb. Keep in mind, the laws we create define how we see our humanity. We must ask ourselves: What are we saying when we go into a womb and snuff out an innocent, powerless, voiceless life?

As a physician, I can say without hesitation: Life begins at conception. While what I have to say may be difficult for some to hear, I am saying it because I am not just pro-life; I am pro–eternal life. I want all of us to end up in Heaven together someday.

A Call into the Public Square

Filled to overflowing, the boundless love of Christ to which Sister witnesses daily spills into the public square and includes the truth that sets us free (see John 8:32). Encouraged by the example of our brothers and sisters before us, let us now follow her example to share Christ's love and take our Faith and voices into the public square, mindful that if the disciples had remained hidden in the Upper Room, only praying, we would never have a Church today. The Holy Spirit called them to emerge from the safety of the Upper Room to live out their faith boldly and courageously in a culture hostile to the gospel message: "Catholics have a duty to act when people's dignity and rights are at stake. Christ expects us to be active [in the public square]: loving our neighbor, engaging the culture, promoting the common good, and defending the dignity and rights of all. This is part and parcel of being a follower of Christ."[188]

Faith is not purely a private matter, and if it fails to inform every dimension of our lives, it is not true faith.[189] Echoing Cardinal Sarah,

---

[188] Bishop Thomas J. Olmsted, quoted in "New Book Challenges Catholics to Play Role in Public Square," Catholic News Agency, https://www. catholicnewsagency.com/news/7784/new-book-challenges-catholics -to-play-role-in-public-square.

[189] Olmsted, "New Book Challenges."

"Let us not be afraid.... The temptation to cowardice is everywhere."[190] Had Sister Dede remained in the chapel that August day in 2020, she would never have taken her place on the national stage to witness to Christ's teaching and to move, strengthen, and inspire a Church and a nation.

It Is Not Enough to Discuss; It Is Necessary to Act

Following Sister's example to witness to her Faith wherever she is called, let us now unapologetically take our faith into the culture, where we may be salt and light (see Matt. 5:13–14). Inspired by the lives of courageous witnesses, such as the apostles, who left the Upper Room, and Sister Dede, who daily speaks words of truth to a troubled world, let us, rooted in prayer, also heed the words of John Paul II: "You, too, be courageous! The world needs convinced and fearless witnesses. It is not enough to discuss, it is necessary to act!"[191]

In a battle for the souls of our children and nation, Sister Dede's messages and exhortations are more relevant today than ever before and will be evergreen into perpetuity. With renewed perseverance, let us resolve to save our souls, strengthen our Church, and imbue the Faith in our children, mindful that the leaders we elect today will forge the nation they will inherit and the cultural battles they will fight.

Let us cultivate virtue and, as citizens of both Heaven and earth (see Phil. 3:20; *CCC* 2796), also lovingly permeate our culture with the truth of the human person for advancing the common good. This includes "electing government leaders who respect and uphold the moral law."[192] For it is precisely "because we are people of both faith

---

[190] Sarah, *The Day*, 17.

[191] John Paul II, *The Meaning of Vocation: In the Words of St. John Paul II* (Princeton, NJ: Scepter Publishers, 1998), 20.

[192] Burke, *On Our Civic Responsibility*, no. 45.

and reason," state our U.S. bishops, that it is "necessary for us to bring this essential truth about human life and dignity to the public square," where we are called to defend life, defend marriage, and promote the well-being and dignity of all.[193]

In his 2009 book, Archbishop Charles Chaput aptly summarized, "If we really love this county, and if we really treasure our faith, living our Catholic beliefs without excuses or apologies, and advancing them in the public square are the best expressions of patriotism we can give to the nation."[194]

It Is the Hour to Awake from Sleep (Rom. 13:11)

Sister Dede Byrne's courageous love now awakens those who have fallen asleep and challenges us to love our neighbors enough to share with them the truths that lead to eternal life. "You know what hour it is, how it is … time now for you to wake from sleep. For salvation is nearer to us now than when we first believed; the night is far gone, the day is at hand. Let us then cast off the works of darkness and put on the armor of light" (Rom. 13:11–12).

As Sister and Father Meeks summarize, "Our struggle is not against flesh and blood. This battle that we face right now is not between Republicans versus Democrats, conservatives versus liberals, the Right versus the Left. No. This battle is between Our Dear Lord and the evil one — the devil."

The real heroism of Sister Dede lies not in her skill as a surgeon or in the many lives she has saved; it lies not in the many abortion pill reversals she has done or in her many brave works as a retired colonel in the army; it lies not in her defense of this great nation or

---

[193] USCCB, *Forming Consciences for Faithful Citizenship*, no. 10.

[194] Charles Chaput, *Render unto Caesar: Serving Our Nation by Living Our Catholic Beliefs in Political Life* (New York: Image, 2009), 219.

her place of honor on a national stage. What makes Sister Dede Byrne a heroine — what makes so many find her inspiring and what makes her example so important today — is the way she loves; the way she demonstrates how to attain sanctity in the small, unseen details of daily life; the way she proclaims her faith without fear or apology; and the way her actions, far more than her words, cry out, "I'm not just pro-life; I'm pro–eternal life!"

Dr. John Stewart aptly reflects, "I've heard it said that the opposite of love is fear [see 1 John 4:18]. Thus, Sister Dede's courage is really a manifestation of her love. It's just natural to her but has also been nurtured by a lifetime of service — service to her patients, service to her country, and service to her community. If she's not a saint, then none of us has any hope!"

For Such a Time as This (Esther 4:14)

Recalling my response to Sister when she asked if I could wait until she was dead to pen this book, people of faith worldwide would echo the same: No, Sister. I'm sorry. The day is now far spent.[195]

The world is desperate for witnesses to Christ's love *now*; the unborn and those nearing death demand that you be their voice *now*; our confused youth are yearning for your affirmation of their dignity as God's children *now*; and, finally, our Church and world are yearning for more courageous leaders unafraid to speak hard truths *now*, mindful that the fate of our Church will greatly impact the fate not only of our nation but of our souls.

So let us put on the armor of God that we may be able to stand against the wiles of the devil, having done everything to hold our ground. For our struggle is not against flesh and blood, but against

---

[195] Robert Cardinal Sarah, *The Day Is Now Far Spent* (San Francisco: Ignatius Press, 2019).

the spiritual forces of evil in the heavenly realms (see Eph. 6:11–12). Let us emerge from the Upper Room, live our faith in the public square, mindful, as Sister Dede stated, that "we do it because no one else will. Because if we don't, we will have to answer to the Lord, who will ask us, 'Why didn't you do more?' " There is hope because we are determined to be God's light when nobody notices Him, His explanation when nobody understands Him, and His mercy when nobody loves Him.[196] There is hope because we are undeterred in our resolve to reclaim the souls of our children and the soul of our nation. Yes, we are weathered and worn from the battle. But this tired, poor, huddled mass, yearning to breathe free,[197] is now poised in grace, strengthened by God, rooted in prayer, with rosary in hand — just like Sister Dede — to become saints and reclaim the truth that is rightfully ours. Be not afraid. You were born for this.[198]

Thank you, Sister Dede, for your witness, faith, service, and love. Your life and courage have blessed our Church and inspired a nation. We love you.

---

[196] Father Mike Schmitz, "Eucharistic Procession through New York City."

[197] Emma Lazarus, "The New Colossus," plaque on the Statue of Liberty, November 2, 1883.

[198] Attributed to one of Sister Dede's favorite saints, Saint Joan of Arc.

Bibliography

"Abortion Pill Reversal." Charlotte Lozier Institute. September 24, 2021. https://lozierinstitute.org/abortion-pill-reversal-a-record-of -safety-and-efficacy/.

"About Us." ACTS XXIX. https://www.actsxxix.org/how-we-think.

"Al Kresta: Build the Church; Bless the Nation." YouTube video. https://www.youtube.com/watch?v=Y5pUhjLOG4A.

Arnaouti, Matthew Keith Charalambos, Gabrielle Cahill, Michael David Baird, Laëlle Mangurat, Rachel Harris, Louidort Pierre Philippe Edme, Michelle Nyah Joseph, Tamara Worlton, Sylvio Augustin Jr., and The Haiti Disaster Response —Junior Research Collaborative. "Medical Disaster Response: A Critical Analysis of the 2010 Haiti Earthquake." *Front Public Health* 10 (November 2022). National Library of Medicine. https://www.ncbi.nlm.nih. gov/pmc/articles/PMC9665839/.

"The Bedouin and the Monastery." Mount Sinai Monastery. https:// sinaimonastery.com/index.php/en/the-bedouin/the-bedouin -and-the-monastery.

Benedict XVI. Address in Barangaroo, Sydney Harbour, Australia. July 17, 2008, https://www.vatican.va/content/benedict-xvi/ en/speeches/2008/july/documents/hf_ben-xvi_spe_20080717 _barangaroo.html.

———. Homily at Yankee Stadium. April 20, 2008.

Bennett, Deacon Geoff. "Catholics, Hear Sister Dede Byrne on Life, Then Vote Your Conscience." Catholic Charities Archdiocese of Denver Respect Life Radio. https://respectliferadio.podbean.com/e/catholics-hear-sister-dede-byrne-on-life-then-vote-your-well-formed-conscience/.

Bernstein, Brittany. "Pro-Life Activists Found Guilty of Violating FACE Act Conspiracy Charges for 2020 Incident at D.C. Clinic." *National Review*, August 29, 2023. https://www.nationalreview.com/news/pro-life-activists-found-guilty-of-violating-face-act-conspiracy-charges-for-2020-incident-at-d-c-clinic/.

"Bishop William D. Byrne." Diocese of Springfield, Massachusetts. https://diospringfield.org/bishop-william-d-byrne/.

Boston, Gabriella. "Nun Serves God and Army." *Washington Times*, January 25, 2009. https://www.washingtontimes.com/news/2009/jan/25/working-miracles/.

Bukuras, Joe. "Brother and Sister Who Are Bishop and Nun Say Faithful Parents Helped Foster Vocations." Catholic News Agency. February 9, 2024. https://www.catholicnewsagency.com/news/256788/brother-and-sister-who-are-bishop-and-nun-say-faithful-parents-helped-foster-vocations.

Burke, Most Reverend Raymond L. *On Our Civic Responsibility for the Common Good.* EWTN. https://www.ewtn.com/catholicism/library/on-our-civic-responsibility-for-the-common-good-3658.

Burle, Sister Philip Marie. *Praying the Scriptures of the Rosary for Family Healing.* CD Baby. 2015. Compact disc.

Byrne, Sister Dede (Deirdre M.). Address to the Arlington Advisory Forum, March 2024.

———. Address at the Basilica of the National Shrine of the Immaculate Conception, Washington, D.C., October 28, 2023.

————. Address to the Catholic Evidence League, Baltimore, Maryland, October 21, 2023.

————. Address to the Catholic Medical Association in Illinois, June 15, 2024.

————. Address to college students at the University of Florida, April 23, 2023.

————. Address to the Legatus chapter in Oklahoma City, June 2024.

————. "Defend Life Lecture Tour." Saint Philip Neri Parish. You Tube video. https://www.youtube.com/watch?v=wuJie 6JaSJI.

————. "Full Text: Sister Dede Byrne's Speech at the 2020 Republican National Convention." Catholic News Agency. August 26, 2020. https://www.catholicnewsagency.com/news/45617/full-text-sister-dede-byrnes-speech-at-the-2020-republican-national-convention.

————. "HHS Says University Hospital Forced Nurse to Assist in Abortions." Interview on *EWTN News Nightly*. YouTube video. August 29, 2019. https://www.youtube.com/watch?v= 7eQ0XCyMuQQ.

————. "In the Service of Christ: My 'Tours' in the Nuba Mountains." In *Sudan's Nuba Mountains People Under Siege: Accounts by Humanitarians in the Battle Zone*. Edited by Samuel Totten, 64–74. Jefferson, NC: McFarland, 2017.

————. "Preparation for Battle." YouTube video. January 21, 2023. https://www.youtube.com/watch?v=GqPb4ePrKVY.

————. "Sister Deirdre Byrne Shares Her Thoughts on the March for Life." January 29, 2021. YouTube video. https://www.youtube.com/watch?v=U5ilmgpYamg.

Caldwell, Zelda. " 'Rosary Rally' outside U.S. Capitol to Unleash Prayers for a 'World Gone Mad.' " *Catholic World Report*, October

7, 2022. https://www.catholicworldreport.com/2022/10/07/rosary-rally-outside-u-s-capitol-to-unleash-prayers-for-a-world-gone-mad/.

Calloway, Donald. *Champions of the Rosary*. Stockbridge, MA: Marian Press, 2016.

———. "Champions of the Rosary and St. Joseph." Parousia Media. YouTube video, 21:23. September 2020. https://www.youtube.com/watch?v=xQ1I8Lab8_M.

Camp, Emma. "Homeschooling Has Increased by Over 50 Percent since 2018." *Reason*, November 1, 2023. https://reason.com/2023/11/01/homeschooling-has-increased-by-over-50-percent-since-2018/.

"Can the Abortion Pill Be Reversed?" Abortion Pill Reversal. https://abortionpillreversal.com/abortion-pill-reversal/overview.

"Catholic Doctor of the Year." Mission Doctors Association. https://www.missiondoctors.org/catholic-doctor-of-the-year/.

"A Catholic Doctor Helping a Million People in Sudan and South Sudan." *EWTN News Nightly*. April 27, 2022. https://www.youtube.com/watch?v=HZJrBZr3_yM.

"Catholic Women Issue Statement Opposing Use of 'Abortion-Tainted Vaccines.'" Catholic News Agency. March 9, 2021. https://www.catholicnewsagency.com/news/246797/catholic-women-issue-statement-opposing-use-of-abortion-tainted-vaccines.

Chaput, Charles. *Render unto Caesar: Serving Our Nation by Living Our Catholic Beliefs in Political Life*. New York: Image, 2009.

Christian, Gina. "Report: Vocations to Religious Life in US Decline, but Key Factors Can Positively Impact Number." *OSV News*, February 3, 2024, https://www.osvnews.com/2024/02/03/report-vocations-to-religious-life-in-us-decline-but-key-factors-can-positively-impact-numbers/.

Deavel, David. "Discovering the Truth through Holiness and Beauty." *Imaginative Conservative*, October 4, 2023. https://theimaginative

conservative.org/2023/10/discovering-truth-holiness-beauty-david-deavel.html.

Dellinger, J. W. "Meet the 'Nun with the Gun' Honored at the 2019 White Mass." *Angelus News*, October 15, 2019. https://angelus news.com/local/la-catholics/meet-the-nun-with-the-gun-honored-at-the-white-mass/.

Desmond, Frawley Joan. "The Unconventional Mission of Sister Dede." *National Catholic Register*, September 3, 2020. https://www.nc register.com/interview/the-unconventional-mission-of-sister-dede.

Deweese, Kate McEntee. "Mass Attendance Rising in Archdiocese of Seattle." *Northwest Catholic*, February 13, 2024. https://nw catholic.org/news/kate-mcentee-deweese/mass-attendance-rising-in-archdiocese-of-seattle.

Donahoe, Jeffrey. "Sister Dede Answers the Call." *Georgetown University Health Magazine*, October 16, 2016. https://today.advancement.georgetown.edu/health-magazine/2016/sister-dede-byrne/.

Etheredge, Craig. "The Pull of Compassion God Can Use to Bring People to Christ." *Discipleship* (blog). https://discipleship.org/blog/the-pull-of-compassion-god-can-use-a-crisis-to-bring-people-to-christ/.

"Eucharistic Procession through New York City." Napa Institute. YouTube video. November 29, 2023. https://www.youtube.com/watch?v=5R-wCd4VSZs.

"The Eucharistic Procession at 10,000 Feet." Diocese of Lansing. March 23, 2020. https://www.youtube.com/watch?v=jMp9aCQZP2A.

"Everything You Need to Know about Dr. Tom." Catholic Medical Mission Board. https://cmmb.org/everything-you-need-to-know-about-dr-tom/.

Fenton, Francesca Pollio. "This Catholic Doctor Provides Care for 1 Million People in Sudan, South Sudan." EWTN Great Britain. April 28, 2022. https://ewtn.co.uk/article-this-catholic-doctor-provides-care-for-1-million-people-in-sudan-south-sudan/.

Ferreri, Eric. "After 9/11, a Short-Lived Rush to Church." *Duke Today*, August 19, 2016, https://today.duke.edu/2016/08/after-911-short-lived-rush-church.

Global Surgical and Medical Support Group. https://www.gsmsg.org/menu.

Hale, Jim. "Abortion Worker Claims Catholic Faith Is Her 'Whole Life' in Testimony at DC FACE Act Trial." LifeSite News. August 21, 2023. https://www.lifesitenews.com/analysis/abortion-worker-claims-catholic-faith-is-her-whole-life-in-testimony-at-dc-face-act-trial/.

"He Must Increase, I Must Decrease." *Diocesan*. January 12, 2019, https://diocesan.com/he-must-increase-i-must-decrease/.

"Help Dr. Tom Save Lives in the Nuba Mountains." African Mission Healthcare. https://www.healthfornuba.com.

"Holy Bush." Mount Sinai Monastery. https://sinaimonastery.com/index.php/en/description/the-monastery/holy-bush.

Horton, Father. "St. Catherine of Siena: The World Is Rotten Because of Silence." Fauxtations. September 4, 2018. https://fauxtations.wordpress.com/2018/09/04/st-catherine-of-siena-the-world-is-rotten-because-of-silence/.

John Paul II. Post-synodal apostolic exhortation *Christifideles Laici*. December 30, 1988.

———. Apostolic exhortation *Familiaris Consortio*. November 22, 1981.

———. Homily. Oriole Park at Camden Yards, Baltimore, Maryland. October 8, 1995.

———. *Letter of Pope John Paul II to Women*. June 25, 1995.

————. *The Meaning of Vocation: In the Words of St. John Paul II.* Princeton, NJ: Scepter Publishers, 1998.

————. Meeting with President Ronald Reagan, Vizcaya Museum, Miami, Florida, September 10, 1987.

Jones, Kevin. "Survey of New Priests: Most Pray Rosary, Go to Eucharistic Adoration, Parents Stay Married." Catholic News Agency. April 26, 2023. https://www.catholicnewsagency.com/news /254179/survey-of-new-priests-most-pray-rosary-go-to -eucharistic-adoration-parents-stayed-married.

Kennedy, Peter. "I Am Called to Be Faithful." Sermon Illustrator. https://www.sermonillustrator.org/illustrator/sermon3a/i_am_ called_to_be_faithful.htm.

Klemond, Susan. "Catholic Schools Held Steady during Heights of COVID, Relying on Faith and Fundamentals." *National Catholic Register,* October 31, 2022. https://www.ncregister.com/news/ catholic-schools-held-steady-during-height-of-covid-relying -on-faith-and-fundamentals.

Kosta, Laura. "Mass Counts Show Slight Increase in Attendance in 2023." *St. Louis Review,* December 2023. https://www.archstl .org/mass-counts-show-slight-increase-in-attendance-in-2023 -9226.

Kresta, Al. "Archbishop Chaput Is Right: We Are Strangers in a Strange Land." *National Catholic Register,* March 8, 2017. https://www. ncregister.com/blog/archbishop-chaput-is-right-we-are-strangers -in-a-strange-land.

Lazarus, Emma. "The New Colossus." Plaque on the Statue of Liberty. November 2, 1883.

Leo XIII. Encyclical *Magnae Dei Matris.* September 8, 1892.

Little Workers of the Sacred Hearts. https://littleworkersofthesacred hearts.com/.

McClarey, Donald R. "Cardinal Carberry and the First Conclave of 1978." *American Catholic,* August 2, 2021, https://the-american

-catholic.com/2021/08/02/cardinal-carberry-and-the-first-conclave-of-1978/.

McKeown, Jonah. "A Doctor Begged a Religious Sister for Help. Last Week, She and Her Family Escaped Afghanistan." Catholic News Agency. February 17, 2022. https://www.catholicnewsagency. com/news/250418/a-doctor-begged-a-religious-sister-for-helplast-week-she-and-her-family-escaped-afghanistan.

———. "American Medical Association Retains Opposition to Assisted Suicide." Catholic News Agency. November 14, 2023. https://www.catholicnewsagency.com/news/256012/american-medical-association-retains-opposition-to-assisted-suicide-amid-catholic-doctors-advocacy.

Meloy, Dan. "Drive-In Masses Offer Creative Solution for COVID-Conscious Faithful." *Detroit Catholic*, July 14, 2020. https://www.detroitcatholic.com/news/drive-in-masses-offer-creative-solution-for-covid-conscious-faithful-video.

"Mildred Jefferson — Trailblazer for Justice." Radiance Foundation. https://radiancefoundation.org/trailblazer/.

"More Than 500 Hate Crimes against Europe's Christians Recorded in 2019." *Catholic World Report*, November 20, 2019. https://www.catholicworldreport.com/2020/11/17/more-than-500-hate-crimes-against-europes-christians-recorded-in-2019/.

"Mother Teresa at the National Prayer Breakfast." February 3, 1994. EWTN. https://www.ewtn.com/catholicism/library/mother-teresa-at-the-national-prayer-breakfast-2714.

Multinational Force and Observers. https://mfo.org.

Mullen, Shannon. "If This Nun-Doctor Can't Get a Vaccine Religious Exemption, Who Can?" Catholic News Agency. March 11, 2022. https://www.catholicnewsagency.com/news/250642/catholic-nun-doctor-deirdre-byrne-vaccine-mandate.

"New Book Challenges Catholics to Play Role in Public Square." Catholic News Agency. https://www.catholicnewsagency .com/news/7784/new-book-challenges-catholics-to-play-role -in-public-square.

"New Poll Finds That Millennials and Gen Z — Now About One-Third of the Electorate — Don't Hold Extremist Abortion Views, Embrace Limits," Demetree Institute for Prolife Advancement, https://www.instituteforprolifeadvancement.org/new-poll-finds -that-millennials-gen-z-now-about-one-third-of-the-electorate -dont-hold-extremist-abortion-views-embrace-limits/.

Newman, John Henry Cardinal. *An Essay in Aid of a Grammar of Assent.* London: Longmans, Green, 1903.

Newport, Frank. "Religious Group Voting and the 2020 Election." Gallup. November 13, 2020. https://news.gallup.com/opinion/ polling-matters/324410/religious-group-voting-2020-election. aspx.

Palumbo, Mario and Trish. *Jesus Christ Is Alive.* The Orchard. 2010. Compact disc.

Paul VI. Apostolic exhortation *Evangelii Nuntiandi.* December 8, 1975.

———. Encyclical letter *Humanae Vitae.* July 25, 1968.

"Poll Shows Large Percentage of Catholics Did Not Vote in 2020." Catholic Vote, May 14, 2024. https://catholicvote.org/poll-shows -large-percentage-of-catholics-did-not-vote-in-2020/.

"The Pope Who Changed Poland." Poland.pl. https://polska.pl/ history/historical-figures/pope-changed-poland/.

Ragheb, Michael, Ashish H. Shah, Sarah Jernigan, Tulay Koru-Sengul, and John Ragheb. "Epidemiology of Pediatric Hydrocephalus in Haiti: Analysis of a Surgical Case Series." *Journal of Neurosurgery* 23, no. 5 (February 2019). https://thejns.org/pediatrics/view/ journals/j-neurosurg-pediatr/23/5/article-p568.xml.

Rausch, Stacy. "Soldier, Surgeon, Sister." *Arlington Catholic Herald*, August 12, 2015.

Reddy, Bob. "Catholic School Numbers Skyrocket." Diocese of Venice in Florida. August 4, 2022. https://dioceseofvenice.org /catholic-school-numbers-skyrocket/.

Ring, Wilson. "US Agency: Hospital Forced Nurse to Participate in Abortion." Associated Press. August 28, 2019. https://apnews. com/article/b4f4dc46734f49f88198bc31f9013506.

Sadler, Ashley. "We Have Lost All Common Sense and as a Result We Are Losing Our Religious Freedom." LifeSite News. August 4, 2021. https://www.lifesitenews.com/news/735731/.

"Saint Catherine." Mount Sinai Monastery. https://sinaimonastery. com/index.php/en/history/saint-catherine.

Sarah, Robert Cardinal. "The Catholic Church's Enduring Answer to the Practical Atheism of Our Age." Napa Institute. June 14, 2024. https://napa-institute.org/cardinal-sarah/.

———. *The Day Is Now Far Spent*. San Francisco: Ignatius Press, 2019.

Schiffer, Kathy. "Sister Deirdre 'Dede' Byrne — Surgeon, Soldier, Sister, Servant." EWTN Great Britain. August 24, 2020. https:// ewtn.co.uk/sister-deirdre-dede-byrne-surgeon-soldier-sister -servant/.

Schmitz, Fr. Mike. "Eucharistic Procession through New York City." *Napa Institute.* November 29, 2023. https://www.youtube.com/ watch?v=5R-wCd4VSZs.

Schweers, Kevin. "Eucharistic Adoration Is on the Rise Locally with a USCCB Campaign Underway." *Arlington Catholic Herald*, October 15, 2023. https://www.catholicherald.com/article/local /eucharistic-adoration-is-on-the-rise-locally-with-a-usccb -campaign-underway/.

Siegel-Itzkovich, Judy. "The Days and Years of the Tichos." *Jerusalem Post*, February 21, 2015. https://www.jpost.com/israel-news /health/the-days-and-years-of-the-tichos-391744.

Bibliography

Snow, McKenna. "Bishop at Catholic Prayer Breakfast: Fauci Perfectly Shows Need for Eucharistic Revival." CatholicVote. February 8, 2024. https://catholicvote.org/national-catholic-prayer-break fast-fauci-perfectly-explains-need-eucharistic-revival/.

"Spanish Catholic Center." Catholic Charities. https://www.catholic charitiesdc.org/about-us/our-locations/spanish-catholic -center/.

"Suing District of Columbia: Sr. Deirdre Byrne." *The World Over*. Interview with Raymond Arroyo. March 10, 2022. https://www.youtube.com/watch?v=uPbFbQqM468.

"Treasures." Mount Sinai Monastery. https://sinaimonastery.com/index.php/en/treasures.

Trump, Donald J. "Remarks by President Trump at the 2019 Salute to America." Trump White House Archives. July 4, 2019. https://trumpwhitehouse.archives.gov/briefings-statements/remarks -president-trump-salute-america/.

Trunkey, Donald, Ronald Maier, Lynette Scherer, David Dawson, and Warren Dorlac. *Military Trauma System Review, US Central Command* (2010). https://jts.health.mil/assets/docs/assessments/Afghan-Trauma-System-Review-18-Mar-2010.pdf.

"2022 National Rosary Rally and National Eucharistic Procession." Rosary Coast to Coast. October 9, 2022. https://www.youtube.com/watch?v=0MrUNud3Rbc.

United States of America v. Lauren Handy. United States Court of Appeals. September 2023. https://www.justice.gov/d9/2023-09/u.s._v._handy_no._23-3143_dc_cir._09.22.23.pdf.

United States Conference of Catholic Bishops. *Forming Consciences for Faithful Citizenship — Part I — The U.S. Bishops' Reflection on Catholic Teaching and Political Life*. 2019. https://www.usccb.org/issues-and-action/faithful-citizenship/forming -consciences-for-faithful-citizenship-part-one.

———. *Living the Gospel of Life: A Challenge to American Catholics.* 1998. https://www.usccb.org/issues-and-action/human-life-and-dignity/abortion/living-the-gospel-of-life.

———. *Understanding Conscience.* 2017. https://www.usccb.org/prolife/understanding-conscience.

"Victory through the Rosary." America Needs Fatima. December 11, 2013. https://americaneedsfatima.org/blog/victory-through-the-rosary.

"The Voice of Women in Support of Unborn Babies and in Opposition to 'Abortion-Tainted Vaccines.'" Edward Pentin. March 8, 2021. https://edwardpentin.co.uk/wp-content/uploads/2021/03/STATE-MENT-The-Voice-of-Women-in-Defense-of-Unborn-Babies-and-in-Opposition-to-Abortion-tainted-Vaccines-WORD-DOC.pdf.

Vulnerable People Project. https://vulnerablepeopleproject.com.

Wolf, Naomi. "What's in the Pfizer Documents?" Hillsdale College. YouTube video. https://www.youtube.com/watch?v=T9Y_W_30hsM.

About the Author

Leisa Marie Carzon, Ph.D. is an assistant professor of education and Catholic School Leadership Graduate Program Director, president and chairman of the board of a Catholic health-care clinic, president of Plymouth Right to Life, and founder of the Aquinas Education Fund. She has served as a development executive for the Dominican Sisters of Mary, Mother of the Eucharist, a consultant for Catholic nonprofit organizations, and a State Director for CatholicVote. She sings opera and oratorio as a coloratura soprano and is a blessed wife and mother.

Sophia Institute

Sophia Institute is a nonprofit institution that seeks to nurture the spiritual, moral, and cultural life of souls and to spread the gospel of Christ in conformity with the authentic teachings of the Roman Catholic Church.

Sophia Institute Press fulfills this mission by offering translations, reprints, and new publications that afford readers a rich source of the enduring wisdom of mankind.

Sophia Institute also operates the popular online resource CatholicExchange.com. *Catholic Exchange* provides world news from a Catholic perspective as well as daily devotionals and articles that will help readers to grow in holiness and live a life consistent with the teachings of the Church.

In 2013, Sophia Institute launched Sophia Institute for Teachers to renew and rebuild Catholic culture through service to Catholic education. With the goal of nurturing the spiritual, moral, and cultural life of souls, and an abiding respect for the role and work of teachers, we strive to provide materials and programs that are at once enlightening to the mind and ennobling to the heart; faithful and complete, as well as useful and practical.

Sophia Institute gratefully recognizes the Solidarity Association for preserving and encouraging the growth of our apostolate over the course of many years. Without their generous and timely support, this book would not be in your hands.

www.SophiaInstitute.com
www.CatholicExchange.com
www.SophiaInstituteforTeachers.org

Sophia Institute Press is a registered trademark of Sophia Institute. Sophia Institute is a tax-exempt institution as defined by the Internal Revenue Code, Section 501(c)(3). Tax ID 22-2548708.